Volume 6

WORDS
for Students of English

A Vocabulary Series for ESL

Holly Deemer Rogerson
Gary Esarey
Carol Jasnow
Suzanne T. Hershelman
Linda M. Schmandt
Dorolyn A. Smith
Courtenay Meade Snellings

Pitt Series in English as a Second Language

Ann Arbor
University of Michigan Press

First published by the University of Michigan Press 1993
Copyright © 1989, University of Pittsburgh Press and
    the English Language Institute, University of Pittsburgh
All rights reserved
ISBN 0-472-08216-7
Published in the United States of America by
The University of Michigan Press
Manufactured in the United States of America

2000   1999   1998   1997   7   6   5

Illustrations by Suzanne T. Hershelman

Words for Students of English

Vocabulary Series Editors
Holly Deemer Rogerson
Lionel Menasche

Contents

Foreword

The objective of this series of vocabulary texts for the student of English as a foreign language is to facilitate the learning of approximately 3,000 new base words. Vocabulary learning has long been deemphasized in language teaching, much to the detriment of the students, who have mostly been left to fend for themselves. We thoroughly agree with Muriel Saville-Troike, who states, "Vocabulary knowledge in English is the most important aspect of oral English proficiency for academic achievement" (*TESOL Quarterly*, vol. 18, no. 2, p. 216).

With the present lack of comprehensive vocabulary texts suitable for both classroom use and home study, this series is intended to support teachers in preparing effective vocabulary lessons so that they can meet their students' urgent need for an increased lexicon. We present here a selection of base vocabulary items and some of their derived forms (i.e., the noun, verb, adverb, and adjective of the same stem) together with a series of exercises designed to help students remember the new words and use them in context.

This text has been used in an experimental edition in the English Language Institute, and modifications suggested by its use have been incorporated in the present version.

Christina Bratt Paulston
Director, English Language Institute
University of Pittsburgh

Acknowledgments

A series such as this depends greatly on the cooperation and hard work of numerous people:

Christina Bratt Paulston and Holly Deemer Rogerson originated the idea for the series.

Christina Bratt Paulston provided ongoing support for the series.

Mary Newton Bruder, Carol Jasnow, Christina Bratt Paulston, and Holly Deemer Rogerson developed the first version of the list of approximately 600 words assumed known.

Holly Deemer Rogerson developed the original pool of words from which the 150 topic word lists were chosen. She also organized the word lists and, with Lionel Menasche, provided general management of the project, including authors' drafts, revisions, editing, illustrations, duplicating, testing, and typing.

Ideas for word lists, format, and exercise types were contributed by Betsy Davis, Gary Esarey, Suzanne T. Hershelman, Carol Jasnow, Carol Moltz, Lionel Menasche, Holly Deemer Rogerson, Dorolyn Smith, and Linda M. Schmandt.

Lionel Menasche and Holly Deemer Rogerson were responsible for final revisions of content with input from classroom testing by Isabel Dillener, Jeanette Courson, Caroline Haessly, Pat Furey, Carol Jasnow, Ken Rose, Linda M. Schmandt, Jill Sherman, Tom Swinscoe, and Lois Wilson.

Courtenay Meade Snellings and Dexter Kimball provided valuable editorial assistance in content revision and proofreading.

JoEllen Walker and Anna Mae Townsend typed several drafts of the manuscript.

Lisa Krizmanich assisted during the testing phase.

Introduction

Volumes 1–7 of *Words for Students of English* present English base words,* with definitions, examples, and exercises. The texts may be used as core texts for vocabulary learning classes or as supplementary texts in reading, speaking, and writing classes. They may also be used for individual study.

Each unit focuses on one topic so that the words being presented can be practiced in meaningful contexts. Some of the new words in each unit are directly related to the topic, while others are less directly connected. Most of the words in a given unit can be used in a variety of contexts.

Volume 1 assumes a knowledge of 600 base words in English. Starting from this point, new words are presented in each unit, with the definitions, examples, and exercises in Volumes 1–6 *containing only vocabulary which has been previously learned.* There are 25 units in each of Volumes 1–6, while Volume 7 has 22 units. The first units in Volume 1 contain only about ten base words each in order to allow the students to become familiar with the format of the units. After the first units, each unit in Volume 1 contains approximately fifteen base words. In Volume 2, there are approximately fifteen base words in each unit. In Volumes 3 and 4, each unit contains fifteen to twenty base words; in Volumes 5 and 6, there are approximately 25 base words per unit; and in Volume 7, there are approximately 32 base words in each unit. On completion of the series of seven volumes, students will have learned approximately 3,700 base words.

Given that Volume 1 assumes a knowledge of 600 base words, the level of Volumes 1 and 2 can be loosely described as beginning, Volumes 3 and 4 as intermediate, Volumes 5 and 6 as high intermediate or advanced, and Volume 7 as advanced.

Selection of Words and Unit Topics

The 600 assumed words upon which Volumes 1–6 are based were chosen by a panel of experienced ESL teachers at the University of Pittsburgh as the group of words which are most typically learned by ESL students during their first two years of middle

---

*"Base" may be defined variously in lexical analysis, but for our present pedagogical purpose it implies any alternant from which other forms are derived. It is frequently impossible to say which form of a word is the most basic.

school or high school ESL classes. The words presented in Volumes 1–7 were selected according to usefulness from a variety of word-frequency lists. The authors and editors added other words to the topics at suitable levels of difficulty. In volumes 5 and 6 special attention is given to two- and three-word verbs.

In many cases students have to learn words with more than one meaning or with meanings that may **vary** according to context. A decision was made in each such instance as to whether the meaning in the new context was different enough to warrant further definition or similar enough for the students to extrapolate from what they had previously learned. These decisions were based on dictionary definitions and authors' or editors' personal judgments. For example, a word such as *beat* might appear in these contexts: (a) beat the opposing football team, (b) beat a drum, (c) a beat of a heart, (d) beat a person. Contexts (b) and (d) (meaning = strike) were judged close enough to allow extrapolation of meaning from one context to another, but (a) and (c) were thought to require separate definitions.

We have assumed that when a student learns a new vocabulary item, an approximate meaning for the word is assimilated, and that meaning is linked to the context in which the word was first encountered. Then, as the student meets the word in other contexts, the initially learned, approximate meaning is expanded and refined. Hence, many words are not only used several times in the unit in which they first appear, but are also used in later units.

The unit topics were chosen and ordered according to their perceived relevance to the students' lives, that is, their communicative usefulness. Most topics are covered in one unit in each volume, but certain broad topics, for example "School," are repeated twice within the same volume, in which case they are marked (A) or (B). A few topics, such as "Religion" and "Banking," due to the difficulty or abstractness of the words associated with them, are not covered in the first volume. Certain other topics whose words were perceived as tangible and easy, for example, "Telephone" and "Post Office," are completed in the first two volumes.

It should be noted that the repetition of each topic, at times within the same volume and always in at least one subsequent volume, allows for review and recycling of the material learned. Thus, long-term retention of the vocabulary is facilitated.

Format and Suggestions for Teachers: Volumes 1–6
(Note: Volume 7 has a different format, described in the introduction to that volume.)

Flexibility in using this vocabulary series has been a prime consideration in planning the format and exercises of the units. Therefore, although suggestions are given in the following paragraphs, it is assumed that teachers in different situations will decide according to their own students' needs whether work should be done in or out of class, orally or in writing, and with or without direct assistance from the teacher. The pace at which classes can proceed through each volume will vary greatly, depending on the students' motivation, study habits, and general workload, as well as the degree of emphasis the teacher wishes to place on productive vocabulary skills.

Each unit in Volumes 1–6 has the same format. The five sections of each unit are as follows.

WORD FORM CHART	STUDY EXERCISES
DEFINITIONS AND EXAMPLES	FOLLOW-UP
INTRODUCTORY EXERCISES	

The WORD FORM CHART presents base words and some or all of their related forms, categorized by part of speech. In Volumes 1 and 2, an effort was made to simplify the charts by omitting many derived or related forms which were either not common, or not useful for students at this level, or not easily recognizable from a knowledge of the base form. After Volume 2, more related forms are added because the students can handle more as they progress in learning the language. Decisions on what forms to omit were made by authors and editors on the basis of experience gained during testing of these materials with linguistically heterogeneous classes. Teachers in different educational contexts should consider supplementing the charts according to their own students' needs and their ability to absorb more material. For example, many words could be added by giving antonyms formed from words already given (planned/unplanned, honest/dishonest).

In the NOUNS column of the charts in Volumes 1 and 2 only, nouns which normally or frequently refer to humans are marked by the symbol ⅄. When a noun, as defined in the unit, can be either human or nonhuman, the symbol is in parentheses: (⅄). Gerunds are not included in the charts. Nouns have not been marked "count" and "non-count" because so many nouns function in both ways.

In the VERBS column, irregular past tenses and past participles are in parentheses following the verbs. In cases where more than one past tense or past participle is acceptable, the more regular one is included in the chart. Thus, for example, in the Volume 1, Unit #4 Word Form Chart no irregular forms are listed for *forecast* because the regular form *forecasted* is also currently acceptable.

In the ADJECTIVES column, we have included any present or past participles that appear prenominally as adjectives, as well as any regular adjectives. We have not included in this column nouns which form Noun-Noun modification patterns.

The next section, DEFINITIONS AND EXAMPLES, gives the meanings of the words as well as example sentences which are usually related to the topic of the unit. The form chosen for definition is not always the base form. Other forms are sometimes chosen for greater ease of definition or learning. In all definitions and examples, only previously learned words are used. This applies also within the set of definitions in each unit. Thus, the words in each set of definitions are presented in an order which allows their definition and exemplification using only previously introduced words.

Grammatical information is given in the definitions by means of the following conventions: "to" is used before a verb to indicate the verb form, articles are used with nouns whenever possible to indicate that the word is a noun, and parentheses enclose prepositions that may follow a verb. Words with more than one meaning are cross-referenced to definitions in earlier units when new definitions are given. Extra information (e.g., irregular plurals and abbreviations) is given within braces ({ }). Separable two- or three-word verbs are labeled while inseparable ones are left unmarked.

This section, together with the Word Form Chart, can be efficiently handled as work assigned for intensive individual study, followed by discussion in class of questions raised by students. At this point the teacher may also wish to elaborate on certain definitions and give further examples.

Writing explicit definitions of words using the intentionally limited vocabulary available results in some rather broad definitions and others that are limited to certain aspects of the meaning. The deliberate compromise here between precision and generality is designed to make the text fully accessible to students by avoiding the major weakness of many other vocabulary texts: defining new items with words that are themselves unknown to the learner. The easily understood broad definitions, which may take the form of a standard verbal definition, a picture, or a list of examples, are then refined by further exposure to appropriate examples in this unit and series and in the students' later reading. Also, students can usefully refer to a bilingual dictionary in conjunction with studying the example sentences given.

After the Definitions and Examples section, there is a three-tiered system of exercises sequenced to take the student from easy, open-book, fairly controlled exercises through more difficult, less controlled exercises to a final phase with communicative exercises.

The first part of the sequence consists of INTRODUCTORY EXERCISES. These are designed to acquaint the students with the new words in the unit and lead them to an initial understanding of the words by using the Definitions and Examples section. We recommend that these brief and easy exercises be done with books open, orally or in writing, immediately after the teacher's first presentation of the new words.

The next section in each unit, headed STUDY EXERCISES, is a longer and more difficult set of exercises designed to be used by the students for individual study or for oral or written work in class. In Volumes 5 and 6, this section includes an analogies exercise similar in format to that of the Graduate Record Examination (GRE).

The final section is the FOLLOW-UP. This includes a dictation and more open-ended communicative exercises designed to be done after the students have studied the words. The latter may be done orally in class, or teachers may request written answers to selected questions.

Each volume also contains an INDEX listing all the base words presented in that volume. Words in the preceding volumes and the assumed words are given in separate appendices in Volume 1–5. With each word is listed the volume and unit where it is presented. In Volume 6, there is both an index for the volume and an appendix combining all the words in the assumed list and in Volumes 1–6.

An ANSWER KEY at the end of each volume provides answers for all the exercises in the Study Exercises sections, except where a variety of answers is acceptable. Answers are not provided for the Introductory Exercises or the exercises in the Follow-Up so that the teacher can choose to use these exercises for homework or testing purposes if desired.

Production and Recognition

Although a distinction between vocabulary known for recognition and that known for production is often propounded, the actual situation is probably best represented by a continuum stretching from mere recognition to production which is accurate both semantically and syntactically. The exercises in Volumes 1–6 cover the full range of this continuum so that teachers wishing to stress productive vocabulary knowledge will have ample opportunity to give their students feedback on the use of the new words in their speech and writing. However, the goal of many teachers will be to increase their students' recognition vocabularies as rapidly as possible, with the expectation that those words which students meet again frequently in other contexts and have a use for will gradually become part of their productive vocabularies. Teachers with this goal of recognition vocabulary development in mind will wish to proceed more rapidly through the units and deemphasize those exercises requiring productive capabilities, for example, by limiting their corrections to semantic errors, rather than correcting syntactic mistakes as well.

In Volume 7 the new words in each unit are classified into two groups: words for production and words for recognition. The rationale for the different format of Volume 7 is given in the introduction to that volume.

Words for Students of English

Government (A)

Word Form Chart

NOUN	VERB	ADJECTIVE	ADVERB
address	address		
addressee			
amendment	amend	amended	
autonomy		autonomous	autonomously
bureau			
bureaucracy		bureaucratic	bureaucratically
bureaucrat			
	call on		
	come up with		
commerce		commercial	commercially
commercial			
commercialism			
confirmation	confirm	confirmed	
		confirming	
		confirmatory	
contribution	contribute	contributory	
contributor		contributing	
council			
councilor			
delegate	delegate		
delegation			
	draw up		
federalism		federal	federally
federalist			
	hold off		
municipality		municipal	
parliament		parliamentary	
point		pointed	
proposal	propose	proposed	

NOUN	VERB	ADJECTIVE	ADVERB
regime			
resolution	resolve		
revenue			
rule	rule	ruling	
ruler			
	stand up for		
	stand up to		

Definitions and Examples

1. **parliament** [a national government assembly with the power to make laws]

   The British **Parliament** is divided into two assemblies which both meet at Westminster.

   England has had a **parliamentary** system of government since the fourteenth century.

2. **delegate** (a) [a representative; a person who acts for another]

   In a democracy, voters elect **delegates** to make laws for them.

   A **delegation** of students visited the university president to request a new examination policy.

   (b) [to give responsibility to another person]

   A good manager **delegates** responsibility to his employees; he does not try to do everything himself.

3. **address** (a) [to communicate directly with someone, especially in a formal speech]

   The queen **addresses** Parliament annually on the day of its official opening.

   The president of the United States delivers an annual **address** to the Congress to summarize the past year and announce plans for the next.

   (b) [1-6: the number and street where a house is]

   The official **address** of the head of England's government is 10 Downing Street.

4. **federal** [belonging to a form of government where the power is divided between a central authority and regional authorities]

   The central authority in a **federation** is sometimes called the **federal** government.

   The U.S. government is a **federal** system. The **federal** government is responsible for defense, and the states are responsible for education.

5. **municipal** [related to a city or local government]

    > A mayor is the head of a **municipal** government.
    > "**Municipality**" is another word for "city."

6. **bureau** [a specialized administrative office, especially a department in a government]

    > The Federal **Bureau** of Investigation (FBI) is a U.S. agency that investigates crimes against federal law.
    > A travel **bureau** is an office that provides information about transportation fares and schedules, hotels, and interesting sights in a local area.

7. **bureaucracy** [the system of all government administrative offices which are staffed by nonelected officials]

    > The people who work in a **bureaucracy** are **bureaucrats**.
    > **Bureaucrats** have a reputation for being inflexible. They may be more interested in papers and rules than in helping people.

8. **amend** [to correct or improve, often by adding or subtracting information]

    > The First **Amendment** to the U.S. Constitution guarantees freedom of speech.
    > Before Parliament passed the law, it was **amended** to include a tax reduction.

9. **confirm** (a) [to state again that something is true or correct]

    > The morning paper announced new tax rates, and the president's noontime radio address **confirmed** the report.
    > We ordered plane tickets by phone and received **confirmation** of the purchase in the mail.

    (b) [to make something certain by giving legal approval]

    > The president announced the appointment of a new ambassador, but the appointment was not official until Parliament **confirmed** it.

10. **propose** [to suggest]

    > A delegation of students **proposed** that their school save money by having fewer hours of class. Their **proposal** was not accepted by the school administrators.
    > A marriage **proposal** is an offer of marriage. Traditionally, in the United States, the man **proposes** to the woman.

11. **resolution** (a) [a plan of action that has been decided on, often the result of a formal vote]

> The members of Parliament voted for a **resolution** to cut taxes by five percent over five years.
> I have **resolved** to exercise more and eat healthier foods.
> People often make New Year's **resolutions** which they do not keep.

(b) [the solution to a complex problem; the conclusion of a complex story]

> Everyone hopes for a **resolution** to the problems in the Middle East.
> People want leaders who will **resolve** their country's problems.

12. **autonomous** [governed by oneself; independent]

> Regional governments may fight to win **autonomy** from a central authority. In Spain, for example, the Basques want to have an **autonomous** government in the north instead of being controlled by Madrid.
> During the Civil War in the United States in the 1860s, southern states declared an **autonomous** government, completely separate from the federal government in Washington.

13. **revenue** [the income of a government]

> A government cannot be autonomous without a reliable source of **revenue**.
> To get more **revenue**, a government can increase taxes.

14. **contribute** [to give or supply, together with others]

> I **contribute** money to my church to maintain the building and to help poor people.
> When the big project was completed, the boss thanked all of his employees for the extra time and effort they had **contributed**.

15. **call on** (a) [to visit, especially in an official way]

> Delegates from the major businesses in the city **called on** the new mayor to ask for his help.
> Good salesmen **call on** their customers regularly.

(b) [to request someone to do something]

> Rich people are frequently **called on** to contribute money to many different causes.
> In times of war or other national difficulty, a government **calls on** all citizens for their support.
> If a student is sleeping in class, the teacher may **call on** him to answer a question in order to wake him up.

16. **come up with** [to think of or find, often in order to give to other people]

> The person who first **came up with** the idea of a personal computer must be very rich.
> I cannot take a vacation unless I can **come up with** $200 to buy a plane ticket.

17. **commerce** [the buying and selling of goods and services, especially between governments or other large organizations]

> The U.S. Department of **Commerce** regulates and advises businesses and industries in the country.
> **Commercialism** is an attitude that emphasizes making a profit.
> The **commercial** areas of many American cities have moved from downtown to the suburban sections.

18. **commercial** [an advertisement on radio or television]

> Television **commercials** are often louder than regular programs.
> Before elections in the United States, voters hear radio and TV **commercials** that try to convince them to vote for certain people.

19. **point** (a) [the sharp end of something]

> Knives, nails, and pins end in a **point**.

(b) [a small round mark, or a location indicated by that mark]

> The shortest distance between two **points** is a straight line.
> The general marked the **point** on the map where the bombs would fall.

(c) [4-21: the purpose; the reason]

> There is no **point** in arguing with him, because he will never change his opinion.

(d) [4-21: to signal with your finger in order to show somebody something]

> The man **pointed** to where our seats were.

(e) [4-21: a number in a score]

> To win a volleyball game you must have fifteen **points**, and you must have two more **points** than your opponent.

20. **regime** (a) [a system of managing a government with strong, central (sometimes military) control]

> Spain was a very conservative country during the **regime** of Francisco Franco.
> In France, the era when the kings still had absolute power is known as the old **regime**.

(b) [a routine]

> After my operation, the doctor insisted that I follow a strict **regime** of exercise and special diet.

21. **ruler** (a) [a person who controls or governs]

> Genghis Khan was the **ruler** of a large area of Asia in the thirteenth
> century.
> The **ruling** party in a country is the one with the most power.

>> (b) [3-1: rule: a law or regulation; what a person is or is not permitted
>> to do]

>>> Many schools have strict **rules** about students' behavior.

22. **stand up for** [to defend; to support in an argument]

> My parents taught me always to **stand up for** the ideas that I believe in.
> Improvements in education often lead to social change; when people
>   learn about their legal rights, they begin to **stand up for** them.

23. **stand up to** [to be brave or strong when challenged or threatened]

> The employee **stood up to** her boss when he asked her to overcharge a
>   customer; she refused to participate in a dishonest policy, even though
>   she might lose her job as a result.

24. **council** [a group of people who are assembled to lead, advise, or discuss
     certain issues]

> Government leaders sometimes appoint special **councils** to investigate
>   problems like drugs or crime.
> My friend Joe Smith is a town **councilor** who is very popular with the
>   citizens.

25. **draw up** {separable} [to prepare a document]

> One of the main responsibilities of a corporation lawyer is to **draw up**
>   contracts.
> After government negotiators decided on the terms of the agreement,
>   their staff members **drew** it **up**.

26. **hold off** (on) {separable} [to delay]

> The mayor **held off on** making a decision until he had talked to his
>   councilors.
> Although the soldiers were tired, they were able to **hold** the enemy **off**
>   until help arrived.

Introductory Exercises

A. Match each word or phrase with its definition.

_____	1. a representative	**a.** addressee
_____	2. a correction or improvement	**b.** amendment
_____	3. a suggestion	**c.** autonomous
_____	4. a national assembly that makes laws	**d.** bureaucrats
_____	5. a plan of action	**e.** call on
_____	6. the sharp end of something	**f.** come up with
_____	7. a person who governs	**g.** commerce
_____	8. to make something certain	**h.** confirm
_____	9. the person to whom you are speaking	**i.** contribution
_____	10. to think of	**j.** council
_____	11. to defend	**k.** delegate
_____	12. buying and selling	**l.** draw up
_____	13. nonelected government officials	**m.** federal
_____	14. related to a city	**n.** hold off
_____	15. income	**o.** municipal
_____	16. to prepare	**p.** parliament
_____	17. to be brave when threatened	**q.** point
_____	18. independent	**r.** proposal
_____	19. to delay	**s.** regime
		t. resolution
		u. revenue
		v. ruler
		w. stand up for
		x. stand up to

B. Answer each question with a word from the word form chart.

1. What person has the most power in a government?
2. What person represents other people?
3. If you believe strongly in an idea, what do you do?
4. What can you do if someone threatens you?
5. What government body can make laws?
6. What does a government get from taxes?
7. What is the system of offices that administers a government?
8. What is a very authoritarian government?
9. What should you do if someone requests money for a good cause?
10. If you are not sure of a decision, what should you do?
11. Who gives advice to the head of the government?
12. What do you do when you decide on a specific plan?
13. What can you do with your finger to show someone directions?
14. What can you see on television to make you buy something?

Study Exercises

C. Write **T** if the sentence is true and **F** if it is false.

_____ **1.** In a federal system, the central authority has complete power.

_____ **2.** A bureaucrat always works in a municipal government.

_____ **3.** Proposals are always accepted.

_____ **4.** A mayor is the head of a federal government.

_____ **5.** If something is proven to be true, it is confirmed.

_____ **6.** If you want something to happen quickly, you should hold off on it.

_____ **7.** A ruler is a prominent person in the government.

_____ **8.** When you participate in a discussion, you contribute your ideas.

_____ **9.** The Bureau of Commerce regulates trade.

_____ **10.** People's heads end in a point.

_____ **11.** Creative people rarely come up with new ideas.

_____ **12.** To stand up for something is the same as to back down.

_____ **13.** Egypt is on a point of land.

_____ **14.** A councilor is one of a group of people.

_____ **15.** A member of Parliament is a government official.

D. Change each underlined word to a word or phrase from the word form chart. Do not change the meaning of the sentence.

_____ **1.** The president's <u>speech</u> to the United Nations was shown on television.

_____ **2.** Many people in the Soviet Union suffered under the <u>powerful government</u> of Joseph Stalin.

_____ **3.** The councilors <u>wrote</u> an official plan to increase the government's <u>revenue</u>.

_____ **4.** Everyone in the office <u>gave</u> time and energy to the project.

_____ **5.** The newspaper editor accused local <u>government workers</u> of being corrupt.

_____ **6.** My landlord will make me move if I do not <u>find and give him</u> the rent before Friday.

_____ **7.** A <u>representative group</u> of citizens called on the president to ask for lower taxes.

_____ **8.** The president <u>asked</u> all of the citizens to help him improve the country's economy.

_____ **9.** A government councilor <u>suggested</u> an amendment to the Constitution.

_____ **10.** A good negotiator must be able to <u>find solutions for</u> disagreements quickly.

E.   Read the passage and answer the questions that follow.

How does an idea become a law in the United States? First, one of the representatives in Congress must propose that the law be considered. This proposal is given to the appropriate committee; for example, the commerce committee would study a
5   resolution to change sales taxes. The committee then makes recommendations to the whole assembly, and there is a period of discussion before the vote. During the weeks of discussion, delegations from groups who are interested in the resolution may call on representatives to stand up for their point of view. In
10 special cases the president may be interested in the proposed law and may make a special address to Congress or the people. With all of these different people coming up with suggestions and making changes, a resolution rarely passes in its original form. Usually some amendments are added to make it more acceptable
15 to more people.
         If a resolution receives enough votes to pass in one assembly, it must then be considered in the other. Delegates from both assemblies may meet to draw up a compromise proposal. If they succeed, and the legislation is approved, it is then the
20 responsibility of the bureaucracy to carry out all of the parts of the laws.

1. Write two words that are used in the passage to mean "a suggested law."

_____

_____

2. What is the role of special delegations? _____

_____

3. What can the president do if he is interested? _____

_____

4. Give two reasons why the final law may be different from the original proposal.

a. _____

b. _____

5. What is the role of nonelected government officials in this process? _____

_____

Follow-up

F.   Dictation: Write the sentences that your teacher reads aloud.

1. _____
2. _____
3. _____
4. _____
5. _____

G.   Answer the following questions.

1. Does your country have a federal system of government? Explain.
2. Name some offices or departments in the bureaucracy of your country.
3. Would you like to have a bureaucratic job? Why or why not?
4. Have you ever been chosen as a delegate from a group you belong to? Explain.
5. Does your country have a parliament? Where does it meet?
6. Who is the head of your government?
7. Have you contributed money to any good cause lately? Which one?
8. Name something that is important for you to stand up for.
9. What is your government's main source of revenue?
10. What proposal would you like to make to the head of this school?
11. What is your favorite commercial on TV or radio?

Education

Word Form Chart

NOUN	VERB	ADJECTIVE	ADVERB
background			
certificate	certify	certified	
certification		certifiable	certifiably
classmate			
comprehensiveness		comprehensive	comprehensively
context	contextualize	contextualized	contextually
degree			
	determine	determining	
dullness	dull	dull	dully
faculty			
	get through		
	get through with		
	go back		
	go on		
	go through with		
ignorance		ignorant	ignorantly
intellect		intellectual	intellectually
intellectual			
	keep up with		
narration	narrate	narrative	
narrator			
narrative			
nursery			
nursery school			
		outstanding	outstandingly
rudiment		rudimentary	
sponsor	sponsor	sponsored	
sponsorship		sponsoring	

NOUN	VERB	ADJECTIVE	ADVERB
suspension	suspend	suspended	
theme		thematic	thematically
vocation		vocational	vocationally

Definitions and Examples

1. **sponsor** [a person or institution which supports a person or idea by arguing for it and/or providing money for it; an advocate]

   > The Saudi Educational Mission is the major **sponsor** of Saudi Arabian students studying abroad.
   > Private television programs are **sponsored** by businesses which buy advertising.
   > A member of Parliament may **sponsor** a resolution that will help his region.

2. **nursery school** [a school for children under age five]

   > Children may go to **nursery school** before they begin elementary school.
   > **Nursery school** is not compulsory, but some parents think that it gives their children an advantage later.

3. **nursery** (a) [a room especially for children]

   > Some babies sleep with their parents instead of in a **nursery**.
   > The **nursery** is usually not the neatest place in a house.
   > The smaller children stayed in the **nursery** during church service.

   (b) [a place where plants are grown for sale or experimentation]

   > **Nurseries** sell both houseplants and small trees.
   > Large universities with agricultural departments may have **nurseries** where special varieties of seeds are developed.

4. **rudimentary** [elementary; related to basic facts]

   > A **rudimentary** knowledge of computers may soon be a requirement for getting a good job.
   > Children learn the **rudiments** of mathematics in their first few years of school.

5. **outstanding** (a) [excellent; superior to others in the same category]

   > Students with **outstanding** academic records may win scholarships.
   > Professor Cary has a reputation as an **outstanding** lecturer. His classes are always well attended.

   (b) [not resolved (used with problems or debts)]

   > At the end of the contract negotiations, there were many **outstanding** areas of disagreement; it was impossible to reach a compromise.
   > People who buy everything on credit always have **outstanding** debts.

6. **vocation** [an occupation, especially one that is very suitable for a person]

>High school counselors sometimes give students advice about choosing a **vocation**.
>
>A **vocational** school gives students technical skills to prepare them for jobs.

7. **degree** (a) [an academic title given to a person who has completed certain studies at the university level]

>Students in the United States receive a bachelor of arts (B.A.) **degree** if they successfully finish four years of study. A master of arts (M.A.) **degree** requires at least one extra year of study. The highest **degree** is the doctor of philosophy (Ph.D.).

(b) [a relative measurement or amount of relationship, progress, or distance]

>The student's bad attitude affected his grades to a greater **degree** than he had expected; in other words, it had more influence than he had thought it would.
>
>Our **degree** of ignorance about how people learn language is surprising, considering how much research has been done.

>(c) [2-15: a measure of temperature]

>>Zero **degrees** Celsius is the same as thirty-two **degrees** Farenheit.

8. **comprehensive** (a) [including a wide range of knowledge or material]

>A final exam in a class may be **comprehensive**, including questions about every subject discussed during the semester.
>
>Newspapers often do not describe events **comprehensively**. Instead, they give only the main facts.

>(b) **comprehend** [5-24: to understand]

>>She did not **comprehend** most of what the teacher said and decided to change to the beginning class.

9. **theme** (a) [a topic (often of a piece of writing, music, or art)]

>A major **theme** in this author's work is the lack of understanding between parents and children.
>
>Religious **themes** are common in European art of the fourteenth century.

(b) [a short piece of writing done as a school exercise]

>When I was studying French, the teacher required us to write a one-page **theme** every week.

10. **suspend** (a) [to take away an advantage or permission, usually as punishment]

> The head of the school **suspended** three students for hitting each other.
>   The students were not allowed to attend school for three weeks.
> If a driver is caught drinking alcohol while he is driving, his license will
>   be **suspended** for one year.

(b) [to hang, usually in a way that allows free movement]

> A lamp may be **suspended** from the ceiling of a room.
> Wet clothing may be **suspended** from a rope to dry.

11. **certificate** [a document that confirms that something is true or that
something has been done]

> If students complete this English course with no more
>   than eight absences, they receive a **certificate** of
>   attendance.
> To get a university identification card, you must have
>   a letter that **certifies** that you are a full-time student.
> Teachers in U.S. public schools must be **certified** by a
>   state Department of Education. To earn **certification**,
>   a teacher must take special courses at a university.

12. **background** (a) [a person's experience and education]

> I have studied music, but my **background** is limited to traditional pieces.
>   I have no experience playing contemporary music.

(b) [ancestry]

> My family's **background** is German, Irish, and Czech. I have ancestors of
>   all of those nationalities.

(c) [the historical or supporting causes for a situation]

> Current political movements in Latin America can only be understood
>   against a **background** of U.S. involvement there.
> To understand the organization of school systems in the United States,
>   you must have political and religious **background** information.

(d) [a noise, picture, or space that is not the main focus]

> It is difficult to understand someone over the telephone if there is a lot of
>   noise in the **background**.
> The photograph showed a small city with distant mountains in the
>   **background**.

13. **dull** (a) [not intelligent or clever; not alert]

> Instructors must have extra patience with **dull** students.
> After the accident, the driver could not stand up. He just looked **dully** around without understanding what had happened.

(b) [not sharp]

> A **dull** knife is not very useful.
> Scissors get **dull** if you do not take care of them.

(c) [1-25: boring, not interesting or bright]

> The student fell asleep during the **dull** class.
> The walls of the classroom were painted a **dull** green.

14. **faculty** (a) [the instructors at a school]

> After a student finishes his Ph.D. degree, he may join the **faculty** of a university.
> The **faculty** of the physics department voted to request a salary increase.

(b) [an ability]

> Good poets have an extraordinary **faculty** of observation.

15. **narrative** [a story; a description of real or fictional events]

> A university course called "The English **Narrative**" might require reading of adventure stories like Huckleberry Finn by Mark Twain.
> History books are usually written in **narrative** style, describing political and social changes in chronological order.

16. **intellectual** [related to the mind and reasoning rather than to the emotions]

> Universities are centers of **intellectual** activity.
> During popular revolutions, **intellectuals** are sometimes forced to do manual work.

17. **keep up with** (a) [to maintain the same speed as; not to fall behind in]

> To **keep up with** the work in this course, you need to study for several hours every night.
> The small child had to run in order to **keep up with** his big brother.
> It is important for doctors to **keep up with** developments in medical technology.

(b) [to maintain contact with]

> It is difficult for me to **keep up with** my friends in other cities because I rarely write letters.

18. **determine** (a) [to be the cause of; to influence]

>   Students' success in school is **determined** by many factors, including
>   attitude and background.
>   The climate and the materials available **determine** the kinds of houses
>   people build.

>   (b) [2-24: to find an answer or explanation]

>>   Using complex tools, astronomers were able to **determine** the
>>   exact temperature of three areas of the moon.

>   (c) **determination** [5-20: a strong and firm purpose or intention]

>>   A winning team needs both skill and **determination**.
>>   Martin was **determined** to win the game, so he cheated.

19. **go back** (to) [to return]

>   Ali came here from Turkey. After earning a degree in computer science,
>   he **went back**.
>   I recently **went back to** the town where I was born, in order to find
>   information about my background.
>   When Frances's new plan did not work out, she had to **go back to** her
>   original one.

20. **get through with** [to finish]

>   Most students **get through with** high school when they are eighteen
>   years old.
>   When the delegate **got through with** his speech, other representatives
>   began to propose amendments to his resolution.

21. **get through** [to endure]

>   It is easy to **get through** a severe winter if you have warm clothing and a
>   well-heated house.
>   Some students **get through** examination periods by drinking a lot of coffee
>   to keep them awake.

22. **go through with** [to carry out; to put a plan into effect despite difficulties or
hesitation]

>   After the first semester of medical school, some students decide not to **go
>   through with** their plans to become doctors.
>   The government will **go through with** the new tax plan although many of
>   the delegates oppose it.

23. **go on** (with) [to continue]

>   Many people **go on with** their education after finishing high school.
>   The professor **went on with** his lecture even after the class time had
>   ended.
>   The graduate student worked hard to complete his studies; however,
>   when his money ran out, he realized he could not **go on**.

24. **ignorance** (a) [lack of knowledge]

> Someone who has little formal education may be **ignorant** of history, but very knowledgeable about practical matters.
>
> Sometimes children do dangerous things out of **ignorance**; the same behavior in adults, who should know better, shows stupidity.

> (b) [3-11: to leave someone out of a group; not to pay attention to someone or something]

> > After the teacher had answered five of Jim's questions, she decided to **ignore** him for the rest of the lesson.

25. **classmate** [a person who is in the same class at school]

> Do you still keep up with your **classmates** from elementary school?
>
> Children in nursery school must learn to share with their **classmates**.

26. **context** [the part of a written or spoken statement where a word occurs; the situation in which an event occurs]

> The **context** in which a word is used can help you understand it; other words and the main idea of the paragraph give clues to the meaning.
>
> It is difficult to understand any historical event with out **contextualizing** it: you must know what happened before, who was involved, and what the common beliefs of the period were.

Introductory Exercises

A.   Match each word with its definition.

_____ 1. the instructors in a school	**a.** background
_____ 2. an academic title	**b.** certificate
_____ 3. a room for children	**c.** comprehensive
_____ 4. a person's experience and education	**d.** degree
_____ 5. a story	**e.** determine
_____ 6. an especially suitable occupation	**f.** dull
_____ 7. a topic	**g.** faculty
_____ 8. including a wide range of material	**h.** get through
_____ 9. superior to others in the same category	**i.** get through with
_____ 10. to endure	**j.** go back
_____ 11. not intelligent or clever	**k.** go on with
_____ 12. to return	**l.** go through with
_____ 13. basic	**m.** ignorant
_____ 14. to finish	**n.** intellectual
_____ 15. to be the cause of	**o.** keep up with
_____ 16. to maintain the same speed	**p.** narrative
_____ 17. related to the mind	**q.** nursery
_____ 18. without knowledge	**r.** outstanding
	s. rudimentary
	t. sponsor
	u. suspend
	v. theme
	w. vocation

B.   Answer each question with a word from the word form chart.

1. What does a student receive after successfully completing four years at a university?
2. Who may pay for a student's education?
3. What kind of student learns very slowly?
4. What kind of school can a student attend to learn television repair?
5. What kind of school may a three-year-old child attend?
6. What kind of person reads many books and thinks a lot?
7. What kind of fiction tells a story?
8. What kind of exam includes all of the information in a course?
9. What part of a picture is not the major focus?
10. Who teaches in a university?
11. What may happen to a student who frequently breaks the rules in school?
12. What is the main idea of a narrative?
13. What can you do if you want to see a place again?
14. How can you describe an extraordinarily good student?
15. What kind of knowledge do you need before you study the advanced areas of a subject?

16. What are the parts of a sentence before and after a particular word?

17. What are people who attend the same classes in school?

Study Exercises

C. Write **T** if the sentence is true and **F** if it is false.

_____ **1.** Outstanding students are usually dull.

_____ **2.** The theme of a narrative is the same as its main idea.

_____ **3.** Someone with a rudimentary knowledge of mathematics could easily be a physicist.

_____ **4.** A certificate is usually a piece of paper.

_____ **5.** Doctors should keep up with current medical technology.

_____ **6.** The amount of moisture in the air determines the number and the type of clouds in the sky.

_____ **7.** There are several kinds of university degrees.

_____ **8.** People of many national backgrounds live in the United States.

_____ **9.** A person who tells a story is a narration.

_____ **10.** A determined person rarely goes through with plans he has made.

_____ **11.** A dull knife cuts things easily.

_____ **12.** Most people go back to high school after they earn their degree.

_____ **13.** Carpets are often suspended from the floor near the windows.

_____ **14.** Students who do not get through with their studies earn a degree.

_____ **15.** One way to keep up with friends is to write letters.

_____ **16.** People get through their lives by dying.

_____ **17.** "Dull," "stupid," and "ignorant" all mean the same thing.

D. Complete the analogies with a word or phrase from the word form chart in this unit.

1. staff : office :: _____ : school

2. university : adult :: _____ : child

3. history : country :: _____ : person

4. physical : body :: _____ : mind

5. certificate : course :: _____ : university

6. complex : advanced :: _____ : basic

7. topic : discussion :: _____ : painting

8. desert : water :: _____ : information

E.   Circle the letter of each word that can complete the phrase. More than one completion is correct in each group.

1. go back
   a. home
   b. the car
   c. to school
   d. there
   e. it

2. go through with
   a. the door
   b. your plan
   c. it
   d. the resolution
   e. a cold winter

3. keep up with
   a. their work
   b. my old friends
   c. them
   d. suspension
   e. out of here

4. get through with
   a. the work
   b. finish
   c. my studies
   d. a pasture
   e. a meeting

5. go on with
   a. your speech
   b. that
   c. the top
   d. to the store
   e. the conversation

F.   Read the passage and answer the questions that follow.

In the United States, teachers in all public elementary and secondary schools are required by the government to be certified. The exact requirements for certification are determined by the state in which a teacher is working, but they always include an
5   undergraduate degree. In addition, teachers must usually get through several semesters of courses in educational methods and child psychology. Many states also require that teachers go back to the university regularly, even after they have joined the faculty of a school. They consider this to be necessary vocational training for
10   teachers to keep up with developments in education.

While most people approve of this system, there are some problems with it. Teachers are not generally required to have comprehensive knowledge of the subject they teach; in fact, some know little more than the rudiments. On the other hand, someone
15   who has an outstanding intellectual reputation will not be allowed to teach in public schools without being certified. In general, however, the system works, and it will probably not be drastically amended in the near future.

Write **T** if the sentence is true and **F** if it is false.

_____ **1.** Teacher certification is required by the government for public school teachers.

_____ **2.** All school faculty must be certified by the schools they work for.

_____ **3.** All teachers in public elementary schools must have a university degree.

_____ **4.** Teachers may be ignorant of advanced ideas in their subject area.

_____ **5.** An outstanding intellectual reputation guarantees a teacher a good job.

Answer the following questions.

6. Who determines the requirements for certification? _____

_____

7. What courses are part of a teacher's vocational training? _____

_____

8. Why do teachers have to go back to school after they have their degrees?

_____

_____

Follow-up

G. Dictation: Write the sentences that your teacher reads aloud.

1. _____

2. _____

3. _____

4. _____

5. _____

H. Answer the following questions.

1. How many years does it take to get a university degree in your country?

2. Must teachers in your country be certified? How do they earn their certification?

3. Do you know of any government agencies or companies that sponsor study abroad? Which ones?

4. How many faculty members does your school have?

5. How many classmates do you have?

6. Are there any vocational schools in your city? What do they teach?

7. What is the educational background of most high school teachers in your country?
8. In your opinion, what should be included in a comprehensive language course?
9. Name something in your life that you would like to get through with.
10. Name a subject you are completely ignorant about.
11. What factors determine whether a person succeeds in school?
12. Do most children in your country go to nursery school? What do children do there?
13. Will you go on with your studies after you finish this course? What will you do?
14. Are students ever suspended from your school? What happens to them?

I. Answer the following questions.

1. Describe an outstanding teacher that you have had.
2. Imagine that you are talking to a student from the United States, and explain the system of education in your country.
3. Think of a recent political event in your country. What contextual information is necessary to fully understand this event?

Food

Word Form Chart

NOUN	VERB	ADJECTIVE	ADVERB
absorption	absorb	absorbent	
artificiality		artificial	artificially
authenticity	authenticate	authentic	authentically
bit			
	cut up		
		daily	daily
digestion	digest	digestive	
digestibility		digestible	
	do without		
	eat up		
economy	economize	economical	economically
economizer			
exaggeration	exaggerate	exaggerated	exaggeratedly
ethnicity		ethnic	ethnically
famine		famished	
nourishment	nourish	nourished	
		nourishing	
undernourishment	undernourish	undernourished	
odor		odorless	
		odoriferous	
perishability	perish	perishable	
preservative	preserve	preserved	
preserve			
protein			
ripeness	ripen	ripe	
		ripened	
		ripening	
rot	rot	rotten	
		rotted	
		rotting	

NOUN	VERB	ADJECTIVE	ADVERB
spread	spread (spread, spread) throw away use up	spreading	
vitamin			

Definitions and Examples

1. **famine** [a severe and comprehensive shortage of food during which people may starve to death]

    In 1985 and 1986, a **famine** in East Africa caused the deaths of millions of people.

    In casual speech, people say "I'm **famished**" to mean that they are extremely hungry.

2. **daily** [every day]

    Good health requires a balanced diet and **daily** exercise.

    Most people in Western countries eat three meals **daily**: breakfast, lunch, and dinner.

3. **do without** [to be able to live without (something)]

    This soup would be good with meat in it, but we can **do without** it.

    During famines people have sometimes **done without** food for several days.

    People who live in the suburbs of large cities in the United States often cannot **do without** a car.

4. **economize** [to use resources (such as income, food, or energy) carefully; to avoid waste]

    Shopping carefully and comparing prices at different stores are good ways to **economize**.

    Eating in an inexpensive restaurant can be as **economical** as eating at home. In other words, it might not cost more.

    If we do not use our energy resources **economically**, we may have a serious shortage in a few years.

5. **rot** [to fall into pieces and become unusable because of age or bad maintenance]

    Rotten fruits turn black and often smell bad.

    Old wood **rots** because of moisture and bugs.

    A **rotten** person is one who has become bad or corrupt.

6. **odor** [a smell, often bad]

> Rotten eggs have a horrible **odor**.
> Many flowers have a very pleasant **odor**; others are **odorless**.

7. **perishable** [likely to rot quickly; easily injured]

> **Perishable** food, such as fresh meat, should be kept cold and used within a few days.
> In many countries, people shop daily for **perishable** foods.

8. **perish** [to die (usually used with people)]

> People **perish** if they have to do without food and water for a long time.
> Thousands of soldiers **perished** in World War II.

9. **Ripe** (a) [completely developed, especially by time or experience; (with food, used for fruit and vegetables)]

> **Ripe** fruit is often soft and has a strong, pleasant odor.
> If a tomato is green, you can put it in the sun to **ripen** it.

(b) [ready for some specific purpose]

> "The country is **ripe** for a change" could be said by a politician during an election. It means that the country is ready for something different.

10. **use up** {separable} [to use completely, to finish the total amount (of a resource, food, or something else with a limited quantity)]

> This fruit is very ripe; we should **use** it **up** before it gets rotten.
> In the 1970s many people were afraid of **using up** all the world's energy resources.

11. **absorb** (a) [to take into itself]

> If you spill water, you can use a cloth or some other **absorbent** material to clean it up.
> These new apartments have special ceilings which **absorb** sounds. People who live there are never bothered by noise from their neighbors.
> An immigrant has to **absorb** a lot of information about his new country's language and culture.

(b) [to get the full attention of; to interest greatly]

> Children sometimes become so **absorbed** in a game that they do not hear someone calling them.
> The newspaper says that this movie is "the **absorbing** story of two people who are looking for a new life."

12. **digest** (a) [to change food into a form that the body can use]

> Kim went to the doctor because of problems with her **digestion**.
> The stomach is part of the human **digestive** system.
> Food must be **digested** so that nutrients can be absorbed into the blood.

(b) [to absorb mentally; to understand and remember]

> This article is very complex. I had to read it twice before I could **digest** its main points.
> Some people cannot easily **digest** information that they hear; they prefer to get information by reading.

13. **authentic** [genuine; real]

> Many people cannot tell the difference between an **authentic**, handwoven Persian carpet and one made in a factory.
> To **authenticate** a painting means to show that it is really the work of a certain artist.

14. **artificial** [made by people; not occurring in nature]

> People who want to lose weight often eat foods with an **artificial** sweetener instead of sugar.
> **Artificial** coloring is added to some foods to make them more attractive to people.

15. **throw away** {separable} [to reject or dismiss something because it is useless; to put something in the garbage]

> We **throw away** food when it gets rotten.
> My grandmother never **threw** anything **away**. Her basement was full of old clothing, letters, and other useless things.

16. **vitamin** [a natural, complex substance that is necessary for the human body to work correctly]

> **Vitamins** are usually identified by letters.
> **Vitamin** C is in oranges, and **vitamin** D is in milk.
> Some people take a **vitamin** pill daily.

17. **nourishment** [the food, vitamins, and other substances that are necessary for life and growth]

> It is especially important for pregnant women to get the proper **nourishment**.
> **Undernourished** children often have very thin arms and legs but large, round stomachs.
> During a famine, many people suffer from **undernourishment**.

18. **protein** [a complex chemical substance that occurs in all living matter and is essential for the growth and repair of animal cells]

> Meat is a good source of **protein**. We can also get **protein** from nuts and eggs.
> If a person's diet is lacking in **protein**, he will become very weak.

19. **spread** (a) [to become more widely known]

> Television is partly responsible for the modern **spread** of knowledge about events and customs in other countries.

(b) [to distribute further]

> To finish the cake, I **spread** a thick layer of cream on the top.
> A good painter **spreads** the paint on quickly and carefully.

(c) [to extend further in place or time]

> After three days of rain, flood waters had **spread** up to a half mile from the river.
> An infectious disease can **spread** quickly to a whole population.

20. **eat up** {separable} [consume; use all of]

> You may have your dessert after you **eat** your vegetables **up**.
> My new project at work is **eating up** all of my time; I am working extra hours and still cannot finish everything.

21. **exaggerate** [to make something seem bigger or more important than it really is]

> People often **exaggerate** when they tell a story in order to make the story funnier or more interesting.
> My neighbor says that the tomatoes in his garden weigh three pounds each, but I think he is **exaggerating**.

22. **bit** [a small amount]

> A **bit** of salt can make a big difference in the taste of food.
> If you can wait a **bit**, I will go with you. I should be ready in twenty minutes.

23. **preserve** (a) [to prepare food in a way that will make it last for a long time]

> Meat may be **preserved** by being dried, smoked, or salted.
> Many packaged foods contain chemical **preservatives** so that we do not have to use them up immediately.

(b) [to keep safe or in an unchanged form]

> It is difficult for people to **preserve** their dignity when they are poor and must beg for food.
> A wildlife **preserve** is a place where wild animals live under the protection of the government.

24. **cut up** {separable} [to cut into pieces]

> Since children cannot eat a large piece of meat, it is often necessary to **cut** it **up** for them.
> My father does not really like that vegetable, but he will eat it **cut up** in a salad.

25. **ethnic** [characteristic of a particular cultural, national, religious, or other socially-defined group in society]

      An **ethnic** restaurant is one that serves the traditional food of a particular national or cultural group.

      The largest **ethnic** groups in the United States are blacks and Hispanics.

Introductory Exercises

A.   Match each word or phrase with its definition.

___ 1. to avoid waste	**a.** absorb
___ 2. to change food so the body can use it	**b.** artificial
___ 3. to use completely	**c.** authentic
___ 4. bad and unusable because of age	**d.** bit
___ 5. to die	**e.** cut up
___ 6. starving	**f.** daily
___ 7. completely developed	**g.** digest
___ 8. to put in the garbage	**h.** economize
___ 9. a natural substance necessary for the body to work	**i.** exaggerate
___ 10. every day	**j.** famished
___ 11. to become more widely known	**k.** nourishment
___ 12. food and vitamins necessary for life and growth	**l.** odorless
___ 13. genuine; real	**m.** perish
___ 14. a small amount	**n.** preserve
___ 15. to make something seem bigger	**o.** ripe
___ 16. without any smell	**p.** rotten
___ 17. man-made	**q.** spread
___ 18. to keep safe	**r.** throw away
	s. use up
	t. vitamin

B.   Answer each question with a word from the word form chart in this unit.

1. What kind of food must be used quickly?
2. What's the matter with smelly, black vegetables?
3. What system in the body includes the stomach?
4. If you cannot have something, what must you do?
5. If fruit is ripe, but not yet rotten, what should you do?
6. What should you do with rotten food?
7. What happens to someone who does not get enough food?

8. How often do people need to eat?
9. Why do people shop carefully and compare prices?
10. How do you put butter on bread?
11. What do salesmen sometimes do when they describe their product?
12. How do people feel when they're very hungry?
13. How much should you eat if you're not very hungry?
14. What happens to the water in the pan when you cook rice?
15. What kind of restaurant serves the typical food of one social group?

Study Exercises

C. Write **T** if the sentence is true and **F** if it is false.

_____ 1. Plastic containers are perishable.

_____ 2. Fruit get ripe before it rots.

_____ 3. You have to cut up rice before you can eat it.

_____ 4. If you want to give a clear description of something you should exaggerate.

_____ 5. You can preserve books by putting them in water.

_____ 6. The sun is not an artificial source of light.

_____ 7. The heart is part of the digestive system.

_____ 8. Candy is not a good source of vitamins.

_____ 9. To economize is to cut down on your spending.

_____ 10. Ethnic food is the same in every country.

_____ 11. Famine is a common problem of wealthy people.

_____ 12. It is hard to spread something solid.

_____ 13. The odor of rotten eggs is terrible.

_____ 14. A piece of metal will absorb water.

D. Match each word or phrase with its opposite.

_____ 1. authentic

_____ 2. economize

_____ 3. preserve

_____ 4. throw away

_____ 5. do without

_____ 6. artificial

_____ 7. bit

a. waste
b. keep
c. plenty
d. fake
e. have
f. destroy
g. natural
h. increase
i. save

E. Complete the analogies with a word or phrase from the word form chart.

1. heart : circulation :: stomach : _____

2. person : corrupt :: fruit : _____

3. eyes : sight :: nose : _____

4. preserve : treasure :: _____ : garbage

5. water : thirst :: food : _____

6. big : vast :: hungry : _____

F. In each blank, write the most appropriate two- or three-word verb from the following list. Add a pronoun to each verb.

call on	draw up	keep up with
come up with	eat up	stand up to
cut down on	get through	throw away
cut up	go on with	use up
do without	hold off on	

1. This produce is rotten. You ought to _____ .

2. I have an appointment tomorrow to sign a lease. My landlord is _____ today.

3. I'm nervous about making a decision, but I cannot _____ any longer—I must decide now.

4. These pears are very ripe. You should _____ before they rot.

5. The child could not eat the large pieces of meat, so her mother _____ .

6. If your neighbor is making you angry, don't be afraid: _____ !

7. I cannot find the information I wanted, but I have to finish this paper, so I will just _____ .

8. Two-year-old children have a lot of energy. It is sometimes hard to _____ .

9. The explorer's trip down the river was very dangerous. He almost didn't _____ alive.

10. When the new ambassador arrived in Geneva, several politicians _____ in his office.

G. Read the passage and answer the questions that follow.

> In much of East Africa in 1984, there was no rain. Because of that lack of rain, complicated by bad government management of scarce resources, there was a famine. By the end of the year, more than 300,000 people had starved or had perished from diseases
> 5 related to undernourishment. At first, the rest of the world knew little about the problem, but finally reports of the disaster began to spread. The governments involved protested that many of the reports were exaggerated, but both journalists and medical personnel confirmed their validity.
> 10 The shortage of food was only the beginning of the problem. When other countries began to contribute food, it could not always be used up fast enough. Doctors discovered that some children had forgotten how to eat because they had done without food for so long. Both children and adults had problems digesting food after so
> 15 much time without it. In addition, some African governments delayed or prohibited shipment of food to needy areas for political reasons. Some ethnic groups received less food, for example, because of conflicts with their country's rulers. In some places, the management was so poor that wheat rotted on boats while people
> 20 did without even one daily meal.

1. Why did 300,000 Africans die? _____

    _____

2. Name two problems that the starving people had after more food arrived.

    a. _____

    b. _____

3. According to journalists, were reports of the suffering true? _____

    _____

4. What happened when wheat stayed on the boats for too long? _____

    _____

Follow-up

H. Dictation: Write the sentences that your teacher reads aloud.

1. _____

2. _____

3. _____

4. _____

5. _____

I.   Answer the following questions.

1. What foods are difficult to digest?
2. What foods are not perishable?
3. What are two things that are easy to spread? Not easy to spread?
4. What are some methods of preserving meat?
5. Is there a good ethnic restaurant in your town? Describe the food there.
6. What are three things that you do daily?
7. Where do you buy clothing if you want to economize?
8. What are three things with a bad odor?
9. What do you eat to get protein?
10. What food must be cut up before you eat it?
11. What is one situation where people tend to exaggerate?
12. What is a material that will not absorb moisture?
13. What are some foods that contain artificial coloring?

J.   You must buy and prepare the food for your family. Describe what you should think about to be sure that they have a healthy diet.

Society

Word Form Chart

NOUN	VERB	ADJECTIVE	ADVERB
	arise		
behalf			
	break in		
	break into		
	call for		
		democratic	democratically
	face up to		
	get ahead		
integration	integrate	integrated	
justification	justify	justifiable	justifiably
movement			
objection	object	objectionable	objectionably
objector			
oppression	oppress	oppressed	
oppressor		oppressive	oppressively
prejudice	prejudice	prejudiced	
		prejudicial	prejudicially
privilege		privileged	
radical		radical	radically
	reciprocate	reciprocal	
rigidity		rigid	rigidly
scope			
tolerance	tolerate	tolerant	tolerantly
intolerance		intolerant	intolerantly
undertaking	undertake		
	(undertook, undertaken)		
unity	unite	united	

Definitions and Examples

1. **get ahead** [to be successful; to advance]

   Getting a good education is one way to **get ahead** in life.
   It is possible to **get ahead** in school if you study hard.

2. **oppress** (a) [to control by force or authority]

   The strong military government **oppressed** the people.
   Sometimes children who feel **oppressed** by their parents run away from home.

   (b) [to cause extreme discomfort]

   The **oppressive** heat made working difficult, and everyone hoped it would soon rain.

3. **justify** [to show or prove to be right or valid]

   The robber tried to **justify** his crime by saying that he needed money to pay his bills.
   The judge did not feel the thief had any **justification** for breaking the law.

4. **object (to)** (a) [to say that you disagree with or disapprove of something]

   John's mother **objects to** the way he dresses; in fact, she does not like the way he does many things.
   Older people **object to** paying a high price for groceries; they remember when food was much cheaper.
   Anyone who has an **objection** to getting up early should never take a class at 8:00 A.M.
   Jim asked if he could smoke in the house, but his roommate **objected**.

   (b) [2-21: something that can be seen or felt]

   There were several interesting **objects** on the table, but the man could not identify them.

5. **prejudice** [a negative feeling toward someone or something, formed without knowledge or factual evidence]

   People are often **prejudiced** against someone of a different race or religion.
   Children learn **prejudices** by listening to older people.

6. **movement** (a) [the activities of a group of people to achieve a specific goal]

   The goal of the American civil rights **movement** in the 1960s was to eliminate prejudicial treatment of blacks.
   The labor **movement** was organized nationally in the United States during the nineteenth century.

   (b) [assumed: motion]

   The **movement** involved in lifting heavy boxes can hurt your back.

7. **radical** (a) [extreme]

> He made a **radical** change in his plans; instead of taking a vacation at the beach, he will go to the mountains.
> Since she lost so much weight, she looks **radically** different.

(b) [extreme social change]

> My political science professor had very **radical** ideas; he thought that severe changes needed to be made in our system of government.

8. **on behalf of** [as the agent of; on the part of]

> One of the teachers spoke **on behalf of** her student who could not speak English and explained the situation to the policeman.
> Parents must often make decisions **on behalf of** their children when they are too young to make decisions for themselves.

9. **face up to** [to recognize the importance of]

> The man finally **faced up to** his smoking problem and decided to give up cigarettes.
> Adults should have the ability to **face up to** their difficulties.

10. **undertake** (a) [to decide to do; to agree to do]

> After many meetings, the engineering firm agreed to **undertake** the project of building the new bridge.

(b) [a task, often difficult and/or complex]

> Finishing a graduate degree can be a long and difficult **undertaking**.

11. **arise** [to result; to begin from]

> Prejudice often **arises** from ignorance.
> It can be a big undertaking to face up to each new problem as it **arises**.

12. **integrate** (a) [to open to people of all races without restriction]

> Although schools, housing, and industry must be **integrated** by law in the United States, prejudice often makes **integration** difficult and unpleasant.
> The **integration** movement partly arose from the many years of oppression experienced by blacks.

(b) [to combine into one]

> A wise employer listens to his employees before he makes a decision and then **integrates** the best parts of their ideas with his.

13. **privilege** [a right which is given as a special advantage]

> Teachers at some universities have the **privilege** of free parking.
> Problems often arise in a society when one group enjoys more **privileges** than another.

14. **reciprocal** [performed, felt, or experienced by both sides]

> Integration in the United States has been difficult because of **reciprocal** hatred between some members of different races.
> A friend invited me to a restaurant for dinner last week; to **reciprocate**, I cooked a very nice meal at home for her.

15. **tolerate** [to allow to happen; to endure]

> I cannot **tolerate** rudeness; it makes me angry when someone is not polite.
> Some people are very **intolerant** of children and do not like to be near them.
> People who are **tolerant** of others do not have prejudices toward them.

16. **unite** [to join together]

> If people of different races **unite** against prejudice, they can abolish it.
> The **United** States was formed when thirteen states **united**.

17. **rigid** [unbending; very firm]

> Mr. Smith had **rigid** beliefs and was never willing to change his mind.
> It is not a good idea to run on a very **rigid** surface because it is bad for the feet; grass and dirt are better running surfaces than streets and sidewalks.

18. **scope** [the area covered by a particular activity or subject]

> The **scope** of the professor's knowledge in her field was very wide; she seemed to know everything about her subject.
> The **scope** of the investigation has not been decided; however, it might include very high government officials.

19. **democratic** (a) [believing in a social equality]

> That wealthy woman is very **democratic**; she treats both rich and poor alike.
> People who are **democratic** do not believe that those with a high social position should have special privileges.

> (b) [2-11: describing a government by the people]

> > The United States has a **democratic** government.

20. **break in (on)** [to interrupt]

> The boy's mother was very angry when he rudely **broke in on** her conversation with her friends.
> Every time the child tried to tell his father what happened, his older sister **broke in** and tried to explain her version of the story first.

21. **break into** [to enter with force]

> While the family was eating dinner downstairs, a robber **broke into** the house through an upstairs window and stole money and jewelry.
> After **breaking into** more than thirty houses, the thief was finally caught.

22. **call for** (a) [to go and get]

> The movie starts at 9:00, so I will **call for** you at 8:30.
> Mr. Edwards always **called for** his daughter at school at 3:15 P.M.

(b) [to be appropriate for; to demand]

> The criminal's actions **called for** a heavy punishment, and the judge
> sentenced him to ten years in prison.
> The racial problems in the United States appeared to **call for** integration;
> however, this policy has not been totally successful in abolishing prejudice.
> The politician who lost the election **called for** another vote.

Introductory Exercises

A. Match each word or phrase with its definition.

_____ **1.** unbending; very firm

_____ **2.** to allow to happen; to endure

_____ **3.** performed, felt, or experienced by both sides

_____ **4.** to open to people of all races without restriction

_____ **5.** to recognize the importance of; to oppose bravely

_____ **6.** to result; to begin

_____ **7.** to decide or agree to do

_____ **8.** extreme

_____ **9.** as agent or support for

_____ **10.** a negative feeling toward someone or something

_____ **11.** the activities of a group of people to achieve a specific goal

_____ **12.** to say that you disagree with or disapprove of something

_____ **13.** to control by force or authority

_____ **14.** to show or prove to be right or valid

_____ **15.** to be successful

_____ **16.** a right which is given as a special advantage

_____ **17.** to join together

_____ **18.** believing in social equality

_____ **19.** the area covered by a particular activity or subject

a. arise
b. on behalf of
c. break in
d. break into
e. call for
f. democratic
g. face up to
h. get ahead
i. integrate
j. justify
k. object
l. oppress
m. movement
n. prejudice
o. privilege
p. radical
q. reciprocal
r. rigid
s. scope
t. tolerate
u. unite
v. undertake

B.   Answer each question with a word from the word form chart.

1. If you succeed in your business, what are you doing?
2. What is a person who controls another by force?
3. If your boss told you he was decreasing your salary, what might you do?
4. What is a person who has a negative feeling toward another person?
5. What word can describe a person who refuses to change his mind?
6. What is a person with extreme beliefs?
7. What do you call a school which is attended by people of different races?
8. What must you do with a problem?
9. If a person does a nice thing for you, what should you do?
10. What word can describe a person who believes that everyone is socially equal?
11. What should you not do if a teacher and another student are talking?
12. What do people hope robbers will not do to their houses?
13. If your clothes are at the laundry and you need them, what must you do?

Study Exercises

C.   Write **T** if the sentence is true and **F** if it is false.

___ 1. Tolerant people usually have few prejudices.

___ 2. A scope is an area where one builds a house.

___ 3. People who face up to their problems must often act bravely.

___ 4. People who are democratic feel that a few small groups should have special privileges.

___ 5. If you invite someone to go to dinner with you, it is rude to call for him.

___ 6. A person who has decided to undertake something has decided not to do it.

___ 7. A company which hires employees of different races is integrated.

___ 8. A friend who wants to help you find a job might speak to his boss on your behalf.

___ 9. Movements are sometimes successful in accomplishing their goals.

___ 10. A red-haired woman who dyed her hair black would probably not look radically different.

D.   Complete the analogies with a word or phrase from the word form chart in this unit.

1. swamp : concrete :: soft : __________

2. write : letter :: __________ : project

3. basic : right :: special : __________

   4. scatter : separate :: _____ : together

   5. size : home :: _____ : problem

   6. break up : fight :: _____ : conversation

   7. positive : negative :: _____ : fail

   8. strong: _____ :: weak : surrender

   9. ignorance : prejudice :: understanding : _____

  10. agree : support :: disagree : _____

E. Match each two- or three-word verb with its synonym. You may use a letter more than once.

____ **1.** cheer up	**a.** to become exhausted
____ **2.** give up	**b.** to collect and store supplies
____ **3.** clear up	**c.** to become less severe; to stop
____ **4.** let up	**d.** to reveal; to show the true situation
____ **5.** use up	**e.** to stop burning
____ **6.** wear out	**f.** to distribute
____ **7.** go out	**g.** to understand
____ **8.** give out	**h.** to make someone's mood improve
____ **9.** handout	**i.** to endure without complaint
____ **10.** put up with	**j.** to clear a surface
____ **11.** carry out	**k.** to surrender; to stop trying
____ **12.** carry on with	**l.** to do
____ **13.** give away	**m.** to become clear
	n. to continue with
	o. to use all of something until it is gone
	p. to build; to construct
	q. to clean a large three-dimensional space
	r. to use until no longer useful

F. In each blank, write the most appropriate word or phrase from the word form chart.

    The second half of the twentieth century has been a time of change for American blacks. From the time that they were brought over from Africa in the nineteenth century by force to work on the large farms in America, many American were (1) _____ against them because of the color of their skin. Some owners treated them well, but others (2) _____ them. As time went on, some Americans found it difficult to (3) _____ the treatment of blacks. In the 1960s, the civil rights (4) _____ became popular with blacks and also with white

Americans with (5) _____ ideas. One of the goals of the
movement was to obtain the same (6) _____ for blacks as white
Americans enjoyed. Another goal was (7) _____ of schools and
business. Although much progress has been made since the 1960s the
(8) _____ of the problem is still much wider than many people
realize.

Follow-up

G. Dictation: Write the sentences that your teacher reads aloud.

1. _____
2. _____
3. _____
4. _____
5. _____

H. Answer the following questions.

1. What would you do if someone behaved oppressively toward you?
2. Are your ideas rigid, or do you have an open mind? How do you know?
3. What kind of behavior do you find objectionable?
4. Are you usually able to face up to your problems, or do you try to avoid them? Give an example.
5. How do you plan to get ahead in life?
6. How do you feel about people who reciprocate evil for evil?
7. Are you conservative or radical in your thinking? Give an example.
8. What would you do if someone broke into your house?
9. Do you plan to undertake any project soon? What?
10. Have you ever been involved in a movement? What kind?

I. What kinds of prejudices do people in your country have? Is there a situation similar to the racial situation in the United States? Describe the scope of the problem and what is being done to solve it.

Family

Word Form Chart

NOUN	VERB	ADJECTIVE	ADVERB
adoption	adopt	adopted	
		adoptive	
bond	bind	bound	
		binding	
	break off		
depth	deepen	deep	deeply
descendant	descend	descending	
descent			
devotion	devote	devoted	devotedly
devotee			
era			
fondness		fond	fondly
frankness		frank	frankly
gene		genetic	genetically
genealogy		genealogical	genealogically
genealogist			
	get along		
	get on		
grounds	ground		
grown-up	grow up		
	have over		
heritage			
interference	interfere	interfering	
interval			
intimacy		intimate	intimately
maternity		maternal	maternally
maturity	mature	mature	maturely
immaturity		immature	immaturely
paternity		paternal	paternally

NOUN	VERB	ADJECTIVE	ADVERB
persuasion persuasiveness	persuade	persuasive	persuasively
	stand up take after talk over wait up		

Definitions and Examples

1. **adopt** [to take and raise or use as one's own]

    If a couple cannot have a child of their own, they may **adopt** one. An **adoption** agency interviews a couple thoroughly before giving them a baby. The **adoptive** parents must be mentally and physically healthy, and they must have enough money to raise a child.
    Many U.S. factories may **adopt** Japanese techniques for manufacturing cars.

2. **bond** [a connection, either emotional or physical; an obligation]

    There is usually a strong emotional **bond** between members of a family.
    The robbers left their victims **bound** to a chair in the basement; the police had to cut through the ropes to free them.
    A lease is a legally **binding** agreement; if you sign it, you must do what it says.

3. **break off** {separable} [to end abruptly]

    The old woman **broke off** all ties with her son when he married someone she did not approve of. The mother had asked him to end the relationship, but he refused to **break** it **off** and went ahead with the marriage.

4. **deep** (a) [extreme; strong]

    His love for his family was very **deep**.
    She had a **deep** interest in photography and took many courses in it.
    It is difficult to wake someone from a **deep** sleep.

    (b) [difficult to understand]

    That professor's lectures are very **deep**.
    My philosophy book is so **deep** that I have to read every chapter twice.

    (c) [dark (used with color)]

    After the sun sets, before it is completely dark, the sky is **deep** blue.

    (d) [low musical range]

    Men generally have **deeper** voices than women.
    Radio announcers often have **deep** voices.

    (e) [**1-23**: far down]

    The hotel swimming pool is twelve feet **deep**.
    Scientists use sound equipment to determine the **depth** of the ocean.

5. **devote** [to give all of one's attention to]

> Carl is a **devoted** child; he never married, but instead spent all of his life caring for his mother.
> Mother Theresa has **devoted** her life to helping the poor in India.
> Some signs of Muslim religious **devotion** are regular prayer and observance of Ramadan.

6. **mature** [fully developed or grown; ripe]

> The oldest child in a family often **matures** quickly, learning early to take responsibility for his siblings.
> Parents may get angry when their children behave **immaturely**.
> **Mature** plants grow more slowly than young ones.

7. **grounds** (a) [the basis for a belief, action, or argument]

> Possible **grounds** for divorce include cruelty and abandonment.
> Scientific arguments are **grounded** in facts, not opinions.

   (b) [the area around and belonging to a building]

> Although their house is small, it was expensive because the **grounds** are extensive.
> The university employs a crew of **grounds**keepers to take care of the grass, trees, and gardens.

8. **grow up** [to develop to maturity; to become an adult (used for people)]

> Children are often asked, "What do you want to be when you **grow up**?" In other words, "What job do you want to have when you're an adult?"
> Children sometimes call adults **grown-ups**.

9. **have over** {separable} [to entertain informally at one's house]

> I seldom **have** the neighbors **over** for dinner because my apartment is very small.
> Who are you **having over** tomorrow?

10. **heritage** [property, a tradition, or something else that is inherited from ancestors]

> Although immigrants must adjust to life in the United States, many groups try to preserve some of their ethnic **heritage**.
> My immigrant grandfather tried to deny his **heritage** by changing his name from Giuseppe to Joe.

11. **descendant** [the person or animal who comes from ones that existed before; the child, grandchild, etc.]

> It is important for us to use resources wisely so that our **descendants** will have enough.
> Some people believe that humans are **descended** from other animals.

12. **interfere** (a) [to be an obstacle]

Bob's father's refusal to lend him the car seriously **interfered** with Bob's plan for the evening.

(b) [to become involved in the life of someone else when you are not welcome]

In the United States, adults expect to be independent of their parents. If the parents try to be too involved in their children's lives, they are accused of **interfering**.

13. **era** [a period of time with some characteristic feature]

Geologists divide time into **eras**. They believe that ice covered the earth during the Pleistocene period of the Cenozoic era.

The colonial **era** of U.S. history was the seventeenth and eighteenth centuries; during that time the United States was governed by England.

14. **fond** [warmly affectionate; loving]

My grandmother was especially **fond** of my younger sister.
Foreigners are often surprised at Americans' **fondness** for their pets.

15. **interval** [the space between two points; the time between two events]

What is a suitable **interval** for a widow to wait before she marries again?
Highways in the United States usually have gas stations or truck stops at **intervals** of every ten or twenty miles.

16. **frank** [honest, direct, and sincere]

People who speak very **frankly** occasionally sound rude.
People who value **frankness** do not believe in hiding their feelings to protect other people.
The councilors reported that their discussions with the president had been **frank**.

17. **gene** [the very small part in a cell in the body that passes characteristics from parents to children]

The color of your eyes is **genetically** determined.
Some current **genetic** research is very controversial. Many people believe that scientists should not be allowed to change the natural organization of **genes**.

18. **genealogy** [the record of the descent of a family, group, or person from its ancestors]

Alfonso's **genealogy** can be found out from these old family papers.
A **genealogist** is a person who helps people locate information about their ancestors.

19. get along (with) [to have a good relationship with]

> High school students do not always **get along with** their parents; they feel that their parents interfere too much with what they want to do.
> My cousins are not really rude to each other, but they have never **gotten along** very well.

20. get on (with) (a) {mostly British} [get along with]

> I have never **gotten on** well **with** my neighbors; their children bother me and my dog bothers them.

> > (b) [5-8: to start; to continue with]

> > > The teacher told me to stop worrying about my assignment and just **get on with** it or I would never finish in time.

21. intimate (a) [related to the most personal and private parts of a person's life; emotionally close]

> **Intimate** friends are very close friends.
> If we say a man and woman are **intimate**, we may mean that they are physically as well as emotionally close.
> It usually takes a long time for **intimacy** to develop between people.

> (b) [private and informal]

> > If a restaurant advertises an "**intimate**" atmosphere, it means that it is small and the customers are treated like special friends.

22. maternal [characteristic of a mother]

> Do you believe that all women naturally have **maternal** feelings?
> The **maternity** floor of a hospital is the area for new babies and their mothers.
> Your **maternal** grandmother is your mother's mother.

23. paternal [characteristic of a father]

> Although he had no children, Michael had a **paternal** attitude toward his friends' children and often gave them advice.
> My **paternal** grandmother died when my father was born.

24. persuade [to convince; to change someone's opinion by argument]

> Parents may try to **persuade** their grown children to live in the same city.
> Politicians who run for office need great powers of **persuasion**; they even study techniques of convincing people to vote for them.
> If you do not believe something, a **persuasive** person can sometimes change your mind.

25. stand up {separable} [to not keep an appointment]

> A classmate said he would meet me at this restaurant at 8:00 P.M., but he never came. He **stood** me **up**!
> After being **stood up** three times, Carlos became very angry.

26. **take after** [to be similar to someone in some characteristic]

> My neighbor's daughter **takes after** her mother; both of them are very smart and very inflexible.
>
> All of my grandchildren **take after** their father; they have blond hair and brown eyes.

27. **talk over** {separable} [to discuss]

> My parents and I have always gotten along well because they are willing to **talk over** problems. If I disagree with something they tell me, we **talk** it **over** and try to reach a compromise.

28. **wait up (for)** [to stay awake at night, waiting for someone to come home]

> I am going to come home very late, so do not bother to **wait up for** me.
>
> When I lived with my parents, one of them always **waited up** to be sure I got home safely.

Introductory Exercises

A. Match each word or phrase with its definition.

_____ **1.** full development	**a.** adopt
_____ **2.** basis for a belief	**b.** bond
_____ **3.** connection	**c.** break off
_____ **4.** to be an obstacle	**d.** deep
_____ **5.** to become an adult	**e.** frank
_____ **6.** to convince	**f.** fondness
_____ **7.** to raise as one's own	**g.** genealogist
_____ **8.** like a mother	**h.** get along
_____ **9.** to not keep an appointment	**i.** grounds
_____ **10.** to have a good relationship	**j.** grow up
_____ **11.** to end abruptly	**k.** interfere
_____ **12.** a person who studies a family's history	**l.** interval
_____ **13.** warm affection	**m.** intimate
_____ **14.** honest and direct	**n.** maternal
_____ **15.** to discuss	**o.** maturity
_____ **16.** personal and private	**p.** paternal
_____ **17.** a period of time or space	**q.** persuade
	r. stand up
	s. take after
	t. talk over
	u. wait up for

B.   Answer each question with a word or phrase from the word form chart.

    1. How are physical characteristics passed from parents to children?
    2. What are the traditions you get from your ancestors?
    3. What do parents do when their children are out late?
    4. What happens to the voices of boys around age fourteen?
    5. Describe a person who is very sincere and open.
    6. Describe a person who has motherly qualities.
    7. Describe a person who can argue convincingly.
    8. Describe a child who takes good care of his elderly parents.
    9. Describe friends who know each other very well.
   10. Describe a person who acts like a child.
   11. What may a couple do for a child whose parents are dead?
   12. What are your children, grandchildren, and great-grandchildren?
   13. If you want to know your neighbors better, what can you do?
   14. Which word(s) name a feeling that you have toward another person?
   15. Which word(s) can describe someone's personality?

Study Exercises

C.   Write **T** if the sentence is true and **F** if it is false.

____   **1.** If you want to keep a secret, you should speak frankly.

____   **2.** You have an intimate connection with your siblings.

____   **3.** A genealogist studies rocks and the physical structure of the earth.

____   **4.** Parents are usually devoted to their children.

____   **5.** Your maternal uncle is your mother's brother.

____   **6.** Children usually have deeper voices than grown-ups.

____   **7.** Most people welcome interference in their private lives.

____   **8.** A ten-year-old child is not grown up.

____   **9.** It should be easy to persuade a devotee of painting to go to an art museum.

____   **10.** Your genes are the main thing that determine your height.

____   **11.** An era is a distance of less than one mile.

____   **12.** Your heritage is what you will leave for your descendants.

____   **13.** Fondness and intimacy are reasonable grounds for breaking off a relationship.

____   **14.** Adopted children take after their parents physically because they are genetically related.

____   **15.** Brothers and sisters sometimes do not get along with each other.

____   **16.** People are usually fond of people who always stand them up.

____   **17.** Talking over a problem is a mature way to try to resolve it.

D.   Match each word or phrase with its synonym.

_____ **1.** bind

_____ **2.** persuade

_____ **3.** get on with

_____ **4.** interfere

_____ **5.** grounds

_____ **6.** era

_____ **7.** talk over

_____ **8.** mature

_____ **9.** have over

_____ **10.** descendant

_____ **11.** fondness

_____ **12.** devoted

a. discuss
b. convince
c. be an obstacle
d. tie up
e. carry on
f. adopted
g. affection
h. child
i. dedicated
j. heritage
k. basis
l. object
m. period
n. ripe
o. invite

E.   Match each word or phrase with its opposite.

_____ **1.** frank

_____ **2.** stand up

_____ **3.** break off

_____ **4.** get along with

_____ **5.** intimate

_____ **6.** adopt

_____ **7.** descendant

_____ **8.** deep

_____ **9.** get on with

_____ **10.** wait up for

a. ancestor
b. authentic
c. dislike
d. high
e. persist
f. reject
g. secretive
h. sleep
i. suspend
j. tolerate
k. uninvolved
l. wait for

F.   Complete the analogies with a word or phrase from the word form chart.

1. future : past :: _____ : ancestor

2. nearby : distance :: _____ : emotions

3. close : intimate :: fond : _____

4. ripe : fruit :: _____ : person

5. zone : distance :: _____ : time

6. resign : job :: _____ : relationship

G. Read the passage and answer the questions that follow.

From 1980 through 1986, approximately forty thousand families in the United States adopted foreign children. Like most adoptive parents, those who choose foreign infants are usually physically unable to have biological children of their own;
5 however, they want a child in order to deepen their feeling of family and to be able to pass on their values to descendants. Couples adopt foreign children because there are not enough babies available for adoption in the United States or because they want to help a child from another country.

10 In many ways the experience of adoptive parents is the same whether or not the child is foreign; in fact, it is shared by all parents. The fact that the child is not genetically related to the parents, and so will not take after them physically, is minor; it does not determine the quality of the emotional bonds between
15 family members. Parents of adopted children, like most others, are devoted to their sons and daughters. They help them learn how to get along in the world, they take care of them when they are sick, and they wait up for them when they are late. Also, adopted children react like many others; as they grow up, they complain
20 that their parents interfere too much in their lives, but once they are mature, they recognize how much they owe their parents.

Despite all these similarities, families which include adopted foreign children face some unique challenges. For example, if the children are Asian or African, they may encounter racial prejudice.
25 The parents must be willing to frankly talk over any problems that arise from this prejudice or from any confusion the child might feel about being different from other members of the family. In addition, the parents must find a way to teach the child about his or her ethnic heritage.

30 Some people object to adoption between races on the grounds that it is usually impossible for adoptive parents to give a child an intimate understanding of his background, if it is different from their own. There is not yet enough evidence to measure the validity of this argument. However, many specialists are persuaded
35 that a child's happiness and success are determined primarily by the amount of love and attention he receives. In this respect, adopted children are among the most likely to be satisfied with their lives.

1. List four reasons why people may adopt a foreign child.

(a) _____

(b) _____

(c) _____

(d) _____

2. In what way do children not take after their adoptive parents? Why not?

_____

_____

3. List three experiences that most families have in common, according to this passage.

(a) _____

(b) _____

(c) _____

4. Name two things that parents should discuss with an adopted child.

(a) _____

(b) _____

5. Why do some people disapprove of the adoption of children who are not of the same race as the parents? _____

_____

Follow-up

H. Dictation: Write the sentences that your teacher reads aloud.

1. _____

2. _____

3. _____

4. _____

5. _____

I. Answer the following questions.

1. Which people in your family are you especially fond of?
2. How does an immature person behave?
3. Do you consider yourself to be a frank person? Give an example.
4. What is one thing that interferes with your progress in learning English?
5. Name some characteristics that are passed on genetically.
6. What are possible grounds for a divorce?
7. What kind(s) of people is it difficult for you to get along with?
8. Whom in your family do you take after? In what way(s)?
9. What kind(s) of decisions do you talk over with your parents? Your children?
10. Do you ever have friends over? How do you entertain them?
11. How does a devoted teacher behave? Describe the behavior of a person who feels religious devotion.

12. Do you know any adopted children? Describe some problems of adopted children.
13. Name one thing that you did not want to do, but that someone persuaded you to do. How did they persuade you?
14. At what age are children in your country considered to be grown-up? Explain.
15. In your opinion, what is a good interval between the birth of children in a family?

J.   1. Describe what happens in your family when people are angry at each other.
2. What factors do you think are the most important in binding members of a family together? In binding friends together?

Economy

Word Form Chart

NOUN	VERB	ADJECTIVE	ADVERB
ampleness		ample	amply
	buy up		
consumer	consume		
consumption			
convert	convert	converted	
conversion			
decline	decline	declining	
durability		durable	durably
durableness			
duration			
economy	economize	economic	economically
		economical	
	ensure		
	fall off		
globe		global	globally
grimness		grim	grimly
interval			
moderate	moderate	moderate	moderately
moderator			
moderation			
	overcome		
	pan out		
	put off		
reserve	reserve	reserved	
reservation			
respect	respect	respected	
		respectful	respectfully
	rule out		
	see to		

NOUN	VERB	ADJECTIVE	ADVERB
	take in		
	take up		
	think over		

Definitions and Examples

1. **economy** (a) [a system for the production and distribution of resources in a city, area, or country]

    > In an agriculturally based **economy**, most people earn their living doing farm work.
    >
    > The United States had an agricultural **economy** until approximately 1900; from then until the 1970s, many people worked in heavy industry and manufacturing.

    (b) [the careful management of money or resources]

    > People who have a limited income must practice **economy**. For example, they must buy clothes and other necessities on sale and must not buy unnecessary luxuries.
    >
    > When you shop for groceries, it's more **economical** to buy food in large amounts. For example, a five-pound bag of sugar costs $2.80 (56¢/pound), but a one-pound bag costs $1.09.

    (c) [related to management of money or resources]

    > This is an **economic** issue, not an educational one.

2. **ample** [enough; sufficient; having plenty or a lot]

    > The new government office building has **ample** space for all the government offices.
    >
    > The city government plans to complete its study of the local economy in three years. This is **ample** time to do a thorough and complete study.

3. **consumer** [a person who buys and uses a product]

    > When **consumers** buy expensive products, such as cars and televisions, they should compare the prices, advantages, and disadvantages of different brands.
    >
    > If a **consumer** feels that a product is defective, he should return the product or write to the manufacturer.

4. **buy up** {separable} [to buy the entire available supply of a product or goods]

    > The university **bought up** all the land around it in order to expand.
    >
    > A large grocery store in my town tried to **buy up** all the smaller stores in order to control the price of food. Fortunately, the effort to **buy** the smaller stores **up** was not successful.

5. **decline** (a) [to decrease]

> The value of the dollar on the world market has **declined** in recent years.
> The number of people who smoke cigarettes in the United States **declined** greatly in the 1980s.

(b) [to refuse politely to do or to accept something]

> We had to **decline** the invitation to visit our friends in another city because we were too busy.
> The government official should have **declined** the free boat that a company offered him. He did not **decline** it, and he was accused of bribery.

6. **ensure** [to guarantee; to make certain that something will happen]

> The student's score of 610 on the TOEFL **ensured** that he would have no trouble being accepted at a university because of his English.
> Money is not enough to **ensure** happiness; a person must be at peace with himself, too.

7. **fall off** [to decline; to become less]

> Certain businesses always **fall off** in the winter; for example, fewer people buy cars and houses in November and December than in other months.
> The number of Americans who travel to Europe usually **falls off** when the value of the dollar declines.

8. **globe** (a) [a round object that represents the earth]

> My nephew is fascinated by other countries, so I bought him a **globe** of the earth so that he can see where different countries are located.
> Most **globes** are round even though the earth itself is not perfectly round.

(b) [any object in the shape of a ball]

> The local newspapers reported a strange blue **globe**-shaped object in the sky around midnight last night; nobody was able to identify it.
> The university's new auditorium is very modern on the inside: the ceiling is covered with large **globes** of colored glass.

9. **global** [international; referring to the entire earth]

> An agreement on nuclear weapons is necessary for **global** peace.
> **Global** understanding will be difficult to achieve while countries are still fighting over territorial space.

10. **durable** [able to last a long time, especially with hard use]

> Blue jeans are popular pants for farmers and factory workers because they are very **durable**; jeans last a long time, and they do not tear easily.
> Cigarette lighters made of metal are more **durable** than lighters made of plastic, but they are also more expensive.

11. **duration** [the period of time during which something lasts or takes place]

> The **duration** of the economic crisis was short; it lasted only six months.

12. **interval** [the duration of time between two events; the amount of space between two objects]

> The label on this bottle of pills says to take one pill at **intervals** of four hours.
>
> During a six-mile race, there is water available to the runners at one-mile **intervals**.

13. **convert (into)** (a) [to exchange for something of equal value]

> If you will be traveling to another country, you should **convert** some money into the currency of the country you are going to.
>
> Before my uncle died last year, he had **converted** all his properties and investments into cash.

(b) [to change something into a different form]

> We **converted** the garage of our house into an extra bedroom.
>
> During the twelfth and thirteenth centuries, chemists were continuously looking for a way to **convert** cheap metals into gold.

(c) **(to)** [to persuade or to be persuaded to adopt a new religion or new belief]

> The first settlers to North and South America **converted** the Indians to Christianity.
>
> When two people from different religious backgrounds get married, one of them often **converts** to the other's religion.

14. **grim** (a) [serious; rigid]

> The teacher had a **grim** look on his face when he saw the poor work of his students.
>
> The policeman **grimly** wrote down the names of the young men who had committed the murder.

(b) [terrible; violent]

> The scene of the accident was a **grim** sight; there were nine dead bodies on the highway.
>
> The predictions for the economy this year are **grim**; unemployment is expected to increase by fifteen percent.

15. **overcome** [to conquer; to defeat]

> The turning point of World War II was when the British, French, and Americans **overcame** the German army at Dunkirk.
>
> Helen Keller, an American who was both blind and deaf, was able to **overcome** her handicaps through hard work and the dedication of a faithful teacher.

16. **pan out** {informal} [to be successful (usually a plan or an idea)]

>   The children wanted to earn money in the summer by selling lemonade.
>   Their efforts **panned out** because they set up their business in an area
>   with a lot of pedestrians.
>
>   The plan to build a new shopping center on the outskirts of our town did
>   not **pan out**; there was ample space, but not enough merchants wanted
>   to invest in the project.

17. **put off** {separable} [to delay something until a later time]

>   I needed a book from the library yesterday, but I **put off** going until it was
>   five o'clock, and by then the library had closed.
>
>   Some students always **put** their homework **off** until it is too late to do
>   it well.

18. **think over** {separable} [to consider seriously]

>   I will **think over** your suggestion to convert the heating system in my
>   house from gas to electricity.
>
>   A: Why don't you come with us to New York city this weekend?
>   B: I have to write a research paper for Monday, but I'll **think** it **over**.

19. **see to** [to ensure that something necessary is done; to take responsibility for
something]

>   When my sister had her third baby, I offered to **see to** the cooking and
>   cleaning plus the care of the other two children.
>
>   A: Who will **see to** the president's duties while he is in the hospital?
>   B: The vice-president is responsible for all official business when the
>   president is not available.

20. **rule out** {separable} [to eliminate]

>   When the company officials were considering whom to hire, they **ruled
>   out** Jim Smith because he did not have enough experience.
>
>   A: What is your diagnosis in the case of this patient, doctor?
>   B: Well, I think we can **rule** cancer **out**; the tests do not show any
>   indications of the disease.

21. **respect** (a) [a particular aspect or detail of something]

>   A large university is good in some **respects**; you meet a wide variety of
>   people, and there are many cultural events. In other **respects**, however,
>   it is easy to feel lost at a large school.
>
>   In one **respect**, the economy of Japan is weak. For example, it is
>   dependent upon other countries for its oil supply. In most other
>   **respects**, however, Japan has a very strong economy.

(b) [to feel or show honor or admiration for a person or thing]

>   It is difficult to **respect** a politician who is not honest.
>   Children should always **respect** older people.

22. **with respect to** [in reference to]

> **With respect to** the new tax law, we can say that fewer people with low incomes will have to pay taxes in the future.

> A: Mr. President, **with respect to** the current state of the economy, how high will unemployment be next year?
> B: We hope unemployment will be less than one percent by the end of the year.

23. **take in** (a) {separable} [to understand]

> I threatened to quit unless I received a raise, but my boss was not able to **take** that fact **in** until I actually resigned.
> My mathematics professor is good, but he speaks very quickly; I can't always **take in** all the points he discusses.

(b) [to include; to consist of]

> The state of California **takes in** the coast, mountains, and desert.
> The Teamsters is a trade union that **takes in** many different professions, including agricultural and industrial workers.

(c) [5-15: {separable} to make smaller (usually clothing)]

> The coat that I bought was too big, so I had to **take** it **in**.

24. **take up** (a) {separable} [to consider a subject (as at a meeting)]

> Congress must **take up** the subject of the decline of the steel industry during this legislative session.
> The tuition increase was the most important issue discussed at the Student Council meeting last week. They will **take** it **up** again when they meet tomorrow.

(b) [to use or consume (especially time or space)]

> Teaching can **take up** a lot of time; a teacher must plan lessons, write materials for class, and correct homework.
> Our new computer **takes up** a lot of space: we need three separate tables for all the equipment.

(c) {separable} [to make shorter]

> The little boy's pants were too long so his mother had to **take** them **up**.

> A: The curtains in the classroom touch the floor. Could you **take** them **up** about six inches?
> B: Sure, that's no problem.

25.   moderate (a) [not excessive or extreme; not radical]

> Someone who supports **moderate** politics wants change to occur a little at
> a time; someone who supports radical change wants to see changes
> made all at once, often through violent means.
> There will be a **moderate** increase in income taxes next year.
> California has a very **moderate** climate, neither too hot nor too cold.

(b) [to be in charge of a meeting or a ceremony]

> The woman who **moderated** the debate about nuclear energy did an
> excellent job. The issue was covered in all respects.

> A: Who is going to be the **moderator** for the graduation ceremony?
> B: The vice-president of the university always sees to that.

26.   reserve (a) [to save for use in the future; to save for a particular person or use]

> People should **reserve** a certain portion of their annual income for their
> future retirement.
> Seats in the front of the bus are **reserved** for elderly or handicapped
> people.

(b) [land or money used for a special purpose]

> National **reserves** have been set up in order to protect animals and plants
> that live in the wild. People have protested attempts by the
> government to convert national **reserves** into private land.
> **Reserves** have been established for American Indians to live on. Indian
> **reserves** are usually called **reservations**. Non-Indians are forbidden by
> law from buying land on **reservations**.

27.   reservation [an arrangement by which a ticket or hotel room can be used in
the future]

> You can sometimes get cheaper airplane tickets if you make **reservations**
> several months in advance.

> A: You're going to Washington? Where are you going to stay?
> B: We have **reservations** at the Economy Inn for Friday and Saturday
> night.

Introductory Exercises

A.   Match each word with its definition.

_____	1. to eliminate	**a.** ample
_____	2. the period of time between two events	**b.** buy up
		c. consume
_____	3. to conquer or defeat	**d.** convert
_____	4. a round object in the shape of the earth	**e.** decline
		f. economy
_____	5. sufficient	**g.** ensure
_____	6. to delay doing something	**h.** fall off
		i. globe
_____	7. a system for the distribution of resources	**j.** grim
		k. interval
_____	8. a decrease	**l.** moderate
_____	9. to discuss at a meeting	**m.** overcome
_____	10. to buy and use a product	**n.** pan out
		o. put off
_____	11. to make sure something is accomplished	**p.** reserve
		q. respect
_____	12. serious	**r.** rule out
_____	13. to consider seriously	**s.** see to
_____	14. to become less	**t.** take in
_____	15. to guarantee	**u.** take up
_____	16. to feel or show honor or admiration	**v.** think over
_____	17. to include; to consist of	
_____	18. land used for a special purpose	
_____	19. to exchange for equal value	
_____	20. not extreme	

B.   Answer **T** if the sentence is true and **F** if it is false.

_____   1. If the consumption of a product falls off, economists consider that it has increased.

_____   2. Throwaway products are not very durable.

_____   3. Governments hope to see their export rates decline.

_____   4. Lawyers and doctors must usually economize on their style of living because of their incomes.

_____   5. A business plan that doesn't pan out is not successful.

_____   6. Government policy should ensure that there is full employment in the economy.

_____   7. A young child with a new toy is a grim sight.

—— **8.** A business may try to overcome its competitors by buying them out.

—— **9.** You should always put off having medical and dental examinations at regular intervals.

—— **10.** It's advisable to travel abroad without ample money.

—— **11.** A government whose economy depends on tourism must see to it that there are ample facilities for entertainment.

—— **12.** A moderate decline in the rate of inflation means that consumer goods cost more.

—— **13.** It's important to wear globes during cold weather to protect your hands.

—— **14.** The coast of Florida takes in two different bodies of water.

—— **15.** **Economic** and **economical** mean the same thing.

Study Exercises

C. In each blank, write the most appropriate word from the word form chart. Some words may be used more than once.

1. It's dangerous for a country to have a(n) _____ that depends upon one agricultural product. The danger is that if consumption of that one product _____ , the economy will suffer. Having a diverse economy means that the country is not dependent upon one item for its foreign reserves.

2. Production by heavy industries, such as the steel and automobile industries, _____ in the United States since the 1970s because of strong competition from foreign companies. Because of this, U.S. industry is trying to _____ to other kinds of production, such as that of computer technology.

3. The explosion of the Challenger rocket in 1986 was a _____ loss to the American space program, but this did not _____ future attempts to develop the space program.

4. The current popularity of small cars in the United States shows that _____ realize the _____ advantages of the smaller cars; until the 1973 oil crisis Americans preferred large cars with _____ space inside even though such cars used a lot of fuel.

5. The price of houses _____ when there are more houses available than people want to buy. On the other hand, the cost of housing increases when a few people try to _____ all available houses to use as rental property.

6. Books with hard covers are more _____ than those with paper covers. Therefore, library books and reference books often have hard covers.

7. I have had a(n) _____ increase in my salary this year, but I must _____ carefully whether it is enough for me to be able to buy a new car.

8. Unfortunately, Eileen's new clothing business did not _____ , and she had to close the store after fourteen months. However, in some _____ the failure was a good thing because she had discovered that she did not like being confined to one place all day.

9. The theory of electricity has been explained to me at least ten times, but I have never been able to _____ it _____ completely. The concept is simply too abstract for me.

10. In order to have true _____ peace, all nations will have to _____ the rights and needs of each of their neighbors. People in each nation will have to _____ dislikes caused by religious and political differences.

D. Circle the letter of the word or phrase which best completes each phrase.

1. put off
   a. a decision
   b. your shoes
   c. the television

2. ensure
   a. your life
   b. a decade
   c. a good result

3. convert to
   a. a new religion
   b. some new clothes
   c. a neighbor

4. overcome
   a. your friend's house
   b. a problem
   c. a mountain

5. take up
   a. an airplane
   b. the garbage
   c. the curtains

6. moderate
   a. the living room
   b. a meeting
   c. a test

7. decline
   a. an invitation
   b. a question
   c. a guest

8. buy up
   a. a chain of stores
   b. a new car
   c. a pair of earrings

9. see to
   a. a view
   b. a problem
   c. a movie

10. respect
    a. your parents
    b. a new book
    c. an interval

11. take in
    a. a moderator
    b. a large area
    c. ampleness

12. reserve
    a. a hotel room
    b. a garden
    c. a favorite meal

E.   Read the passage and answer the questions that follow.

Three years ago my grandfather died, and my sister and I
received an inheritance. It was not a large amount of money, but it
was ample for us to set up a business. A business of our own had
been a dream of ours since we were children. The only problem
5   was that we did not know what kind of business to begin. After
thinking the matter over for quite some time, and after ruling out
such suggestions as a cleaning service, a clothing store, and a toy
store, we ultimately decided to open a small restaurant. My sister
and I both love to cook, and we often cook for our friends.

10 When we began, neither of us had any idea what having your
own business meant. I simply did not take in how much work was
involved in establishing a restaurant or how much time would be
taken up with small details. There are a million details to see to—
state licenses; regulations and laws from both the city and the
15 state, health regulations to follow closely; tax information to learn
about—not to mention learning about the restaurant trade itself.
Both my sister and I quit our jobs to work on establishing our
restaurant. I did not like to think about what would happen if this
effort did not pan out.

20 The first step, after we had made all the necessary legal
arrangements, was to find a space for our restaurant. After a
seemingly endless interval spent searching and searching, we
found the perfect place. It was located between the downtown area
and the university. The building had originally contained an old
25 clothing factory, but it had stood empty for many years. The inside
of the building was run-down and very grim looking, but the rent
was economical. There was a small kitchen, and we converted the
main factory room into a dining room for customers. The theme of
our restaurant was international, since we wanted to serve food
30 from around the world, so our decorations were from many
different countries. We bought up all the antique maps and globes
that we could find.

Finally, after buying the necessary equipment and advertising
at the businesses downtown and at the university, we were ready
35 to open for business. The first day was great in one respect because
we had over 75 customers, but in another respect it was a disaster.
We ran out of food! We thought we had plenty of everything, but
we even had to use all of our reserves. That day taught us that a
restaurant is more than a decorated dining room.

40 However, we learned. After we overcame our initial tendency
to prepare too little food, we had quite a successful restaurant. We
have developed a set of regular customers, which ensures some
income even during the low periods. Business tends to fall off a
little during the summer, but we do not mind because it allows us
45 a break. We have had the restaurant for three years now, and I
cannot imagine doing anything else. How else could I have so
many friends over for dinner every day?

1. Where did the sisters get the money for their business? _____

2. How did they decide what kind of business to open? _____

3. What were some details that had to be seen to at the beginning? _____

4. Why was the rent of the building economical? _____

5. How did the sisters decorate the dining room? _____

6. In what respect was the first day a disaster? _____

7. Why do you think business falls off during the summer? _____

Follow-up

F.   Dictation: Write the sentences that your teacher reads aloud.

1. _____
2. _____
3. _____
4. _____
5. _____

G.   Answer the following questions.

1. What are the most important consumer products in your country?
2. What has been the biggest fear that you have had to overcome when traveling?
3. How do you convert temperature readings from Celsius to Fahrenheit?
4. Describe a nature reserve in your country.
5. What responsibilities do you have to see to at your job?
6. What will you do if your grades fall off?
7. What is the grimmest scene that you have ever seen?
8. What do you plan to do for the duration of your stay here?
9. What do you consider to be a moderate amount of exercise?
10. What types of jobs would you completely rule out for yourself?
11. What is an economical way to travel?
12. What is an ample income for students in your city?

13. What responsibilities do you most often put off?
14. What is the conversion rate of your currency to dollars?
15. Describe some economic issues that are problems for your country.

H. Answer one of the following questions.

1. Do you or does your family have a business? Tell about the business.
2. Describe the national economy of your country. What are the most important industries? What is the role of the government with respect to planning?

Science (A)

Word Form Chart

NOUN	VERB	ADJECTIVE	ADVERB
application	apply	applied	
		applicable	
beam	beam	beamed	
		beaming	
breakdown	break down		
	come across		
component		component	
cylinder		cylindrical	cylindrically
	dilute	diluted	
	dissolve	dissolved	
		dissolving	
file	file	filed	
		filing	
friction			
graph	graph		
	hand in		
input	input		
lever			
	make out		
mammal		mammalian	
mechanic	mechanize	mechanical	mechanically
property			
	randomize	random	randomly
	read up on		
relevance		relevant	
irrelevance		irrelevant	
scale	scale		
	shut off		
sophistication		sophisticated	
		unsophisticated	

Definitions and Examples

1. **applied** [put in practice]

   When we talk about **applied** science, we mean the use of general theories and laws of science to solve practical problems. For example, in **applied** physics, scientists use the laws of physics to discover how to send a rocket into space.

   Courses in education are sometimes more theoretical than **applied**; that is, the philosophy of education is studied instead of actual activities for use in the classroom.

2. **component** [a simpler part of something more complex]

   Most things are made of **components**. Some things have many **components**; some have only a few. For example, a car has many **component** parts: tires, brakes, windows, seats, mirrors, pipes, and the engine (which itself is made of many **components**).

   Water has two chemical **components**: oxygen and hydrogen.

3. **break down** {separable} (a) [to analyze or separate something into its component parts]

   One method for solving a scientific problem is to **break** the problem **down** into a series of smaller problems. This can also work for solving personal problems. A problem that seems too large to be overcome can be effectively handled if it is **broken down** into smaller parts.

   A large component of any beginning chemistry class is studying the chemical **breakdown** of different materials. Salt, for example, can be **broken down** into two different chemicals, but oxygen cannot.

   (b) [to become unusable because of breaking or other failure]

   On our vacation in Texas, our car **broke down** in the middle of a desert, about 30 miles from the nearest town.

   If you take good care of equipment, it should last a long time and not **break down**.

4. **beam** (a) [a ray of light]

   Some sources of light send out **beams** while others send out general light. For example, a fire omits a very general light, but a searchlight sends out a single, concentrated **beam** in search of something. A lighthouse, which is a tall tower on the coast, sends out a strong **beam** to warn sailors that they are near land.

   (b) [a piece of metal or wood used to support a building]

   My grandmother lives in a very old house in which the **beams** of the ceiling are open to view.

   Most commercial buildings are made with steel **beams**.

5. **come across** [to meet or find by chance]

> The biologist **came across** an unknown type of cancer during his latest experiment.
>
> While I was cleaning out the attic, I **came across** some old baby pictures of my father that I had never seen before.

6. **cylinder** [an object whose shape is long and round and which is empty on the inside]

> The **cylinders** are important parts of a car engine.
>
> Large cars have eight **cylinders** while smaller cars have four.
>
> Cans that have food in them are **cylindrically** shaped.

7. **dilute** [to make a liquid weaker in flavor or strength by adding another liquid (usually water) to it]

> If coffee is too strong, you can **dilute** it by adding a little water to it.
>
> A **diluted** acid is safer to work with than a strong acid.

8. **dissolve** (a) [to disappear gradually into a liquid]

> Sugar and salt both **dissolve** in water; that is, they both are gradually broken down by the liquid until they seem to disappear.
>
> My father puts so much sugar in his coffee that half of it does not **dissolve**.

(b) [to bring to an end (usually an organization)]

> The telephone company in the United States was **dissolved** by Congress because it was felt to be unfair to have a company with no competition.
>
> In a parliamentary form of government, the prime minister has the power to **dissolve** the parliament in order to hold new elections.

9. **mammal** [any of a class of warm-blooded animals, including humans, who give birth to live young and nurse them]

> Any animal who nurses its young is a **mammal**. This includes rats, dogs, cats, monkeys, and people, but not birds or fish.
>
> **Mammals** are considered warm blooded because their blood temperature remains constant.

10. **file** (a) [a container, such as a cabinet, used to keep records and information in order; the records themselves]

> A scientist's **files** must be well organized so that she can find records when she needs them.

> Student: Where can I find information about Peter the Great of Russia?
> Librarian: It's **filed** under *p* for Peter.

(b) [a tool with a rough surface that is used for shaping solid objects]

> The mechanic used a **file** to smooth the rough edges of the pipe he had cut.
> After the heavy rain, the wooden door of our house was so swollen we could not close it, so we **filed** about a half inch of wood from the bottom.

(c) [a line of people or things arranged one after another]

> When children at elementary school wait in line to go into lunch, they must stand single **file**, which means they must stand in a line, one student after another.
> About 1,000 people a day **file** past the body of Lenin at Red Square in Moscow.

11. **mechanic** [a person who repairs machines, especially cars]

> I am very lucky to have found a good **mechanic**. He is very reliable and trustworthy as well as inexpensive. Every six months he checks my car for minor problems.
> The heating system of our school broke down just when the temperature dropped to zero degrees Fahrenheit. It took the **mechanic** two days to repair the heater.

12. **mechanical** (a) [as if by machine; impersonal and without feeling]

> The salesclerk at the department store was very busy. Her smile was so **mechanical** that it looked as if it had been painted on her face.
> The chemistry teacher at my high school did not really enjoy teaching. His lessons were always very **mechanical**, and the students certainly did not enjoy them.

(b) [relating to machines; made or operated by a machine]

> A **mechanical** toy is one that has a small machine inside it to make it move. **Mechanical** dolls can walk by themselves.
> A **mechanical** engineer studies how machines work.

13. **lever** [a simple machine consisting of a rigid body, such as a board, balanced on a fixed point]

> A **lever** can be used to lift an object that would otherwise be too heavy for a person to lift. For example, if you want to move a heavy stone from your garden, put a smaller stone next to it, and then put a board on top of the smaller stone but partially under the heavy stone. The board serves as a **lever** to raise the large stone up.
>
> The construction workers used a **lever** to remove an old tree from their construction site.

14. **graph** [a diagram that shows change in one factor compared to another or that shows the points of a mathematical formula]

> Businesses use **graphs** to show how well their products are selling. For example, in this **graph** we see that a lot more cars are sold in December than in January or February.
>
> Scientists also use **graphs** to demonstrate the results of their experiments.
>
> Mathematicians use **graphs** to represent different formulas. A **graph** of two parallel lines looks like this:

15. **hand in** {separable} [to give or deliver to someone; to give schoolwork to a teacher]

> The students in the writing classes have to **hand in** a composition every week.
>
> Teachers expect students to **hand** homework **in** on time.
>
> Student A: When do we **hand** our research papers **in**?
> Student B: The teacher wants them **handed in** next Monday.

16. **relevant** [related or important to the matter at hand]

> When people apply for a job, their age, race, or sex is not **relevant**. What is **relevant** are their qualifications for the job.
>
> Professors in American universities often give essay tests; when you answer an essay, do not write everything you know about a topic. Write only the information that is **relevant** to the specific question.

17. **read up on** [to read all the latest information about a particular subject]

> Before students write research papers, they need to **read up on** the topic they are going to research.
>
> My cousin John decided to buy a sailboat last year. Before he bought a boat, however, he **read up on** the different types of boats available; he also took a course in boating safety.

18. **input** [anything put into a system in order to reach a conclusion or achieve a result]

> Any information that you put into a computer is referred to as **input**. Mathematicians and chemists also put **input** into their chemical and mathematical formulas.

> Companies make business decisions based upon the **input** that they receive from their employees about different aspects of the business.

19. **property** (a) [a special quality or characteristic of an object]

> Sweetness is a **property** of all sugars. Another **property** is the ability to dissolve in water.

> A: What are the **properties** of wood?
> B: It swells when it gets wet, and it floats.

(b) [anything that is owned; a piece of land]

> The house where I live, and all the furniture in it, is the **property** of Mr. Herbert.

> My parents have some **property** near a river. It is not a very big piece of land, but it is pretty in the summer because of all the trees.

20. **make out** {separable} (a) [to understand or see by trying hard]

> My biology teacher's handwriting is impossible to read; I can never **make out** what he writes on the board.

> A: Do you see the store across the road? Is that a pharmacy? What does the sign say?
> B: I don't know. I can't **make** it **out** very clearly.

(b) {separable} [to write out facts, usually on a form]

> A: Whom should I **make** this check **out** to?
> B: **Make** it **out** to "The Acme Company."

(c) {informal} [to try to prove or imply that something is true]

> The student had not done his homework, but he **made out** that he had done it and lost it.

> The accused thief **made out** that he had been at a friend's party the night of the robbery.

21. **friction** (a) [the resistance to motion that exists when two touching surfaces move against each other]

> The box of tools was a little heavy, but the reason we could not move it was that the **friction** of the box itself against the sidewalk was too much. We had no trouble moving it when we put the box on wheels.

> You can make a fire by rubbing two sticks together because the **friction** created by the rubbing action causes heat.

(b) [disagreement and unpleasant feelings between two people]

> My father and my brother do not get along well. There is always **friction** between them.

> It is difficult to work in an office in which there is **friction** between two employees.

22. **shut off** {separable} (a) [to stop something from operating]

> Please **shut off** the lights when you leave the room.
>
> After I had locked the door to my house this morning, I realized that I had forgotten to **shut** the television **off**.

(b) {separable} [to automatically stop operating]

> My alarm clock **shuts off** after five minutes.
>
> The British have electric machines for boiling water that **shut** themselves **off** after the water has boiled.

(c) {separable} [to isolate]

> Many people **shut** themselves **off** from their family and friends after their husband or wife has died.
>
> Some religious groups are **shut off** from the outside world. They believe they can worship God best by not having contact with other people.

23. **random** [having no specific pattern or plan]

> When a psychologist does a general experiment about the human mind, he selects people at **random** and asks them questions. He tries to get a **random** sample of people, so that he does not have too many people who are from the same group.
>
> When I am on vacation, I like to explore new cities by walking **randomly** through the downtown streets.

24. **sophisticated** (a) [complicated and complex (usually said of equipment)]

> Doctors often use a lot of **sophisticated** equipment. Unfortunately, such equipment is very expensive, and doctors in some countries do not have access to many **sophisticated** instruments.
>
> A lever is a very **unsophisticated** piece of machinery, but it is the most appropriate instrument for certain jobs, such as lifting heavy objects.

(b) [experienced; wise in the ways of the world]

> Susan is a very **sophisticated** dresser; she always knows the most recent fashions and is the first person in our area to wear them.
>
> Despite his millions of dollars and great **sophistication**, Mr. Jones prefers simple things in life. He would rather spend a quiet evening with his family than go to the most **sophisticated** dinner party.

25. **scale** (a) [a system of gradually increasing measurement or classification of size, amount, importance or rank]

>   Animals can be classified biologically on a **scale** ranging from very primitive, such as one-celled animals, to very complex, such as mammals.
>
>   Professor Denyer is not only a brilliant researcher, but he is also an excellent teacher. In fact, on a **scale** of one to ten, I would give him a nine as a teacher.

(b) [the size of a picture or plan in relative size to itself]

>   Plans for building a house are always drawn to **scale**, which means they are drawn in exactly the same shape as the building they represent but much smaller than the actual size.
>
>   Architects use an instrument called a **scale** to draw plans for a house.

(c) [one of the small, flat, rigid plates that form the outer covering of some animals, such as fish and snakes]

>   Snakes have **scales** as a protective covering in the same way that mammals have hair and birds have feathers.
>
>   After you catch a fish, you must remove the **scales** before you cook it.

(d) [a machine or instrument for determining weight]

>   **Scales** in the United States measure a person's weight in pounds. In most of the rest of the world, weight is measured in kilos, except in England. In the United Kingdom, **scales** measure weight in "stones"; one stone equals fourteen pounds.
>
>   The most accurate type of **scale** is a balance **scale**.

Introductory Exercises

A. Match each word with its definition.

_____	1. a system of gradually increasing measurement	**a.**	applied
_____	2. to give schoolwork to a teacher	**b.**	beam
_____	3. a cabinet to keep records in	**c.**	break down
_____	4. to understand by trying hard	**d.**	come across
_____	5. a ray of light	**e.**	component
_____	6. a board balanced on a fixed point, used for lifting things	**f.**	cylinder
_____	7. to analyze something into its component parts	**g.**	dilute
_____	8. a characteristic	**h.**	dissolve
_____	9. put into practice	**i.**	file
_____	10. an animal that bears live young and nurses them	**j.**	friction
_____	11. to meet or find by chance	**k.**	graph
_____	12. having no specific plan or pattern	**l.**	hand in
_____	13. to make a liquid weaker by adding water	**m.**	lever
_____	14. complicated and complex	**n.**	make out
_____	15. a long, round object that is empty on the inside	**o.**	mammal
_____	16. a diagram that shows change in one factor compared to another	**p.**	mechanic
_____	17. related to the matter under discussion	**q.**	property
_____	18. to disappear gradually into a liquid	**r.**	random

s. read up on
t. relevant
u. scale
v. sophisticated

B. Answer each question with a word from the word form chart.

1. What is one thing you should do to prepare for studying a new subject?
2. What do you call information fed into a computer?
3. What happens to soap when you put it into a washing machine?
4. What do you do to the television when you finish watching it?
5. What is created when two sticks are rubbed together?
6. If a teacher is discussing the properties of a certain chemical and a student asks a question about mammals in Australia, how do we describe the question?
7. What do you call the parts which a system is broken down into?
8. What kind of engineer studies machines?
9. How do people enter a movie theater?

10. What do you call anything that is owned?

11. What are fish covered with?

12. If a person tries to convince people that he has a college degree, but he really does not, what is he doing?

13. If you find something accidentally that you weren't looking for, what have you done?

14. What do you have if your car stops working?

15. What can economists use to show the state of an area's economy?

16. What happens to a cup of tea if you add more water to it?

17. How can you describe a person who has traveled a lot in other countries?

Study Exercises

C.   Write **T** if the sentence is true and **F** if it is false.

_____ **1.** Doctors and all professionals, including teachers, should read up on the latest developments in their fields.

_____ **2.** A composition cannot be broken down into component parts.

_____ **3.** A happy family has a lot of friction.

_____ **4.** A mailman hands in letters from door to door.

_____ **5.** Some alarm clocks shut themselves off automatically.

_____ **6.** A mechanical smile is the sign of a friendly person.

_____ **7.** One of the properties of oxygen is that it is colorless.

_____ **8.** Graphs are useful for visually showing the financial state of a company.

_____ **9.** The police destroy files on criminals after two months.

_____ **10.** A person's shoe size is not relevant to whether that person should be considered for a job.

_____ **11.** Teachers give grades on homework randomly.

_____ **12.** An X ray is a beam of light.

_____ **13.** A mechanical clock does not use electricity.

_____ **14.** Scientists are always concerned about the practical application of their theories.

_____ **15.** Sophistication is a sign of intelligence.

D.   Paraphrase the underlined words in each sentence using a word from the word form chart.

1. People often do not realize that theoretical mathematics has many practical <u>uses</u>, especially in the field of engineering.

  2. A navy search plane uses a strong <u>ray</u> of light to look for people who are lost at sea at night.

      _____

  3. Although a whale looks like a large fish, it is in fact a <u>warm-blooded</u> <u>animal</u> <u>that</u> <u>gives</u> <u>birth</u> <u>to</u> <u>live</u> <u>young</u>.

      _____

  4. Many older cities in the United States developed and grew <u>without</u> <u>any</u> <u>specific</u> <u>plan</u>; one exception is Washington, D.C., which was <u>planned</u> by a Frenchman.

      _____

  5. I always do my homework, but sometimes I forget to <u>give</u> <u>it</u> <u>to</u> <u>the</u> <u>teacher</u>.

      _____

  6. What are the <u>characteristics</u> of plastic?

      _____

  7. When our car broke down, we had to find a strong <u>board</u> to lift the car high enough for the <u>car</u> <u>repairman</u> to lie under it.

      _____

  8. The first record player, which was invented by Thomas Edison, consisted of a needle and a <u>long</u>, <u>round</u> <u>object</u> <u>that</u> <u>was</u> <u>empty</u> <u>inside</u>.

      _____

  9. Some high school chemistry labs have very <u>complex</u> <u>and</u> <u>advanced</u> equipment for students to use in experiments.

      _____

10. At the museum there were copies of old Greek and Roman buildings that were the actual size; they were not built to <u>the</u> <u>relative</u> <u>size</u> <u>of</u> <u>the</u> <u>buildings</u>.

      _____

11. I can not <u>read</u> the words on the sign from here—it is too far away.

      _____

12. The President of the United States does not have the authority to <u>end</u> a labor union in this country.

      _____

13. Jim was unhappy at his job because of all the <u>disagreements</u> among his fellow employees.

      _____

E. Complete the analogies with a word or phrase from the word form chart.

  1. ice : melt :: salt : _____

  2. hair : dog :: _____ : fish

  3. bee : insect :: man : _____

  4. meet : a friend on the street :: _____ : a picture in a drawer

5. gate : iron :: _____ : wood

6. sugar : sweeten :: water : _____

7. box : cube :: can : _____

8. doctor : people :: _____ : cars

F. In each blank, write the most appropriate word or phrase from the word form chart.

High school students in some states in the United States have the opportunity to spend summer vacations in an unusual manner. The Departments of Education in those states have recently begun organizing four- to six-week concentrated programs in the sciences each summer. The programs, called the "Governor's School for the Sciences," are for high school students who have a special interest in the natural sciences. The participating students—far from being chosen (1) _____—are specially chosen for their demonstrated interest and ability in the sciences. Instead of spending their summer vacation at the swimming pool, these students spend it (2) _____ the latest developments in chemistry and physics. They are almost completely (3) _____ from the outside world as they surround themselves ten hours a day with the world of science.

A Governor's School for the Sciences is always held at a major university, where students have access to very (4) _____ equipment. They spend part of each day in classes, but a large part of their time is spent doing laboratory work. In chemistry classes, for example, students must do experiments in which they analyze unidentified liquids and materials and must (5) _____ them _____ into their (6) _____ chemicals. They must, in addition, determine what (7) _____ chemicals have by doing different tests, such as (8) _____ a chemical in acid or by (9) _____ a liquid with another and noticing the reaction. Students must write the results of the experiments and (10) _____ them _____ to the professors.

In the physics classes, students examine the mechanical and physical properties of different phenomena. Using a ball and a tipped surface, for instance, students can determine the effect of (11) _____ on the speed of an object rolling downhill. In many programs students have access to laser (12) _____ and are able to determine the effects that such a concentrated (13) _____ of light has on different objects.

These are just a few examples of the opportunities available to some high school students. It is to be hoped that soon such opportunities will be open to students in each state in the country, and in fields other than the sciences.

Follow-up

G. Dictation: Write the sentences that your teacher reads aloud.

1. _____
2. _____
3. _____
4. _____
5. _____

H. Answer the following questions.

1. Name several objects that are cylindrical in shape.
2. What are some practical applications of chemistry in the home? of physics?
3. How would you describe a sophisticated traveler?
4. From how far away can you make out a street sign?
5. Name some things that dissolve in water.
6. How are novels filed in the library? How are nonfiction books filed?
7. What are some properties of cement?
8. When do the street lights shut off in the morning?
9. Name five mammals that aren't pets.
10. On a scale of one to ten, how would you rate the U.S. president? the leader of your country? a movie star?
11. What kinds of things do you expect to come across when you clean your closet?
12. What can cause friction between friends?
13. What are the component parts of a book? of a classroom?
14. Think of two random numbers between one and twenty. See if one of your classmates can guess the numbers you are thinking of.

I. Describe a science experiment that you did in one of the following.

1. elementary school
2. high school
3. university

Recreation

Word Form Chart

NOUN	VERB	ADJECTIVE	ADVERB	PREPOSITION
anchor	anchor	anchored		
astonishment	astonish	astonished		
		astonishing	astonishingly	
	calm down			
dynamism		dynamic	dynamically	
exception	except	exceptional	exceptionally	except
grin	grin	grinning		
hook	hook	hooked		
illusion				
disillusion	disillusion	disillusioned		
disillusionment		disillusioning		
melody		melodious	melodiously	
		melodic	melodically	
net	net	netted		
notion				
rhythm		rhythmical	rhythmically	
		rhythmic		
shock	shock	shocked		
		shocking	shockingly	
simultaneity		simultaneous	simultaneously	
slope	slope	sloping		
	stick to			
swing	swing	swinging		
	(swung,			
	swung)			
	take up			
	turn in			
	turn on			
wonder	wonder	wonderful	wonderfully	
		wondering	wonderingly	
	write out			

Definitions and Examples

1. **anchor** [a heavy metal object attached to a ship and thrown into the water in order to keep the ship in place]

    All ships and boats must have an **anchor** in order to keep the ship from moving when it has stopped. When the sailors of a sailboat, for example, are ready to stop, they simply throw the **anchor** over the side of the boat.

    Many people in Florida, California, and the Caribbean have sailboats as a hobby. For people who spend their vacations sailing, there are places, usually in protected harbors, where sailors can **anchor** their boats to stay overnight.

2. **wonder** (a) [something which causes great admiration]

    The Taj Mahal in India is one of the great **wonders** of the world. People travel from all over the world to see it.

    One of the most **wonderful** sights I have ever seen is Machu Picchu, the ancient ruins of the Inca Indians in Peru.

    (b) [to want to know more about something or to have doubts]

    Children often **wonder** about many things of nature: How do birds fly? Why does the wind blow? What happens to people after they die?

    A: I **wonder** where my dictionary is.
    B: Isn't it on your desk?
    A: I thought it was, but it's not there now.
    B: I **wonder** if someone borrowed it?
    A: Oh, that's it. John borrowed it because he's writing a composition for English class.

3. **calm down** {separable} [to become quiet and calm from a state of extreme emotion]

    When children become very excited in the evening, it can be difficult to **calm** them **down** before they go to bed.

    If my brother plays very actively with his three-year-old daughter before bed, it takes an hour for her to **calm down** and be ready to sleep.

    My mother was so nervous after hearing about my accident that she did not **calm down** for two days.

    We often talk about the weather or the wind as "**calming down**" after a particularly rough storm.

4. **grin** [a wide smile that shows the teeth]

    There are several types of **grins**: some are **grins** of embarrassment when a person has just done something silly, some are **grins** of newly discovered pleasure, and some are just **grins** of pure enjoyment of life.

    When I went to Germany as a high school exchange student, I wondered how my German family would receive me. The first time I met them, they looked very serious, but when I said my first German sentence in my American accent, they **grinned**, and I knew everything would be all right.

5. **astonish** [to fill with sudden surprise, amazement, or wonder]

> The speed with which Ali learned to speak English **astonished** his teachers.
>
> Travelers to the American West are always **astonished** by the grandness of the Rocky Mountains.
>
> A: Did you hear the news that the president of the United States just resigned?
>
> B: Yes, I was quite **astonished**. I never expected him to do that.

6. **net** (a) [an object, made of loosely woven thread or string, which is used to catch animals or to divide two things]

> The word **net** can refer to a fabric, or it can be the name of an object that is made from **net** fabric. For example, people who fish in the ocean can catch large quantities of fish in huge **nets**. "**Net**" is also the name of the object that separates the two halves of a tennis court.
>
> When my brother was around ten years old, his hobby was to go to the fields near our house to catch insects with a small **net**.

(b) [the total gain or loss, as of profit]

> The **net** gain for our new company last year was $5,000. We took in $50,000, and we spent $45,000.
>
> My town has had a **net** loss in population. Although approximately 1,000 people have moved here in the last two years, over 4,000 people have moved away.

7. **hook** [a piece of (usually) metal with a sharp bend that is used to catch, drag, close, or hang something]

> Fishermen use **hooks** at the end of a line to catch fish.
>
> People also use **hooks** to hang pictures on the wall.
>
> Women's skirts often have **hooks** to close the waist.
>
> My father and my two uncles spent Sunday fishing on the river near our house. In one hour my father **hooked** three fish and caught two more with a net. He couldn't stop grinning when he got home.

8. **simultaneous** [happening or existing at the same time]

> There was a symphony concert on the radio last night and a **simultaneous** showing of the concert on television.
>
> The two children were so excited by the circus that they **simultaneously** tried to tell their mother what they had seen.

9. **turn on** {separable} [to cause to start operating]

> When I come home from work in the evenings, sometimes I am too tired to even **turn on** the television.
>
> We stayed at a nice hotel on our vacation last summer, but it was extremely hot. We wondered why no one had **turned** the air conditioner **on** in our room the first night. We later learned that it had broken down.

10. **exception** [a case that does not follow normal rules]

> Most tourists really enjoy visiting Disney World in Florida; the few who do not are **exceptions**.
>
> It is possible to make rules about English spelling but there are so many **exceptions** that the rules are not always helpful. For example, i goes before e, **except** after c, as in **piece** and **receipt**.

11. **exceptional** [better than average; superior]

> There is a wonderful vacation spot in an area called Cinque Terre on the northwest coast of Italy. The views of the mountains and the Mediterranean Sea are **exceptional**, the hotels are inexpensive, and the food is good but astonishingly cheap.
>
> Train service in Japan is said to be **exceptionally** efficient; trains are frequent and are never more than two minutes late.

12. **turn in** (a) [to go to bed]

> People who spend the day in vigorous physical activity usually need to **turn in** early.
>
> When we went camping and mountain-climbing, we got up at five o'clock in the morning and always **turned in** around eight o'clock in the evening.

  (b) {separable} [to hand in (an assignment or a form)]

> Teachers sometimes lower the grade of an assignment that is **turned in** late.
>
> A: When is our history assignment due?
> B: We have to **turn** it **in** next Tuesday.

13. **dynamic** (a) [having a lot of energy; very active]

> Rock and roll singers must be very **dynamic**; their fans want to see a performance with a lot of energy and movement.
>
> Different cultures have differing ideas about what makes a good teacher. Although being **dynamic** is not enough, Americans value **dynamism** as one desirable characteristic of a teacher.

  (b) [continually changing]

> An economy which is not **dynamic** is one that is dying.
>
> People who study languages know that all languages are **dynamic**: languages are constantly changing.

14. **melody** [the arrangement of sounds in a song]

> **Melody** refers to the musical sound of a song. All songs and musical works have a **melody**, but not all **melodies** have words. If someone has a **melodious** voice, it means we think he or she has a very pleasant-sounding voice.

15. **notion** (a) [a general impression or feeling]

> Americans who live in the north of the United States, where winters are severe, often have the wrong **notion** that people in the South spend all year outside in recreational activities.

> Before I traveled in East Asia, I had no **notion** that Japanese, Chinese, and Korean art were so beautiful.

(b) [intention or wish to do something]

> When we planned our holiday in Spain, we had a **notion** to spend all our time lying in the sun at the beach, but there were so many interesting museums, castles, and historic sites to visit that we did not spend even one day at the beach.

> A: What are you going to do this weekend?
> B: I have a **notion** to visit a friend in Washington, D.C., but on Monday I need to turn in a ten-page report which I haven't started yet.

16. **rhythm** [any kind of movement or music that has regularly occurring strong and weak elements]

> The **rhythm** of moving a baby's bed can help make a baby sleep. In fact, any kind of steady **rhythm**, such as the tick-tock noise of a clock, can put a child to sleep.

> In dance music, the melody of a song is not as important as the **rhythm**. Music that is easy to dance to needs a strong **rhythm** that is easy to feel.

17. **write out** {separable} [to write something completely]

> When taking notes in class, it is best not to **write** everything **out** completely. Use as many abbreviations and symbols as you can in order to save time.

> Patient: Should I write my name on the first line?
> Nurse: Yes, please **write out** your complete name; do not use any initials.

> A: Can you tell me how to get to your house for the party?
> B: Yes, I'll **write** the directions **out** for you after class.

18. **swing** (a) [to hang or be suspended from a point while moving rhythmically from one point to another (and sometimes back again)]

> Monkeys that live in trees often travel by **swinging** from one branch to another.
>
> My grandmother's hobby is gardening, and she has many plants and flowers suspended from the ceiling of her front porch. They look very pretty when they **swing** gently in the wind.

    (b) [a seat suspended from above for the enjoyment of someone who sits on it and swings]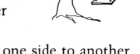

> When my brother and I were small, our father built us a **swing**.
>
> The other kids in the neighborhood used to come to our house to **swing** because you could go much higher than on most other **swings**.

    (c) [the manner in which a person moves an object from one side to another, especially in order to hit a ball in sports]

> A player's **swing** is particularly important in golf and in baseball. In both sports a player must hit a ball with a stick-like instrument, and that instrument must be **swung** with force and accuracy.

19. **slope** [any line or surface (such as the ground) that is at an angle between 0 and 90 degrees]

> A hill used for skiing needs to have a steep **slope**.
>
> A: Where do you want to put your new table?
> B: I'd like to put it by the window, but the floor **slopes** right there, so we'd better put it against the opposite wall.

20. **stick to** (a) [to continue to do a job; to remain in a situation or place]

> I tried to learn to play tennis several years ago, but I did not **stick to** it long enough to become good.
>
> John is a bright student, but if he does not **stick to** his studies better, he will not graduate this year.

    (b) [to hold to something by (or as if by) glue]

> If a stamp won't **stick to** the envelope, put a little glue on the back of the stamp.
>
> I did not realize that several leaves had **stuck to** my dress this morning. I spent the entire day with leaves on my back.

21. **take up** {separable} [to develop an interest in (especially a hobby)]

> My father has lived his entire life near the sea, and he always enjoyed watching sailing, but he did not **take** it **up** himself until he was almost 50 years old.
>
> When people retire, they should **take up** some kind of hobby; otherwise, they might find their retirement rather grim if they have too much free time.

22. **shock** (a) [a severe offense to someone's sense of decency and what is proper or morally right; something that disturbs the mind or emotions as if by a sudden, violent blow]

> It was a **shock** for us to learn that our kind, old, next-door neighbor had killed two men when he was a young man.
>
> I was **shocked** by the fact that a student would turn in a composition that had clearly been copied from another student.
>
> The news of my uncle's death was a **shock** to the family because he was in apparent good health.

(b) [a physical reaction to bodily injury or stress, usually characterized by loss of blood pressure and other physical signs]

> The young girl was not hurt by the car accident, but she was in a state of **shock** as a result.
>
> If you are with a person who goes into **shock**, you should first have the person lie down and then call a doctor.

23. **illusion** (a) [an inaccurcate idea or impression of reality]

> It is an **illusion** to think that you would be happy if only you had more money or a nicer car.
>
> Students sometimes have the **illusion** that teachers assign homework because they want students to be busy; however, teachers assign homework to help students concentrate on the material covered in class.

(b) [a figure or pattern capable of being interpreted in several ways]

> These two lines are actually the same length;
>   it is an **illusion** that line A is bigger.
> Another visual **illusion** is this one, which can
>   be either a vase or two faces, depending upon which lines
>   your eyes focus on.

24. **disillusion** [loss of illusions or hopes]

> Many immigrants to America were **disillusioned** when they realized the streets were not really made of gold.
>
> The young actor went to Hollywood to try to become successful in movies, but his **disillusion** with the shocking lifestyles of many actors caused him to quit the acting profession completely.

Introductory Exercises

A.   Match each word with its definition.

____ 1. superior	**a.** anchor
____ 2. to go to bed	**b.** astonish
____ 3. happening at the same time	**c.** calm down
____ 4. a heavy metal object attached to a ship	**d.** dynamic
____ 5. energetic	**e.** exceptional
____ 6. the sounds in a song	**f.** grin
____ 7. to have many questions	**g.** net
____ 8. to continue to do a job	**h.** notion
____ 9. a general impression or feeling	**i.** rhythm
____ 10. a wide smile that shows the teeth	**j.** shock
____ 11. an object used to catch animals	**k.** simultaneous
____ 12. to fill with sudden surprise or amazement	**l.** slope
____ 13. an inaccurate idea of reality	**m.** stick to
____ 14. to become quiet after a state of extreme emotion	**n.** swing
____ 15. any regularly occurring movement	**o.** take up
____ 16. to begin a hobby	**p.** turn in
	q. wonder
	r. write out

B.   Complete each sentence with a word from the word form chart and any other necessary word.

1. When you go fishing, you should be sure to take a line and a

   _____ .

2. A standard piece of equipment on American playgrounds is a set of

   _____ .

3. Requirements for downhill skiing are a pair of skis, snow, and

   a(n)_____ .

4. For a man who weighed 220 pounds before he began a diet, and who now weighs 180 pounds, 40 pounds represent his _____ loss.

5. If your friend has a sudden desire to eat ice cream, she might have a

   _____ to go to an ice cream shop.

6. If you come across someone who has fallen to the ground, has no color in her face, and who has low blood pressure and a slow heartbeat, she

   might be in a state of _____ .

7. When you walk on wet grass that has just been cut, the grass will
   _____ your shoes.

8. Before you can turn something off, you have to _____ .

9. Americans as a rule do not learn foreign languages easily. Therefore, an
   American who can speak seven or eight languages is considered quite

   _____ .

10. If a doctor normally charges $50 per visit but doesn't charge a patient
    who is unemployed, for that patient he makes a(n) _____ .

11. A politician who is very energetic and is an exciting, emotional speaker
    can be described as _____ .

12. The appearance of a small pool of water in the desert is an example of
    a(n) _____ .

13. It's possible to have music without words, but a song is not a song if
    there is no _____ .

14. If you found out that you were unexpectedly to receive one million
    dollars, you would probably have an expression of _____ on
    your face.

15. After you received the million dollars, it would probably be quite a while
    before you _____ .

16. If you want to hold a boat in one place, you try to _____
    it with something heavy.

Study Exercises

C.   Write **T** if the sentence is true and **F** if it is false.

_____ **1.** Children playing on a swing may be grinning and laughing as they swing higher and higher.

_____ **2.** Dance music should have a distinct rhythm.

_____ **3.** When you go fishing with a fishing pole, you must first put a small piece of food on the hook in order to attract the fish.

_____ **4.** Be careful when going swimming in cold water: if your body is warm and you jump all at once into very cold water, you could suffer shock.

_____ **5.** People in the desert often have the illusion of seeing small pools of water.

_____ **6.** If you want a hobby that doesn't require much money, you could take up running.

_____ **7.** During a major sports event such as the Olympics, many competitions take place simultaneously.

_____ **8.** A steep slope is a good place to set up a tent when you are camping.

_____ **9.** Commercial fishermen catch large quantities of fish with nets.

_____ **10.** If you use checks when you are paying for something, you should write out the information on the checks very clearly.

_____ **11.** You shouldn't turn on your radio at a party or at the beach unless you are sure it won't annoy other people.

_____ **12.** A golfer may have to swing the ball a long distance.

D.   Match each word or phrase with its opposite.

_____ **1.** abbreviate	**a.** turn on
_____ **2.** still	**b.** wonder
_____ **3.** fall off	**c.** sloped
_____ **4.** shut off	**d.** net
_____ **5.** ordinary	**e.** stick to
_____ **6.** know	**f.** write out
_____ **7.** reality	**g.** simultaneous
_____ **8.** flat	**h.** exceptional
_____ **9.** angered	**i.** grin
_____ **10.** straight	**j.** dynamic
_____ **11.** frown	**k.** illusion
	l. hooked
	m. astonished
	n. calmed down

E. Circle the letter of word that is associated with each sport or hobby.

1. golf
   a. net
   b. rope
   c. ball

2. baseball
   a. water
   b. music
   c. swing

3. fishing
   a. grin
   b. hook
   c. notion

4. camping
   a. tent
   b. illusion
   c. hook

5. dancing
   a. wind
   b. rhythm
   c. hook

6. swimming
   a. water
   b. melody
   c. astonishment

7. tennis
   a. anchor
   b. disillusionment
   c. net

8. sailing
   a. shock
   b. anchor
   c. music

9. skiing
   a. slope
   b. court
   c. tent

10. mountain climbing
    a. ball
    b. slope
    c. beam

F. Read the passage and answer the questions that follow.

Last summer my family had a visit from Jim, a fourteen-year-old cousin from Colorado. He is from a mountainous part of the state and could ski at the age of three, but he had never seen the ocean before. We live on the Gulf Coast (that is, the Gulf of
5   Mexico) of Florida, so I grew up by the ocean. My cousin was very excited at the notion of seeing the sea, and it was fun to watch him make new discoveries. His first reaction was one of shock, however; he couldn't believe how flat the gulf was. (Did he expect the waves to form slopes like the mountains?) The day after he
10 arrived, we went sailing in our family boat. He was so excited by the idea of a boat ride that when my father let him adjust the

anchor, he fell over the side into the water! His enthusiasm was
not lessened by his "bath" although he did calm down a little.
Once we were actually sailing, he received his next surprise. The
15 rhythm of a boat really does cause some people to be seasick; Jim
was one of them. We sailed for about an hour, and he was so sick
that he turned in as soon as we got home and stayed in bed
all day.
   The next day, however, we were astonished when he
20 announced that he was ready to go out in the sailboat again, this
time to go fishing. (About two years ago my parents took up deep-
sea fishing as a hobby.) Early the next morning we sailed about
two miles out into the gulf and dropped anchor. Jim had never
been fishing before, and I was afraid he would be disillusioned.
25 Ocean fishing can be slow, and Jim is such a dynamic, energetic
boy that I thought he would be bored. However, he seemed to
enjoy himself. He especially liked swinging the pole to throw the
hook and line into the water. Many boys his age would have been
bored after a half hour, but he stuck to his pole for three hours.
30 Finally, he felt a pull on the line, and we knew he had hooked a
fish. First Jim pulled back until he was almost on the other side of
the boat; then the fish pulled until Jim was almost out of the boat.
This continued for about twenty minutes until we could see the
fish near the surface of the water. I grabbed a net to help bring the
35 fish in. We were all astonished to see the biggest fish anyone in
our family had ever caught. It weighed almost thirty pounds! Jim's
astonishment was greater than ours, I think, and he could not say
anything at first. He just grinned. When he had recovered from his
shock, he declared this the most wonderful vacation anyone could
40 ever take.

Write **T** if the sentence is true and **F** if it is false.

_____ **1.** Jim took up waterskiing when he was very young.

_____ **2.** The author is from Mexico.

_____ **3.** Jim was shocked the first time he saw the Gulf of Mexico.

_____ **4.** The waves in the Gulf form slopes that resemble mountains.

_____ **5.** When Jim adjusted the anchor, he fell out of the boat.

_____ **6.** The rhythm of the boat sailing made Jim sick.

_____ **7.** He turned in immediately after the sailboat ride.

_____ **8.** Jim did not want to go sailing again.

_____ **9.** Jim was disillusioned by deep-sea fishing.

_____ **10.** Deep-sea fishing is a very dynamic hobby.

_____ **11.** Jim had trouble sticking to his fishing.

_____ **12.** Jim's cousin helped him bring in the fish with a net.

_____ **13.** Jim was at first too astonished by his catch to speak.

Follow-up

G. Dictation: Write the sentences that your teacher reads aloud.

1. _____
2. _____
3. _____
4. _____
5. _____

H. Answer the following questions.

1. What would you do if you were camping with a group of people and someone went into shock?
2. What notions do Americans have about your country?
3. What is the first thing you turn on in the morning when you wake up?
4. What hobby (or hobbies) have you taken up?
5. What time do you usually turn in during the week? On the weekend?
6. What is more important to you in a song, the melody or the words? Why?
7. If you are nervous about a test, what do you do to calm yourself down?
8. What is your favorite dance rhythm?
9. What has astonished you most about this city?
10. What illusions did you have as a child? What disillusioned you as an adult?
11. What things cause you to grin?
12. Do you have ski slopes in your country? If so, describe them.
13. Describe a dynamic teacher you have known.
14. Name two actions you cannot do simultaneously.
15. Describe a promise to yourself that you have had trouble sticking to.

I. Answer one of the following questions.

1. Describe a fishing/camping/skiing trip you have been on.
2. Describe the most wonderful trip you have taken.
3. Describe the most dynamic person you have known.

Environment

Word Form Chart

NOUN	VERB	ADJECTIVE	ADVERB
abuse	abuse	abused	
appreciation	appreciate	appreciative	
composition	compose		
constituent	constitute	constituent	
corrosion	corrode	corrosive	
		corroded	
counter	counter		
delicacy		delicate	delicately
deterioration	deteriorate	deteriorated	
		deteriorating	
figure	figure		
		grave	gravely
implement	implement		
implementation			
means			
ore			
outlet			
		partial	partially
precaution		precautionary	
	stick up for		
submersion	submerge	submerged	
	tear down		
thoughtlessness		thoughtless	thoughtlessly
		tremendous	tremendously
	turn off		
	turn out		
		vital	vitally
washout	wash out	washed out	

Definitions and Examples

1. **abuse** [to hurt or injure; to use wrongly or improperly]

   People **abuse** the natural resources of the earth by wasting or polluting them. The industrialized countries are particularly guilty of this—wastes from large factories are poured into rivers and the air.
   Small children should be watched when they are around pets because children may **abuse** small animals without realizing it.

2. **composition** (a) [the combining of parts or elements to make a whole]

   The **composition** of air is approximtely 78% nitrogen and 21% oxygen.

   A: What is the student **composition** of your English class?
   B: About 40% of my class are from the Middle East, about 30% are from Latin America, and about 30% are from Asia.

   (b) [a short essay]

   A well-written **composition** has an introductory paragraph, a clearly stated conclusion, and several paragraphs in between.

   A: What homework do you have to do?
   B: We have to write a **composition** about our favorite summer vacation.

3. **grave** (a) [extremely serious or important; critical and perhaps dangerous]

   The destruction of much of the world's green areas, for example, those in the tropical forests of Brazil, might be creating a **grave** problem for the future: the overall supply of oxygen is decreasing.
   The family across the street from us was in a car accident caused by a drunk driver. Every one of them was in **grave** condition, the doctor said, especially the mother; he is not sure if she will live.

   (b) [3-22: a place of burial; the stone or sign that marks a place of burial]

   Americans traditionally mark **graves** with a stone with the name and years of birth and death of the person who has died. Some people leave flowers on the **grave** of family members on special occasions.

4. **deteriorate** [to become lower in quality or value]

   The quality of the water in our river has **deteriorated** greatly because of industrial pollution.
   Severe inflation causes the standard of living of the middle and working classes to **deteriorate**.
   Their relationship **deteriorated** to such an extent that Mike finally broke it off.

5. **corrode** [to dissolve or deteriorate gradually, especially by chemical action]

   Certain chemicals and acids **corrode** metals.
   Cities that have a lot of snow in the winter use salt on the roads to melt the snow, but unfortunately the salt has a **corrosive** effect on automobiles.

6. **counter** (a) [opposite; against]

Americans are accustomed to receiving their groceries from most grocery stores in free paper bags. Some conservation groups have suggested that they should reuse their bags in order to save trees, but this suggestion runs **counter** to Americans' ideas of convenience.

Private oil companies argue that they should have full permission to drill for oil along the coast of the United States, but the environmental groups **counter** with the argument that oil spills resulting from the drilling are too dangerous for sea life.

(b) [a flat surface on which business takes place, money is counted, or food is served]

At fast-food restaurants such as McDonald's, the customer stands on one side of the **counter** and the server stands on the other side. All food is served over the **counter**.

When I got home yesterday, I did not have my bookbag, and then I remembered that I had left it on the **counter** at the bank.

7. **appreciate** [to be thankful or grateful for something]

People often do not **appreciate** the beauty of their local scenery until they travel to another part of their country.

Older people **appreciate** young people's taking the time to visit and talk with them.

A: Thank you for your help and efforts. I'd like to show my **appreciation** with this small gift.

B: Oh, it was no trouble to help you, but thank you for the present.

8. **delicate** (a) [pleasingly fine, usually small or thin]

The linden tree has a very **delicate** flower; it is long and thin and can be picked very easily. Its smell is also **delicate**—very fresh and light.

Cold weather may have many disadvantages, but one of the advantages is the beautiful, **delicate** patterns made by ice on the windows.

(b) [easily damaged or broken; not strong in health]

The wires in my tape recorder are so **delicate** that the repairman broke a wire when he opened it. My old recorder, on the other hand, had wires that could not be broken, even when the repairman tried!

My friend Allison is quite **delicate**; she gets sick if she gets too hot or does too much exercise.

9. **means (of), (to)** [a method, course of action, or instrument by which some act can be accomplished]

A good education can be a **means to** a better job and a higher social position.

A: By what **means** can we protect our national parks from becoming industrial sites?

B: By writing to our congressmen to let them know we want strong laws prohibiting business in national parks.

10. **outlet** (a) [a means of letting something out]

> Writing poetry is Peter's **outlet** for creative self-expression.
> When there is too much water in the pond, an **outlet** is needed for it.
> Playing provides an **outlet** for a child's energy.

(b) [the source of electricity in a house or building, usually in the form of a small hole in the wall to which wires from the outside are run]

> In order to turn on a lamp, it must be connected to an electrical **outlet**.
> Older houses usually do not have many **outlets**, but today's houses often have three or four **outlets** per room.

11. **precaution (against)** [an action taken in advance to protect against possible failure or danger]

> When you go camping and build a fire, you should keep some water nearby as a **precaution against** the fire's spreading.
> Trees are often planted along roads as a **precautionary** measure **against** the road washing out during a heavy rain.

12. **implement** (a) [a tool or instrument; any means used to reach a desired end]

> An **implement** can be a tool that you use to accomplish a task. A knife is an **implement** for cutting meat; a screwdriver is an **implement** used to remove a screw or put one in place.

> A: What kind of **implement** will you need to repair the outlet?
> B: Only a screwdriver to remove the covering plate.

(b) [to provide a plan or procedure to ensure the fulfillment of a goal]

> The U.S. Environmental Protection Agency is responsible for **implementing** national policy about pollution and the protection of the environment in general.
> It is easy to make a law to address a problem. It is much more difficult to **implement** regulations that will carry out that law.

13. **constituent** (a) [a component; part of a whole]

> Oxygen is a **constituent** of water.
> The Environmental Protection Agency is a **constituent** of the Department of the Interior; that is, the agency is under the direction of this department.

(b) [someone represented by an elected official]

> **Constituents** are the people in a district who elect a representative or a senator.
> There are 5,000 **constituents** in Senator Smith's district, and 80% of them voted in favor of regulations about air pollution.

14. **ore** [a mineral (or combination of minerals) from which a valuable constituent, usually a metal, can be mined]

> The process by which a metal is taken from an **ore** is not complicated. To get iron from iron **ore**, the **ore** must be heated until the iron in it melts and drains off.
>
> A lot of iron **ore** is mined in the states of Minnesota and Wisconsin.

15. **turn off** {separable} [to shut off; to stop the operation of something]

> Never forget to **turn off** the lights of your car after you park, or you will return to a dead battery!
>
> A: Did you **turn** the oven **off** when you finished making dinner?
> B: No, I forgot. So that's why it's so hot in the house!

16. **turn out** (a) {separable} [to turn off a light]

> When I go out in the evening, I **turn** all the lights **out** except one in the living room. I do not like to enter a dark house.

(b) [to result; to be found to be, as after an experiment or experience]

> The experiments about the effects of acid rain on plants **turned out** to be successful from the scientists' point of view. It was found that rain with a high acid content causes decreased production in food crops.
>
> The children thought spending their vacation on their uncle's farm would be boring, but it **turned out** to be the best vacation they had ever had. They learned to milk cows and feed chickens, and they made several new friends.

(c) [to arrive or assemble, as for a public performance]

> More than 5,000 people **turned out** to protest the new nuclear power plant in New Mexico.
>
> Last semester almost 150 people **turned out** for the international dinner held by the foreign students at the university.

17. **partially** (a) [partly; in part; not completely]

> Much of the forest land in California was **partially** destroyed by a forest fire in 1985.
>
> You are **partially** correct if you think air pollution is caused by factories, but a great deal of pollution is also caused by cars.

(b) **part** [assumed: a portion]

> He only ate **part** of the apple; he threw the rest away.

18. **wash out** {separable} [gradual deterioration of land or a road by a stream of water]

> Heavy rains last week **washed out** a section of the road near our school.
> The flooding of the river **washed** fifty square feet of our yard **out**.

(b) {separable} [to wash a small quantity of clothes by hand]

> Delicate clothing must be **washed out** by hand, not in a washing machine.
> You should **wash** this blouse **out** in cold water.

19. **washout** {informal} [a total failure or disappointment]

> Our camping trip was a **washout**; it rained the entire weekend, and our tent leaked.
> The campaign to get people to separate the glass and metal from their garbage will probably be a **washout**. Many people will only make the effort if they are forced to by law.

20. **stick up for** [to defend or support]

> Someone must **stick up for** endangered animals who cannot protect themselves from being killed on a large scale by man. The Greenpeace movement attempts to do this, for example, by fighting the hunting of whales and seals.
> Franklin Roosevelt was a popular president because he **stuck up for** the rights of the average person.

21. **submerge** [to place under water or other liquid; to cover with water]

> The waters from the spring flood were so high that all the houses in the neighborhood were completely **submerged**.
> Sea mammals, such as whales and dolphins, can remain **submerged** for long periods of time.

22. **tear down** {separable} [to destroy completely, usually to destroy something built by man]

> The city wanted to **tear** 25 beautiful old homes **down** in order to build a highway through the middle of the town, but the citizens protested, and the homes were saved.
> The park along the river in our town is about 30 years old. On the same site there had previously been some deteriorated old factories which the local government **tore down** in order to create the park.

23. **thoughtless** [careless; unthinking; inconsiderate]

> It only takes one lit cigarette, **thoughtlessly** thrown on the ground, to start a forest fire.
> My cousin does not mean to be cruel, but he frequently makes **thoughtless** comments that hurt his sister's feelings.

24. tremendous (a) [extremely large in amount or degree]

> The force of a tornado is **tremendous**; for example, a tornado can pick up an entire house and carry it for several miles.
>
> Although birds are small, they eat a **tremendous** amount daily: about ten times their own weight.

(b) [wonderful]

> Our boating trip on the river was **tremendous**: we saw lots of birds and animals, and the scenery was amazing.
>
> Professor Davids is a **tremendous** teacher. He is very dynamic, and his explanations are clear as well as entertaining.

25. vital [essential; having immediate importance]

> It is **vital** that our government take immediate precautions to prevent the continued deterioration of our air and water.
>
> Because hospitals in the United States are so expensive, it is **vitally** important that a person have medical insurance.

26. figure (a) [the shape or form of a body]

> Although it was dark, we could make out the **figure** of a deer about ten yards away.
>
> Large sailing ships used to have the **figure** of a woman on the front.

(b) [an individual, especially a well-known person]

> Rachel Carson was an important **figure** in the environmental movement. She wrote a book called *The Silent Spring*, which is about the effects of pollution on animal life in the wild.
>
> The president is the most important political **figure** in the U.S. government.

(c) [2-24: a symbol representing anything other than a letter, especially a number]

> A mathematician works with **figures**.

(d) [2-24: to find an answer, usually using numbers]

> To **figure** the annual cost of a special bus fare, multiply the monthly fee by twelve.

Introductory Exercises

A. Match each word with its definition.

_____ **1.** essential

_____ **2.** an action to prevent danger

_____ **3.** a tool

_____ **4.** very fine and small

_____ **5.** careless

_____ **6.** to become lower in quality or value

_____ **7.** to hurt or injure

_____ **8.** very serious and important

_____ **9.** to defend or support

_____ **10.** large amount

_____ **11.** to be thankful for something

_____ **12.** to result

_____ **13.** the shape of a body

_____ **14.** to place under water

_____ **15.** a component

_____ **16.** a mineral from which a metal is taken

_____ **17.** opposite or against

_____ **18.** a means of releasing energy

_____ **19.** to dissolve gradually

_____ **20.** a total failure

a. abuse
b. appreciate
c. composition
d. constituent
e. corrode
f. counter
g. delicate
h. deteriorate
i. figure
j. grave
k. implement
l. means
m. ore
n. outlet
o. precaution
p. stick up for
q. submerge
r. tear down
s. thoughtless
t. tremendous
u. turn out
v. vital
w. washout

B. Answer each question with a word from the word form chart.

1. If you have an old wooden fence around your farm and you want to build a new one, what do you do with the old one?
2. What kind of papers do you write in writing class?
3. How do you describe a person who blows cigarette smoke in the faces of other people without realizing it?
4. If you are half finished with a test, and the teacher asks you if you have finished, what can you answer?
5. What's the relation between a good education and a good job?
6. If you're driving your car at night, what should you do before you get out of the car?
7. If part of your street has been destroyed by rain, what has the rain done to it?
8. How do you describe a person whose health is not very strong?
9. What do you call the tablelike surface where you order hamburgers at McDonalds?

10. What is the source of electricity in your house for your lamps and television?
11. If something is absolutely necessary for good health, what is it?
12. What do you call the people in a particular voting district?
13. If the air quality in a city has deteriorated to the point where the streetlights are turned on in the afternoon, how would you describe the pollution situation?
14. What does water do to unprotected iron?
15. If you have a plan to improve something, what else do you need?
16. If a person beats a pet and doesn't feed it, what does he do to it?
17. If you put something under water, what do you do to it?

Study Exercises

C. In each blank, write the most appropriate word from the word form chart. You may use some words more than once.

1. The efforts to raise money to protect the Hudson River

   _____ well; over one million dollars was raised.

2. Last year the town of Warren, Ohio, was _____ destroyed

   when over half the homes and many of the roads were _____
   by the flooded river. However, the townspeople have done a(n)

   _____ job of rebuilding the town. It is difficult to see any
   signs of damage.

3. The _____ of the coal mined in the mountains of
   Pennsylvania is mostly carbon; there is little sulfur in the coal.

4. Once a month I visit the grave of my father and leave flowers on it. I was

   very upset during my last visit to see that some _____
   person had thrown papers and an old soft drink can on the ground nearby.

5. People who work in mines should take _____ against
   accidents by wearing the proper protective equipment.

6. People who use a picnic site after you will _____ it if you
   leave the table and area clean.

7. An unknown person in the oil industry has given the astonishing

   _____ of three million dollars for the establishment of a park
   for wild animals.

8. The Society for the Prevention of Cruelty to Animals (SPCA) was begun

   as a(n) _____ of helping homeless or _____
   animals.

9. My father decided to _____ the old wooden garage behind our house because it had _____ to the point that it hardly had a roof on it. Now we need a new garage because we used to keep all our gardening _____ in the old one.

10. Over ten thousand people _____ to hear the president speak on the _____ need for new laws to protect the country's parks and forests.

11. The _____ mined in Minnesota is rich in iron.

D. Complete the analogies with a word or phrase from the word form chart in this unit.

1. rain : wash out :: acid : _____

2. seed : fruit :: gold : _____

3. doctor : pills :: banker : _____

4. turn off : water :: _____ : light

5. for : against :: supportive : _____

6. all : complete :: half : _____

7. quality : deteriorate :: metal : _____

8. ground : bury :: water : _____

9. reach : conclusion :: _____ : plan

10. tiny : large :: small : _____

11. clean : dirty :: preserved : _____

12. appreciative : nice :: annoyed : _____

E.   Write the letter of the phrase that best completes the sentence.

_____ **1.** I'm fortunate to have a supervisor who

_____ **2.** The composition of the work force in the United States

_____ **3.** John's grades deteriorated greatly after he

_____ **4.** My niece is a delicate child who doesn't play outside much and always

_____ **5.** A ballet costume is delicate and

_____ **6.** Education is often considered a means to an end, but it also

_____ **7.** Some people argue that smoking should be prohibited in all public places, but the counterargument

_____ **8.** We are looking for a figure of national importance to

_____ **9.** One of the vital constituents of the human body

_____ **10.** The "Adoptive Grandparents" program is a good outlet

a. can be an end in itself.

b. for the emotional needs of our senior citizens.

c. lead the fight against child abuse.

d. sticks up for me when the boss thinks I'm wrong.

e. changed tremendously after World War I.

f. has a grave expression.

g. is water.

h. began to spend evenings at the disco.

i. has to be washed out by hand.

j. says that people have a right to smoke where they please.

F.   Read the passage and answer the questions that follow.

       There has recently been much attention given to the effects of acid rain on the environment. What is acid rain? It is the rain that has been falling in the Midwest and north of the United States, in much of Canada, and in much of central and northern Europe. The
5   chemical composition of this rain is highly acidic: the rain is composed (mostly about two-thirds) of sulfuric acid (H_2SO_4) and partially (about one-third) of nitric acid (HNO_3). The sulfuric acid comes from factories that burn coal; the nitric acid comes from any source that burns oil, usually automobiles.
10   Acid rain has caused a grave upsetting of the delicate balance of

nature in the environment. The area of nature most abused by acid rain has been the animal life in rivers and lakes, mainly fish. The acid composition of water is vital to anything that lives in the water because such life is continually exposed to the acidity. Thus when 15 the acid content of a river becomes too high, the fish in the river die. The second area most abused by acid rain is any building or statue made of limestone, a soft stone whose main constituent is calcium (chemical symbol: Ca). Acid rain corrodes and destroys anything made of this material. A third area of concern is the plant life in 20 forests; the health of trees in particular has been deteriorating to the point that entire wooded areas are dying. Scientists have not been able to prove that acid rain is the cause of the deterioration of forests, but they do feel that perhaps "acid fog" is the cause.

What can be done about acid rain, and what precautions can 25 be taken against its deteriorating effects? One means of controlling the acid content in rain is by preventing, through the use of certain antipollution processes, the emission of the harmful sulfuric and nitric acids into the air. However, these processes are very costly. A congressman from the Midwest, an area high in acid 30 rain, has recommended that the government implement a plan in which factories are required to control the amount of sulfuric acid emitted into the air. Recently the constituents in this congressman's district protested the pollution produced by a local factory. The factory removes the iron from iron ore; to do this, 35 they melt the ore by burning coal with a high sulfur content. As a result, the factory emits a lot of sulfuric acid into the air. Over 2,000 people turned out to demonstrate against the factory's increase in output and to demand that production be reduced until the proper pollution controls are implemented. The 40 counterargument made by the factory's management was, of course, that the factory provides employment and that to decrease output would mean decreasing the number of people employed. The factory management further maintains that the cost of such pollution control is too great, and if the factory is forced to install 45 such pollution controls, it will have to close completely, and over 600 people will then lose their jobs.

The solution to the acid rain problem is not an easy one. There are means to control the contaminants in the rain, but these means are very expensive. It seems that we will need government 50 regulations—and perhaps government financial support—in order to implement an effective policy against acid rain.

1. What is the composition of acid rain? _____

_____

2. Where is it found? _____

_____

3. What causes it? _____

_____

4. What aspect of the environment has been most gravely affected? _____

_____

5. What suggestion has been made as a precaution against acid rain? _____

_____

6. Why did so many people in the Midwest turn out to protest a certain factory's production? _____

_____

7. What was the factory's counterargument? _____

_____

8. What do you think the solution to the acid rain problem should be? _____

_____

Follow-up

G. Dictation: Write the sentences that your teacher reads aloud.

1. _____
2. _____
3. _____
4. _____
5. _____

H. Answer the following questions.

1. What is one means to developing good English?
2. What is the most vital export (or exports) of your country's economy?
3. What qualities do you most appreciate in a friend?
4. Who stuck up for you when you were a child and got into trouble?
5. What kind of ore does your country have?
6. What are your outlets for creative energy?
7. What are two thoughtless actions by people in public places which irritate you?
8. Who is the most important political figure in your country? In the United States? In the world?
9. Name something that you often forget to turn off in your house.
10. What is the most tremendous natural phenomenon in your country?
11. What is the composition of student nationalities in this class?
12. What is the religious composition of your country?

I. Do you think that there are certain customs in your country that are good for the nation? Are there any that are causing some deterioration in public and private values? Compare some of these good and bad customs.

Media (A)

Word Form Chart

NOUN	VERB	ADJECTIVE	ADVERB
appendix			
atlas			
catalog	catalog		
dot	dot	dotted	
flash	flash	flashing	
gesture	gesture	gesturing	
	hear of		
hint	hint		
image			
matter	matter		
		novel	
objectivity		objective	
panel			
penetration	penetrate		
preliminary		preliminary	preliminarily
reason		reasonable	reasonably
		unreasonable	unreasonably
	renew	renewable	
		renewed	
significance	signify	significant	significantly
	spell out		
	stand for		
standpoint			

Definitions and Examples

1. **appendix** {plural: appendices} [extra material or information attached to the end of a book or other piece of writing]

   Our history book has an **appendix** that lists all the countries in the world and their capitals.

   A: Where can I find out the number of people who speak Swahili?
   B: I have a book about languages that has several **appendices**; one is an **appendix** of the major languages in Africa and the number of speakers.

2. **dot** [a small spot or point]

   The student did not put a **dot** over the letter i in bit, and the word looked like bet.

   A very common expression that people hear when they are about to sign a contract is "Please sign on the **dotted** line."

3. **catalog** [a list of names, titles, or articles arranged according to a system]

   You can find out what books a library has by looking in the card **catalog**; this is usually a cabinet with cards that have information about a book. The books are **cataloged** according to title, author, and subject.

   Stores also have **catalogs**, especially department stores or stores where people shop by mail. These **catalogs** are usually books with pictures and descriptions of things that are for sale.

   I saw a clock radio that I'd like to buy in a **catalog** from Sears.

4. **flash** (a) [a sudden bright light]

   There was a **flash** in the sky when the plane exploded.
   The sailors **flashed** a light three times in a row to signal that they were in trouble.
   Unfortunately, the reporter's **flash** on his camera broke just when the ambassador entered the room.

   (b) [a brief piece of very recent news]

   We were watching a movie on TV when the program was interrupted with a news **flash** about the president's accident.
   A news **flash** on the radio announced sudden flooding in our neighborhood.

   (c) [to appear or pass suddenly]

   The car **flashed** by so quickly that I could not see the license number.
   The policeman **flashed** his identification card at me, but I could not read his name.

5. **stand for** (a) [to be a symbol for; to represent]

   In the American flag, the color blue **stands for** justice, the color red **for** bravery, and the color white **for** purity.

   A: What does "AP" **stand for**?
   B: It **stands for** "Associated Press," which is an organization that collects news from around the world.

   (b) [to tolerate; to permit]

   American teachers will not **stand for** cheating on examinations or direct copying of other people's work.
   "I will not **stand for** your behavior" means that I absolutely will not permit, accept, or tolerate such behavior under any circumstances.

6. **gesture** (a) [the use of a hand or body movement as a means of communication]

   The same **gesture** may have completely different meanings in two different cultures. For example, nodding your head means "yes" in the United States, but in China it can mean "hello".
   The policeman **gestured** for the journalist to stop, but the journalist did not see him and kept going.

   (b) [something done or said as a symbol]

   The businessman donated one hundred dollars for a war memorial as a **gesture** in support of the men who had fought in the war.
   My brother offered to lend me money to buy a new car; that was a very kind **gesture** on his part.

7. **novel** (a) [new or unusual]

   In Saturday's newspaper there was an editoral which suggested a **novel** approach to the problem of feeding the poor; the author suggested that every family with an income over $50,000 "adopt" a family and contribute to their food bills.
   The theme of the movie I saw last night was certainly not **novel**; there have been at least five movies in the last year with the same idea.

   (b) [3-1: a book with imaginary characters and events]

   In the eighteenth century in England it was considered a waste of time to read **novels**. People were supposed to read essays in order to improve their minds.

8. **hear of** [to have some knowledge about; to be aware of; to recognize a name or some other information]

   Many Americans have never **heard of** Rwanda or Burundi because the newspapers do not report much on that part of the world.

   A: Have you read The Winds of War?
   B: I've **heard of** it, but I've never read it.

9. **atlas** [a book of maps, often with descriptive information]

> I was not sure where Mauritius was until I looked in an **atlas**, where I saw that it is in the Indian Ocean between Africa and India.
>
> My grandfather has an old **atlas** which lists Austria as part of the Austro-Hungarian Empire.

10. **hint** [a suggestion for action or advice that is communicated briefly or indirectly]

> There is a weekly column in the newspaper that gives **hints** and advice about gardening. One helpful **hint** I learned recently was that if you plant tomatoes near flowers, the flowers will be protected from certain harmful insects that avoid tomato plants.
>
> The employee did not want to tell her boss directly that he had made a mistake, so she **hinted** that there might have been a better solution to the problem.

11. **standpoint** [a position from which objects or ideas are viewed and judged]

> From the taxpayer's **standpoint**, the government spends too much money on the military. From the military's **standpoint**, the government does not spend enough money.
>
> The worker's **standpoint** on the new tax law is that businesses and people with large incomes still do not pay enough taxes.

12. **objective** (a) [treating facts without the interference of personal prejudices or feelings]

> A newspaper editorial is not an **objective** account of the news; each editorial reflects the political opinions of the paper's editors about a particular issue.
>
> It is difficult to be completely **objective** when reporting the news. Journalists try to be **objective**, but it is almost impossible at times to prevent their personal feelings from influencing their standpoint on a piece of news.

(b) [an aim or goal]

> An **objective** of the 1987 immigration law was to cut down on the number of illegal workers in the United States.
>
> The missionary's **objective** in going to Africa was to convert people to his religion.

13. **panel** (a) [a group of people who discuss a topic before an audience, judge a contest, or participate in a television or radio game show]

> I saw a **panel** of scientists on TV last night discuss the nuclear weapons situation.
>
> The **panel** of judges for the ice-skating show disagreed about the winner.

(b) [a separate or distinct part of a surface, as a rectangular and raised or sunken surface of a door or wall]

> We bought a new front door for our house. It is made of light wood, but it has four **panels** of dark wood.
>
> The tourists visited an old French house in which the interior walls and ceilings had **panels** edged with gold.

14. **image** (a) [a concept of someone or something held by the public]

> John F. Kennedy had the **image** of being a dynamic man with a lot of energy.
>
> Supporters of the Vietnam War said that its unfavorable public **image** was created by the media.

(b) [a mental picture of something or someone not present]

> The young man's life as an artist was a hard one, but whenever he felt like quitting, he remembered the **image** of his mother on her deathbed saying, "You'll be a great artist some day, son; don't ever give up."

(c) [a picture of an object produced by a camera, mirror, or any electronic system]

> The **image** of a small bullet was visible on the X-ray of the soldier's arm.
>
> The camera on the rocket in space sent back **images** of a new star that scientists did not know existed.

15. **matter** (a) [to be of importance]

> The cost of heating a home does not **matter** to someone with a lot of money, but for families with low incomes, it is a **matter** of great importance. Not being able to pay a gas bill can result in not having any heat at all.
>
> In a composition, teachers are concerned that students express themselves grammatically, but what also **matters** is that the thoughts be complete and well organized.

(b) [a subject of action or difficulty]

> The school office break-in was a **matter** for the police to handle.
>
> A: What's the **matter**? Why do you look so depressed?
> B: I've just found out that I've lost my job.

16. **reasonable** [fair; not extreme or excessive]

> The employee's request for a raise was **reasonable**; he had made many improvements in the project he was working on, and he was a dedicated worker.
>
> Many people feel that a 55-mile-per-hour speed limit is **unreasonable**. The United States is the only country with such a limit, and very few people drive at this speed.

17. **penetrate** [to pass into or through, often by overcoming resistance]

> The army **penetrated** the enemy's defense by having more and superior weapons.
>
> We put plastic covers on our outdoor furniture to protect it from the rain, but during the last heavy rain, water somehow **penetrated** the plastic, and now the furniture is completely wet.

18. **preliminary** [something that precedes or is introductory or preparatory]

> Before Ph.D. students take their main exams, they must take **preliminary** exams to see if they are qualified to finish the degree.
>
> Most companies provide a **preliminary** training session for new employees before they begin their official work.

19. **renew** (a) [to repeat or begin again]

> The two countries **renewed** their peace efforts after a break of two and a half years.
>
> The journalists **renewed** their complaints about the government's attempts at censorship.

(b) [to give or obtain an extension]

> In many states people must **renew** their driver's licenses every four years; in other states the **renewal** period is every two years.
>
> These library books are due tomorrow, but I still need them for my research. I am going to **renew** them for two more weeks.

(c) [to make new or fresh again]

> The travelers were exhausted from their long day's walk, but after dinner they felt **renewed** again.
>
> The city's urban **renewal** efforts have completely changed the looks of the downtown. Old, deteriorated, and unused buildings have been either torn down or redone.

20. **signify** [to mean; to show by a word, signal, or gesture]

> The size of the headline in a newspaper **signifies** the importance of the news that a headline represents: the bigger the letters, the more important the news.
>
> A facial expression in which the eyes are wide open **signifies** different things in different cultures; in the West it **signifies** surprise, but in the East it often means anger.

21. **significant** [having a special meaning; important]

> One **significant** fact about American newspapers today is that most of them are not locally owned but are owned by corporations in other cities.
>
> A **significant** ingredient in many breakfast foods is sugar, which means that many Americans begin their day with a high concentration of sugar.

22. **spell out** {separable} [to make very clear or emphatic]

> The president mentioned in a news conference a new plan for renewing the steel industry. Today there was an article in the paper which **spelled out** the details of the plan.
>
> If you want my brother to do something for you, you must be very clear and direct. It is not enough to give him a hint that you want a favor; you have to **spell** everything **out**.

Introductory Exercises

A. Match each word or phrase with its definition.

_____ 1. a hand or body movement

_____ 2. new or unusual

_____ 3. a position from which an idea is viewed

_____ 4. to be of importance

_____ 5. a book of maps

_____ 6. to give an extension

_____ 7. a small point

_____ 8. an indirect or brief suggestion

_____ 9. not extreme or excessive

_____ 10. a bright, sudden light

_____ 11. treating facts without personal feelings

_____ 12. a concept of someone held by the public

_____ 13. to make very clear

_____ 14. extra information included at the end of a book

_____ 15. to pass into or though by overcoming resistance

_____ 16. a list of names or articles arranged according to a system

_____ 17. to be a symbol for

a. appendix
b. atlas
c. catalog
d. dot
e. flash
f. gesture
g. hear of
h. hint
i. image
j. matter
k. novel
l. objective
m. panel
n. penetrate
o. preliminary
p. reasonable
q. renew
r. significant
s. spell out
t. stand out
u. standpoint

B.   Answer **T** if the sentence is true and **F** of it is false.

_____ **1.** Students take preliminary tests at the end of a course.

_____ **2.** An <u>i</u> that is not dotted may be mistaken for the letter <u>e</u>.

_____ **3.** A novel experience is an experience that you've never had before.

_____ **4.** A writer that most people have never heard of is probably not very significant.

_____ **5.** The winners of Olympics sporting contests such as ice-skating are decided by a panel of judges.

_____ **6.** The appendix of a book contains a list of the book's chapters and corresponding page numbers.

_____ **7.** The objective of most advertising campaigns is to give a certain product a desirable image.

_____ **8.** A news flash is a complete analysis of a recent item of news.

_____ **9.** "U.S.A." stands for "Union of States of America."

_____ **10.** A country's constitution is an attempt to spell out the national laws and ideals.

_____ **11.** It is reasonable to expect a newspaper to print an objective account of the news.

_____ **12.** Many stores print an atlas with pictures and descriptions of their products.

_____ **13.** A leak in your apartment is a matter of concern for your landlord.

_____ **14.** If you decide you want to stop receiving a subscription to a newspaper, you should renew the subscription.

Study Exercises

C.   Paraphrase the underlined words in each sentence using a word from the word form chart.

    1. In a newspaper column, I read a <u>suggestion</u> about how to save money when shopping for a car.

    _____

    2. The <u>light</u> on my camera broke, so I am not able to take any pictures indoors.

    _____

    3. From the <u>point of view</u> of the unemployed workers, the government's position on imports is <u>unfair</u>.

    (a) _____   (b) _____

4. I enjoy the <u>books</u> of Ernest Hemingway because his writing gives me such a clear <u>mental</u> <u>picture</u> of the characters he is describing.

(a) _____ (b) _____

5. It <u>is</u> <u>not</u> <u>important</u> if you do not understand every word that you read in a foreign language. What <u>is</u> <u>important</u> is that you have understood the main ideas.

(a) _____ (b) _____

6. The dining room in my grandmother's old house has walls covered with <u>pieces</u> <u>of</u> <u>wood</u>. Behind one of them is a secret safe.

_____

7. What is the <u>meaning</u> of the president's firing of the Secretary of Education?

_____

8. There is a graph in this <u>book</u> <u>of</u> <u>maps</u> that <u>makes</u> <u>clear</u> the population figures of all the countries in <u>the</u> world.

(a) _____ (b) _____

9. There are two systems of <u>organizing</u> books in libraries in the United States. One is the Dewey <u>Decimal</u> system, and the other, more commonly used, is the LC system. "LC" <u>represents</u> "Library of Congress," and this system was developed <u>by</u> <u>the</u> Library of Congress in Washington, D.C.

(a) _____ (b) _____

10. Something strange happened to today's newspaper; the ink on the front page <u>passed</u> <u>through</u> the paper, and it is impossible to read the second page.

_____

11. There was a television program last night with a <u>group</u> discussion by all of this year's presidential candidates. One candidate was exceptionally noticeable because his <u>hand</u> <u>movements</u> were very exaggerated.

(a) _____ (b) _____

12. I prefer the news on Channel 3 because the reporting seems <u>less</u> <u>influenced</u> <u>by</u> <u>personal</u> <u>opinion</u>.

_____

13. The students have <u>repeated</u> their attempts to get the university administration to <u>change</u> <u>the</u> policy of <u>introductory</u> exams.

(a) _____ (b) _____

D.   Match each word with its synonym.

_____	**1.** novel	**a.** explain
_____	**2.** dot	**b.** introductory
_____	**3.** gesture	**c.** picture
_____	**4.** spell out	**d.** light
_____	**5.** hint	**e.** jury
_____	**6.** renew	**f.** new
_____	**7.** atlas	**g.** important
_____	**8.** preliminary	**h.** suggestion
_____	**9.** flash	**i.** tolerate
_____	**10.** objective	**j.** point
_____	**11.** standpoint	**k.** maps
_____	**12.** stand for	**l.** motion
_____	**13.** significant	**m.** subject
_____	**14.** panel	**n.** point of view
_____	**15.** image	**o.** goal
_____	**16.** matter	**p.** repeat
		q. represent

E.   Circle the letter of the word or phrase which best completes each phrase.

1. hear of
  a. the radio
  b. an author
  c. a voice

2. spell out
  a. a set of instructions
  b. a sentence
  c. a newspaper

3. penetrate
  a. a net
  b. a check
  c. a piece of wood

4. dot
  a. an envelope
  b. an i̅
  c. a p̅icture

5. a gesture
  a. of sympathy
  b. of a matter
  c. of a catalog

6. a panel
  a. a hint
  b. of a tree
  c. of experts

7. look up
  a. in an atlas
  b. to a standpoint
  c. a flash

8. stand for
    a. cheating in business
    b. sitting down
    c. a plant

9. signify
    a. a gesture
    b. a new era
    c. a red light

F. In each blank, write the most appropriate word or phrase from the word form chart in this unit. Some words may be used more than once.

If you have watched any American television, you have probably seen a game show. In a game show a(n) (1) _____ of contestants— "contestants" are people who participate in a contest—compete for prizes by participating in a variety of games. The prizes may be cash or they may be products from a very fashionable (and expensive) (2) _____ . The (3) _____ of such game shows is not very serious, and the shows are meant to be pure entertainment.

There is another class of game shows, however, whose (4) _____ is meant to be more intellectual. The (5) _____ of these shows is to see which member of the participating (6) _____ can answer the most questions about a wide range of (7) _____ ; from the (8) _____ of sophisticated, Hollywood-style entertainment, these shows are quite dull. If you have never (9) _____ this type of show it is not surprising; there are not many of them since they are not popular with a majority of people. The most popular show of this type, "Jeopardy," was canceled but later (10) _____ because so many of its fans requested that it be continued.

Who participates in such shows, and how? "Jeopardy," like many shows, holds a(n) (11) _____ contest off-camera—that is, a contest that the audience does not see—to determine who will appear on the show. The participants must prepare for the show on their own. The show is not a test of intelligence, but it is certainly a test of knowledge, so participants should have a strong familiarity with a(n) (12) _____ of the world and should know about geography, countries and their capitals, and so on. They should have a general knowledge of science and medicine, including the important people of each field. Participants should also know about literature and art; they should know recent and classical authors and their

(13) _____ ; they should also be able to recognize

(14) _____ works of art.

Once on the show, participants compete to answer as many questions as possible. On "Jeopardy," contestants must provide their answers in the form of a question. If a participant's answer is not specific enough, the host of the show will give the participant a(n) (15) _____ or will ask the contestant to "Please (16) _____ your answer." There is a(n) (17) _____ of judges to decide if an answer is acceptable. It does not (18) _____ if an answer is not exactly the same as the judges', but it must be (19) _____ close.

Participants in these shows do take home prizes, even the losers. The winners usually take home a cash prize, but everyone takes home the satisfaction of having been intellectually challenged, which is something that even the audience at home wins!

Follow-up

G. Dictation: Write the sentences that your teacher reads aloud.

1. _____
2. _____
3. _____
4. _____
5. _____

H. Answer the following questions.

1. What gesture(s) indicate(s) "thank you" in your country?
2. What was the most significant event in your country's history?
3. Have you ever heard of Helen Keller? William Randolph Hearst? Pearl Buck? Who were they?
4. What do the initials "U.S.A." stand for? "L.A."? "U.K."?
5. Do you know of anything that can penetrate solid steel?
6. If someone were having trouble understanding English, what hints would you give him or her?
7. How much homework do you think is reasonable for students?
8. From the standpoint of being a foreign student in the United States, what is the most difficult thing for you to adjust to?

9. What image does the U.S. president have in your country? What image does your own leader have in your country?

10. In your country, do you have to take a preliminary exam to enter a university? Describe the exam if you do.

11. What system of cataloging is used in libraries in your country?

12. Have you ever ordered anything from a catalog? Describe the catalog.

13. What matters the most to you in selecting a university?

I. 1. Describe a game show in your country.
    2. Describe a game show you have seen in another country.

Vacation

Word Form Chart

NOUN	VERB	ADJECTIVE	ADVERB
	be bound for		
chief		chief	chiefly
cluster	cluster		
	come by		
	fall through		
	figure on		
	figure out		
	give in		
	go without		
hindrance	hinder		
hut			
interaction	interact	interactive	interactively
manner			
manners			
	mount	mounted	
		overall	overall
stuff			
strip	strip	stripped	
supernatural		supernatural	supernaturally
urgency		urgent	urgently
vessel			
	wait on		
wave	wave	wavy	

Definitions and Examples

1. **wave** (a) [to move back and forth]

    A flag **waved** on top of the building.

    (b) [to signal with the hand]

    We **waved** good-bye to our friends as we left.

    (c) [movement of the water in the ocean or other body of water]

    Waves pounded on the beach.

2. **chief** (a) [the leader; the head of some group]

    The **chief** of the village invited us to stay at his house.
    The **chief** of police spoke to the officers.

    (b) [most important; influential]

    The **chief** reason we came was for adventure.

3. **chiefly** [mostly]

    It is **chiefly** tourists who come here at this time of year.

4. **urgent** [calling for immediate attention; very important]

    The telegram said it was **urgent** that I return home immediately.
    She came up to us with an **urgent** message.

5. **come by** (a) [to make a visit]

    Come by and see us sometime.
    Why don't you **come by** and pay us a visit?

    (b) [to acquire something]

    Somehow we were able to **come by** two tickets to Hawaii.
    When Brittany's grandmother died, she **came by** a large amount of money.

6. **fall through** [to not happen as planned; to fail to happen]

    When he tried to raise the price, the deal **fell through**.
    Our travel plans nearly **fell through** because we could not get time off
       from work.

7. **figure on** [to plan for; to take into consideration]

    You have to **figure on** extra expenses, like meals in restaurants.
    We **figured on** $1,000 per person for a one-week vacation.

8. **figure out** {separable} [to find a way; to solve a problem]

    She **figured out** how we could visit some of the local people on the island.
    We **figured out** a way to save money on travel costs.
    The map was very complicated. I could not **figure** it **out**.

9. **be bound for** [going to, traveling to]

> The plane was **bound for** Australia.
> We were **bound for** Hawaii, but the ship had to turn around.

10. **go without** [not to have something; to do without]

> They **went without** food and water for 24 hours.
> Let's drive out there tonight. We can **go without** sleep if we have to.

11. **hinder** (a) [to slow the progress of something or someone]

> A strong wind **hindered** our progress.

    (b) [to prevent or delay something from happening]

> The headwind **hindered** us from reaching the island before dark.
> A lack of money **hindered** her from taking a vacation this year.
> Not speaking the language was a great **hindrance** to us.

12. **give in** [to submit; surrender]

> I did not want to go, but I finally **gave in**.
> The travel agency **gave in** to our demands and returned our money.
> The hotel people just want more money. Do not **give in** to them.

13. **cluster** [a group of similar things which are collected together]

> We bought a **cluster** of grapes at the market.
> A **cluster** of people gathered outside the chief's door.
> The people **clustered** around the bus stop.

14. **hut** [a small dwelling of simple construction]

> There was a small **hut** near the beach where people could change clothes.
> Several **huts** were built near the river bank.

15. **mount** (a) [to get on; to climb on]

> He **mounted** the platform and looked around.
> **Mounting** their horses, they rode off.

    (b) [to organize]

> They **mounted** a search for the missing tourist.

16. **interaction** [mutual action or influence; communication]

> There was little social **interaction** between the villagers and the townspeople.
> Several chemicals **interacted** to produce a terrible smell.

17. **manner** (a) [a personal characteristic, habitual behavior]

> She dropped her **manner** of boredom when the journey began to get
> interesting.

    (b) [a way]

> I do not object to the plan itself, but I do object to the **manner** in which it
> was forced on us.

18. **manners** [social behavior]

> Good **manners** will help you succeed in many ways.
> His bad **manners** irritated the hostess.

19. **vessel** (a) [a hollow utensil used to hold something, especially liquid]

> The man poured the water into an earthen **vessel** which rested on the
> table.

(b) [a ship]

> Our ship was an ancient **vessel** but still safe to sail.

20. **strip** (a) [a long narrow piece of material or land]

> He put a **strip** of cloth around his head.
> There was a **strip** of farmland between the river and the mountain.

(b) [to remove something, especially clothing]

> He **stripped** off his clothing and jumped into the water.

21. **stuff** (a) [to fill something up]

> She quickly **stuffed** her clothes into the suitcase.

(b) {informal} [personal property; a collection of objects]

> I left my **stuff** on the bus.
> Let's pick up this **stuff** before we go.

22. **stuffy** [making it difficult to breathe]

> The room was **stuffy**, so we opened a window.

23. **supernatural** [something beyond the known laws of nature; something that
     cannot be explained according to the known laws of nature]

> They were trained as scientists and did not want to believe in the
> **supernatural**.
> It was a place of almost **supernatural** beauty.

24. **overall** (a) [as a whole; generally]

> **Overall**, I felt the trip was a success.

(b) [including everything]

> The **overall** impression was of a small, quiet, ordinary town.

25. **wait on** [to serve someone]

> One old gentleman **waited on** all the guests in the hotel restaurant.
> A servant **waited on** the king.

Introductory Exercises

A.   Match each word with its definition.

_____ 1. a small dwelling	**a.** bound for
_____ 2. mostly	**b.** chiefly
_____ 3. a ship	**c.** cluster
_____ 4. personal property; things	**d.** come by
_____ 5. traveling to	**e.** fall through
_____ 6. mutual action or influence	**f.** figure on
_____ 7. to climb on something	**g.** figure out
_____ 8. calling for immediate attention	**h.** give in
_____ 9. to surrender	**i.** go without
_____ 10. to plan for; to take into consideration	**j.** hinder
_____ 11. to slow the progress of something	**k.** hut
_____ 12. a personal characteristic	**l.** interaction
_____ 13. a long narrow piece of material or land	**m.** manner
_____ 14. beyond the laws of nature	**n.** manners
_____ 15. as a whole; generally	**o.** mount
_____ 16. to fail	**p.** overall
_____ 17. collection of similar things	**q.** strip
_____ 18. to make a visit	**r.** stuff
	s. supernatural
	t. urgent
	u. vessel
	v. wait on
	w. wave

B.   Answer each question with a word from the word form chart.

1. What can you do if you do not have money to buy the things you need?
2. Who leads a group of people?
3. What is a name for a container of water?
4. What is a narrow piece of land?
5. What do you lack if you behave badly in public?
6. What should you do if you cannot resist any longer?
7. What do you call a group of similar things that are collected together?
8. What is a name for a very small building?
9. What describes the air in a room with no windows?
10. What does a waiter do?
11. What do you do when you leave your friends?
12. What do you do with a problem in mathematics?
13. What word describes an important message?

Study Exercises

C.   Write **T** if the sentence is true and **F** if it is false.

      ———   **1.** If you are returning from a journey, you are bound for home.

      ———   **2.** When their travel plans fell through, the tourists were able to go on their trip.

      ———   **3.** A stuffy room is probably very cold.

      ———   **4.** If a matter is urgent, it should be ignored.

      ———   **5.** Vessels are generally not flat.

      ———   **6.** A boss has to wait on his employees.

      ———   **7.** Physics makes use of supernatural explanations.

      ———   **8.** After stripping and putting on swimsuits, swimmers can jump into the water.

      ———   **9.** You can mount stairs down to a lower floor.

      ——— **10.** Having no money is a great hindrance.

      ——— **11.** A business could fail if the management does not figure on all necessary expenses.

      ——— **12.** A woman who comes by a large amount of money is probably rather poor.

      ——— **13.** A single grape can be a small cluster.

      ——— **14.** Manners can be good or bad.

D.   Complete the analogies with a word or phrase from the word form chart.

    1. president : nation :: _____ : village

    2. collection : individual :: _____ : one

    3. plan : fail :: business deal : _____

    4. give orders : leader :: _____ : servant

    5. box : thing :: _____ : water

    6. important : news :: _____ : message

    7. shake : hand :: _____ : flag

    8. find : solution :: _____ : problem

E. In each blank, write the most appropriate word or phrase from the word form chart.

It is (1) _____ tourists who come to this part of Hawaii.

They (2) _____ cheap air tickets and low rates in the hotels.

Mostly, they (3) _____ around the hotel, and they pass our house

sometimes on their way to the beach. Earlier this summer, my brother and I

had just come home from school and had not found jobs yet, but that did not

(4) _____ us from having some fun.

We built a small (5) _____ at the side of the road and put up

a sign:

HAWAIIAN DANCER—FREE—EVERY HOUR

Sometimes a bus or cars full of people would stop. Having

(6) _____ off his shirt, my brother Paul assumed his most

traditional (7) _____ . Loudly he sang out some words that

sounded like Hawaiian, as he (8) _____ the steps by the hut. My

little sister (9) _____ the guests, selling lemonade.

More loudly and more (10) _____ , Paul's voice rang out

until he raised his wooden stick and stopped suddenly. An almost

(11) _____ quiet and beauty came over the scene. That was the

time for my sister to turn on the stereo. And I had to come out of the hut to

jump around like a Hawaiian (12) _____ . As soon as the tourists

(13) _____ our little game, they turned and left.

In this way we collected a few dollars a day from the sale of lemonade.

Paul wanted to sell souvenirs and other (14) _____ , but his deal

(15) _____ when my father heard about the business. He put a

stop to it.

Follow-up

F. Dictation: Write the sentences that your teacher reads aloud.

1. _____

2. _____

3. _____

4. _____

5. _____

G.   Answer the following questions.

1. Is tourism an important industry in your country? What places are especially attractive for tourists?
2. When people in your country want to take a vacation, where do they like to go?
3. Do people in your country believe in the supernatural? Explain.
4. When something hinders you from doing what you want, do you usually give in, or do you keep trying? Give an example.
5. Do people in your country have many opportunities to travel?
6. Where would you like to travel?
7. Do you prefer to travel alone? Why?
8. What is the best (worst) vacation you have ever had?
9. Do you think it would be enjoyable to have a job in the tourist industry? If not, why not? If so, what kind of job?

I.   Complete the story.

George was on his way to work. He stopped for a moment in front of the window of a travel agency. A brightly colored picture caught his eye. . . .

Crime

Word Form Chart

NOUN	VERB	ADJECTIVE	ADVERB
aggression		aggressive	aggressively
anonymity		anonymous	anonymously
appeal	appeal	appealing	appealingly
badge			
	break up		
bullet			
coincidence	coincide	coincidental	coincidentally
condemnation	condemn	condemned	
		condemnable	
distress	distress	distressed	
		distressing	distressingly
		distressful	distressfully
	hang around		
indignation		indignant	indignantly
officer			
peculiarity		peculiar	peculiarly
penalty	penalize		
plotter	plot	plotting	
	pound	pounding	
revolver	revolve	revolving	
reward	reward	rewarding	
	take back		
	think about		
trace	trace		
vice			

Definitions and Examples

1. **bullet** [a small piece of shaped metal that is shot from a gun]

    The man loaded the gun with six **bullets**.
    That store sells **bullets** and other hunting supplies.

2. **revolve (around)** (a) [to turn around a central point]

    The earth and the other planets **revolve** around the sun.
    This part of the machine constantly **revolves**.

    (b) [to be especially concerned with or interested in something]

    Sally's life **revolves** around her home and family.

3. **revolver** [a small gun with a revolving cylinder which holds bullets]

    The suspect grabbed his **revolver** and shot the policeman.
    Because a **revolver** is a small weapon, it is easy to conceal.

4. **officer** (a) [a policeman or policewoman]

    The **officer** told the man to throw his revolver on the ground.
    Police **officers** have very dangerous jobs.

    (b) [2-8: an important person in the military, in business, etc.]

    The **officers** in the army make important decisions.

5. **badge** [a small flat item, often of metal or plastic, which shows rank or membership in an organization]

    The elderly woman refused to open her door until the officer showed her his **badge**.
    In some companies, employees must wear plastic **badges** with their pictures on them.

6. **anonymous** [without the person's name]

    No one knows who wrote this book; the author is **anonymous**.
    The newspaper will not publish **anonymous** letters; each writer must sign his name.

7. **coincide** [to happen at the same time]

    My friend's birthday **coincides** with the celebration of New Year's Day.
    Unfortunately, our vacations do not **coincide**; hers is in August, and mine is in June.

8. **coincidence** [a combination of events that seem to be related or that happen accidentally at the same time]

    By **coincidence**, the two brothers met at the museum; they had not made plans to see each other.
    It was a strange **coincidence** that Emma and Joan bought the same dress to wear on their trip together.

9. **plot** [a secret plan to do something bad; a scheme]

> The two thieves **plotted** to rob the bank. However, their **plot** failed; by coincidence, a police officer heard their plans and arrested them.

10. **trace** [a small mark or amount left by something]

> The clever criminal stole the officer's badge and revolver and disappeared without a **trace**.
> I tried to wash the paint from my skirt, but there is still a **trace** left.

11. **vice** [an immoral or bad habit]

> The murderer was an evil man and had many **vices**.
> Eating too much every day is a **vice**, but it is not immoral.

12. **take back** {separable} [to take something from the person you gave it to; to return something]

> Larry **took back** the ring he had given Jenny because she decided not to marry him.
> Bob did not need the couch his mother lent him anymore, so she **took** it **back**.
> We need to **take** this television **back** to the store; it is not working.

13. **break up** (a) {separable} [to stop someone from fighting]

> Someone called the police, and they came and **broke up** the fight.
> "**Break** it **up**! Why are the two of you always fighting?"

> (b) [5-17: to end a relationship]

>> John was sad to see his family **break up** when his parents divorced.

14. **penalty** [a punishment]

> The **penalty** for buying a revolver illegally is very severe.
> Mr. Jones was **penalized** for failing to stop at the stop sign.

15. **hang around** {informal} [to spend time idly; to spend time with someone]

> Teenagers often spend time **hanging around** with their friends.
> The young men didn't have jobs, so they **hung around** on the street corner every day.

16. **think about** [to consider]

> Janice **thought about** the idea for a long time before she decided not to do it.

> A: Have you decided to buy my piano?
> B: I'm still **thinking about** it.

17. **distress** [to cause unhappiness or grief]

> The police officer told Mr. and Mrs. Jones that their son had been arrested for carrying a revolver. This news **distressed** them very much.
> The old lady felt great **distress** after her dog died.

18. **indignant** [angry, especially at cruelty or injustice]

> When the woman saw the boys beat the cat, she was **indignant**.
> The man was **indignant** when the store took back his furniture; however, he did not have enough money to pay for it.

19. **peculiar** [strange]

> I saw a **peculiar** thing today: a dog was walking down the street wearing a pink hat.
> "Officer! Please arrest that man. He has been hanging around my store all day and acting **peculiarly**."

20. **reward** [something given for good behavior; money offered for a special service]

> I hear there is a big **reward** for the capture of the escaped convict.
> The father **rewarded** the little boy for cleaning his room.

21. **pound** (a) [to hammer; to beat]

> The indignant woman **pounded** on the table with her glass.
> Two officers arrested that peculiar man; he was **pounding** on the president's car with a revolver.

> (b) [1-13: a unit of measurement used for weight]

>> The baby weighed only three **pounds** when it was born.

22. **aggressive** (a) [attacking, sometimes without cause]

> If hockey players are too **aggressive**, they are penalized.
> Children often play **aggressively** and hit each other for no reason.

(b) [showing great energy]

> **Aggressive** executives climb the ladder of success quickly.
> Susan is certainly an **aggressive** saleswoman; she has sold more cars than anyone else this week.

23. **condemn** (a) [to judge someone guilty]

> The judge **condemned** the suspect for his aggressive behavior.

(b) [to judge something unfit for use]

> The unsafe building was **condemned** by the building inspector.

24. **appeal** (a) [to attract]

> The dress **appeals** to me because of its pretty color.
> Italian food doesn't **appeal** to Jack; he only likes Chinese food.

(b) [to make an urgent request for help]

> The officers **appealed** for witnesses of the terrible crime.
> The frightened woman **appealed** to the crowd to help her find her lost child.

(c) [to send a case to a higher court in an attempt to reverse a lower court's decision]

> When the man was found guilty, he wanted to **appeal** his case.

Introductory Exercises

A. Match each word or phrase with its definition.

_____ 1. money offered for a special service	**a.** aggressive
_____ 2. to hammer	**b.** anonymous
_____ 3. to return something	**c.** appeal
_____ 4. to spend time idly	**d.** badge
_____ 5. a small mark left by something	**e.** break up
_____ 6. to happen at the same time	**f.** bullet
_____ 7. a secret plan to do something bad	**g.** concide
_____ 8. without the person's name	**h.** condemn
_____ 9. a punishment	**i.** distress
_____ 10. a policeman or policewoman	**j.** hang around
_____ 11. to consider	**k.** indignant
_____ 12. to turn around a central point	**l.** officer
_____ 13. to cause unhappiness or grief	**m.** peculiar
_____ 14. strange	**n.** penalty
_____ 15. to stop someone from fighting	**o.** plot
_____ 16. angry, especially at cruelty or injustice	**p.** pound
	q. revolve
	r. reward
	s. take back
	t. think about
	u. trace
	v. vice

B. Answer each question with a word from the word form chart.

1. How do we feel if we see someone do a cruel thing?
2. What word do we use to describe a person who is acting strangely?
3. What is put in a gun?
4. How can we describe a child who hits other children?
5. What must you have if you work for some companies?

6. What are young people doing when they spend their time idly?
7. What do we do if we stop a fight?
8. What is another word for policewoman?
9. If we consider an idea, what do we do?
10. What do we give someone who finds and returns our wallet?
11. How may you feel if your best friend moves far away?
12. If we don't know who wrote a book, how can we describe the author?
13. What does a judge give a criminal who is found guilty?

Study Exercises

C. Write **T** if the sentence is true and **F** if it is false.

———— 1. A coincidence is always planned.

———— 2. A judge will condemn a boy for helping his mother.

———— 3. Teachers are usually pleased when their students make plots.

———— 4. A mother will be indignant when her child hits his little sister.

———— 5. Before arresting a suspect, an officer shows his badge.

———— 6. Children are rewarded for fighting.

———— 7. A man with flowers on his head is peculiar.

———— 8. We prepare bullet sandwiches for our guests.

———— 9. Our birthdays always coincide with those of our parents.

———— 10. A little girl will be distressed when her dog dies.

———— 11. When young people are bored, they hang around with their friends.

———— 12. After you step in red paint, there will not be a trace on your white shoes.

———— 13. Usually, we don't think about important decisions.

D. In each blank, write the most appropriate two-word verb from the following list. There may be several possible answers.

come by	figure out	come up with	stand for
fall through	give in	break up	spell out
figure on	go without	hear of	turn down
think up	think about	take back	wait on

1. Jim ————————— a new idea for his project. After —————————
   it carefully for a few days, however, he decided it wouldn't work out.

2. Several teachers ————————— a job opening in another school; they
   all applied, but all were ————————— .

3. A: How did you _____ your new radio?

   B: My parents bought it for me. Unfortunately, it's having

   mechanical problems, and I'll have to _____ it

   _____ to the store.

4. The two friends _____ taking a vacation to Florida this year.
   However, they were not able to get airplane reservations, so their

   plans _____ .

5. I tried hard to _____ the argument between Ed and John, but

   neither one would _____ .

6. The university administrators tried to _____ how they could
   buy new sports equipment this year. They were unable to get additional

   money, however, so they will have to _____ new equipment
   until next year.

E. Complete the analogies with a word or phrase from the word form chart.

   1. _____ : unhappiness :: reward : happiness

   2. bad : immoral :: sad : _____

   3. little : much :: _____ : a lot

   4. vehicle : bus :: plan : _____

   5. disgust: appeal to :: condemn : _____

   6. planned : coincidental :: famous : _____

   7. stand up for : support :: _____ : hammer

   8. praise : kindness :: condemn : _____

   9. strange : _____ :: major : chief

  10. certificate : qualification :: _____ : membership

F. In each blank, write the most appropriate word or phrase from the word form
   chart.

   It was no surprise to people in the neighborhood when Ron Long and Bob

   Brown were arrested for trying to rob the jewelry store. Both young men had

   been very violent and (1) _____ as children and had acquired

   many (2) _____ as they grew older. After they graduated from

   high school, neither man found a job. Instead, they spent long afternoons

   (3) _____ together, making plans to get money without working

   for it. Finally, one day they thought of a (4) _____ to rob the

   town jewelry store. Long bought a (5) _____ and some

   (6) _____ . One Saturday night, they went to break into the store.

   They broke the glass in the window by (7) _____ on it with the handle of the (8) _____ . This made so much noise that a police (9) _____ who was in the area came quickly to investigate. He showed them his (10) _____ and arrested them. The two young men were later found guilty by the judge and (11) _____ to five years in prison. Long and Brown are not pleased with the (12) _____ and hope to (13) _____ , but their lawyer doesn't think there is much hope.

Follow-up

G. Dictation: Write the sentences that your teacher reads aloud.

1. _____
2. _____
3. _____
4. _____
5. _____

H. Answer the following questions.

1. What are typical penalties for murder in your country? For robbery?
2. Under what circumstances can people appeal the penalties they receive?
3. Do people in your country ever use badges? Who uses them?
4. In what kinds of situations do you feel distressed?
5. Are girls in your culture condemned for aggressive behavior more than boys? Give examples.
6. What kinds of situations make you feel indignant?
7. Describe the most peculiar sight you have ever seen.
8. What kinds of activities appeal to you?
9. Have you ever broken up a fight? What was it about?
10. What is the most interesting coincidence that has ever happened to you?

I. Complete the story.

Mark was walking down the street when he noticed two men fighting. . . .

Housing

Word Form Chart

NOUN	VERB	ADJECTIVE	ADVERB
accommodation	accommodate	accommodating	
	add up		
adjacency		adjacent	adjacently
architecture		architectural	architecturally
architect			
barrel			
chest			
	clear off		
	clear out		
design	design		
designer			
displacement	displace	displaced	
endurance	endure		
generation	generate		
	go out		
junk	junk		
lot			
misery		miserable	miserably
		prime	
program			
	put up		
	put up with		
rag		ragged	
rod			
spare	spare	spare	sparingly
wiper	wipe		

Definitions and Examples

1. **lot** (a) [a piece of land]

   > Mr. Jones went to buy a **lot** so that he could build a new house.
   > His **lot** measures 700 feet by 1,200 feet.

   > (b) [assumed: much; many]

   >> He drank a **lot** of milk at dinner.

2. **clear off** {separable} [to remove unwanted objects from a surface]

   > Before he can build, he needs to **clear** trash and garbage **off** his lot.
   > Please **clear off** the table so that we can have dinner.

3. **junk** [something of poor quality; trash]

   > Let's clean out some of the cabinets today and throw away the **junk**.
   > Before he can have a garden behind his house, he needs to clear all the
   > **junk** off his lot.

4. **spare** (a) [extra]

   > I have a **spare** pair of socks you can use.
   > Everyone should carry a **spare** tire in his car; you never know when you
   >   might get a flat tire!

   (b) [to do without]

   > A: I forgot to bring any money for lunch. Can you **spare** three dollars?
   > B: No. I'm sorry. I can't **spare** any, but maybe Jim has some extra money.

5. **clear out** {separable} (a) [to remove the contents (especially junk) from an
   enclosed place.

   > Mrs. Meade wants to **clear out** the spare room so that she can paint it.
   > John is **clearing out** his desk. He needs to **clear** it **out** before tomorrow.

   > (b) [5-25: to leave quickly]

   >> The frightened children **cleared out** before their parents arrived.

6. **adjacent** [next to]

   > A: Have you seen her new house?
   > B: Yes. It's very nice, but unfortunately it's **adjacent** to a vacant lot
   >   which is full of junk.
   > A: Maybe she can ask the owners of the lot to clear it off.

   > A: Is your property near mine?
   > B: Yes. I believe our lots are **adjacent** to each other.

7. **accommodate** (a) [to give someone a place to live or stay]

> A: I need a room for the night, please.
> B: I'm sorry sir; we can't **accommodate** you. The hotel is full.

> Our trip to Italy might be canceled. We haven't been able to find **accommodations**.

(b) [to do a service for someone]

> A: I would like to make an appointment to have my hair cut today.
> B: I am afraid we cannot do it today; we close in fifteen minutes. However, we can **accommodate** you tomorrow.

(c) [to adjust]

> She has **accommodated** herself well to her new job.
> Michael broke his right hand last week. However, he has **accommodated** himself very well and is learning to rely on his left hand.

8. **rod** [a straight, thin piece or bar of metal, wood, or other material]

> Bill washed his curtains and hung them back on the curtain **rod**.
> A fishing **rod** has a long piece of string with a hook at the end. It is used for catching fish.
> Lightning **rods** are attached to houses; their purpose is to prevent lightning from striking the house.

9. **put up** {separable} (a) [to build; to construct]

> The builder **put up** a lightning rod and attached it to the house.
> They are **putting up** a new library in that part of town and we hope they **put** it **up** quickly.

(b) [to provide money in advance]

> In order to buy the lot, he had to **put up** twenty thousand dollars.

(c) [to provide accommodations]

> Can you **put** me **up** tonight? I don't feel like driving home.

10. **rag** [a small piece of cloth, often used for cleaning]

> The old dress was torn up into **rags**.
> I need some clean **rags** to dust my furniture.

11. **ragged** [ripped, often old]

> The poor children were dressed in **ragged** and dirty clothes.
> Please don't wear that old sweater; the sleeves have **ragged** edges.

12. **wipe** [to rub something clean or dry]

> After I wash my car, I like to **wipe** it with a clean rag.
> His mother told him to **wipe** his feet before he entered the house.

13. **prime** [first in excellence or value]

> This television program is on during **prime** time, when advertisers have to pay the most for their advertisements.
>
> **Prime** pieces of meat are always the most expensive.

14. **go out** (a) [to stop burning]

> Jim poured water on the fire, but it wouldn't **go out**.
>
> The lights **went out** just when we started to read.

(b) [to leave a place]

> I'm too tired to **go out** tonight.

(c) [to see a member of the opposite sex socially]

> They have been **going out** together for over a year. Maybe they will get engaged soon.

15. **endure** (a) [to continue despite difficulties]

> The first immigrants to America three hundred years ago had to **endure** bitterly cold winters and a shortage of food.
>
> He **endured** many financial problems in order to finish his education.

(b) [to continue unchanged]

> There are buildings in Egypt which have **endured** for hundreds of years.
>
> Some insects have **endured** for a million years with their original shape and structure.

16. **put up with** [to endure or suffer without complaint; to tolerate]

> Myra **put up with** her broken lock for two weeks, but finally she went to her landlord for help.
>
> I can't **put up with** all this snow any longer; I'm moving to Florida!

17. **add up** {separable} [to add]

> Please **add up** these numbers for me. Every time I **add** them **up**, I get a different answer.
>
> In order to find out your monthly expenses, you need to **add up** what you spend for food, heat, electricity, and housing.

18. **design** (a) [to make a plan or pattern for something]

> My father is a talented carpenter; he **designed** and built our kitchen cabinets.
>
> Mr. Robinson is a fashion **designer**; he **designs** beautiful clothes.

(b) [the pattern in something]

> I like the **design** in that fabric.
>
> The kitchen floor had a **design** of white and red squares.

19. **architect** [a person who designs buildings]

> Before we build our house, I want to find a good **architect**.
>
> My brother studied **architecture** in college; now he designs houses.

20. miserable [very unhappy]

> My friend has been **miserable** since that ugly house was put up on the lot adjacent to hers.
> Tom caught a cold last week, and he still feels **miserable**.

21. program (a) [a plan to accomplish something; a procedure for solving a problem]

> Many schools have lunch **programs** to provide hot lunches for poor children.
> Several architects participated in the city **program** to clean up junk-filled vacant lots.

> (b) [**1-9**: a show]

>> I like to watch funny **programs** on television.

> (c) [**5-20**: list of events]

>> The **program** for this evening includes dinner and dancing.

22. barrel [a large, cylindrical container, usually made of wood or metal]

> A pile of rusty **barrels** and other junk filled the vacant lot.
> **Barrels** are often used to mark areas during road construction.
> The wine was stored in large wooden **barrels**.

23. chest (a) [a large, strong box with a lid; a piece of furniture with drawers for storing clothes]

> Valuables are often kept in a locked **chest**.
> We fold our shirts and put them in a **chest** in the bedroom.

> (b) [**3-19**: the top front part of the body]

>> A cold in the **chest** can make a person feel miserable.

24. displace [to change the place or position of]

> Many people were **displaced** from their homes as a result of recent floods.
> A ball placed in water will **displace** some of the water.
> The chair, which I had very carefully positioned for our game, was **displaced** by someone who walked into it as he came into the room.

25. generate (a) [make or produce, especially electricity]

> The Valley Electric company **generates** power for the whole area.
> Fast-moving water is often used to **generate** electricity.

(b) [to bring into existence]

> The young politician **generated** a good program to use vacant city-owned lots to make gardens for the poor.

Introductory Exercises

A. Match each word or phrase with its definition.

——	1. extra	**a.**	accommodate
——	2. to remove the contents from an enclosed place	**b.**	add up
		c.	adjacent
——	3. to endure without complaint	**d.**	architect
——	4. to bring into existence	**e.**	barrel
——	5. to stop burning	**f.**	chest
——	6. to rub something clean or dry	**g.**	clear off
——	7. a person who designs buildings	**h.**	clear out
		i.	design
——	8. first in excellence or value	**j.**	displace
——	9. next to	**k.**	endure
——	10. to build; to construct	**l.**	generate
——	11. to make a plan or pattern for something	**m.**	go out
		n.	junk
——	12. a piece of land	**o.**	lot
——	13. something of poor quality	**p.**	miserable
——	14. to give someone a place to live or stay	**q.**	prime
		r.	program
——	15. to remove unwanted objects	**s.**	put up
		t.	put up with
		u.	rag
		v.	rod
		w.	spare
		x.	wipe

B. Answer each question with a word from the word form chart.

1. If a house is next to yours, where is it?
2. What do you use to wipe the dust from your furniture?
3. What do you call things that you don't want?
4. Where can you keep your clothes?
5. Where can you build a house?
6. If you go to a hotel, what might you want?
7. If you fail your classes, what are you?
8. How do you find the sum of some numbers?
9. Who can help you if you want to build a house?
10. If you have a room with a lot of junk in it, what should you do?
11. What do you do if you need a fence around your lot?
12. What room do you use to accommodate guests who come to stay?
13. When a fire stops burning, what does it do?

Study Exercises

C.   Write **T** if the sentence is true and **F** if it is false.

_____   **1.** An architect designs clothes.

_____   **2.** It is a good idea to be sure a fire has gone out before you go out.

_____   **3.** Stores provide accommodations for travelers.

_____   **4.** If you have extra food, you can spare it.

_____   **5.** People always like to keep junk.

_____   **6.** A pattern in a floor is called a design.

_____   **7.** People make rags from their new clothes.

_____   **8.** If a person lives adjacent to you, it is difficult to visit him.

_____   **9.** Many states have programs to improve the roads.

_____ **10.** If you add up nine and three, the answer is six.

_____ **11.** It is a good idea to put a lightning rod up when you build a house.

_____ **12.** People enjoy putting up with their problems.

_____ **13.** It is a bad idea to clear off a lot before you build a house on it.

_____ **14.** Smart scientists usually do not generate new ideas.

_____ **15.** If you put up with an unpleasant situation, you endure it.

D.   Match each two- or three-word verb with its synonym.

_____ **1.** put up	**a.** to happen; to occur
_____ **2.** put up with	**b.** to think of; to find
_____ **3.** put across	**c.** to visit
_____ **4.** catch on	**d.** to become popular; to understand
_____ **5.** catch up with	**e.** to succeed in doing or providing something
_____ **6.** come to	**f.** to present to the public
_____ **7.** come out	**g.** to become sick with
_____ **8.** come by	**h.** to continue with
_____ **9.** come up with	**i.** to build; to construct
_____ **10.** come through	**j.** to explain adequately
_____ **11.** come down with	**k.** to do
_____ **12.** come out with	**l.** to endure without complaint
_____ **13.** come about	**m.** to become conscious
_____ **14.** carry on with	**n.** to make a visit; to acquire
_____ **15.** carry out	**o.** to be published
	p. to reach the level of others who have done more than you have

E.   Complete the analogies with a word or phrase from the word form chart.

    1. garbage : junk :: distressed : _____

    2. clean out : wipe off :: clear out : _____

    3. spoon : stir :: _____ : wipe

    4. angle : bent :: _____ : straight

    5. house : build :: fence : _____

    6. extra : spare :: pattern : _____

    7. ruins : houses :: _____ : clothes

    8. add up : subtract :: _____ : come back

    9. food : refrigerator :: clothes : _____

    10. clear off : remove :: think up : _____

F.   In each blank, write the most appropriate word or phrase from the word form chart.

       After thinking it over for a long time, Sarah and Bob decided to have a house built. First, they bought a large (1) _____ which was (2) _____ to some beautiful woods. Next, they chose a(n) (3) _____ to design their house. They wanted to have three bedrooms and a(n) (4) _____ room to (5) _____ visiting friends. After some time, the architect finished his (6) _____ , and the building work began. Sarah and Bob hired a contractor. Before he could begin to build, he had to (7) _____ the lot. One corner was filled with old tires, broken machines, and other (8) _____ . Unfortunately, it began to rain as soon as the contractor was ready to build, and it rained for several weeks. Sarah was (9) _____ and did not think she could (10) _____ any more delay. During one of the storms, lightning struck a large tree, and it caught on fire. Everything was so wet, however, that the fire soon (11) _____ . Finally, the weather improved, and the house was finished quickly. You can be sure that Sarah and Bob asked the contractor to (12) _____ a lightning (13) _____ !

Follow-up

G. Dictation: Write the sentences that your teacher reads aloud.

1. _____

2. _____

3. _____

4. _____

5. _____

H. Answer the following questions.

1. What kind of accommodations do you like when you take a trip?
2. Do you have any junk that you need to clear out of your apartment or house? What kind?
3. What is your apartment or house adjacent to?
4. When you feel miserable, do you endure your problems well?
5. Have you ever designed anything? What?
6. Would you like to be an architect? Why or why not?
7. Describe the architecture in your city. Is it similar to the architecture you see in other cities?
8. Add up 39 and 54.
9. Have you ever put up anything? What?
10. If a fire doesn't go out, what can you do?
11. What kinds of items can you keep in a chest?

I. Discuss several programs that were tried in your country. Describe them, and tell whether they were successful and why.

Banking

Word Form Chart

NOUN	VERB	ADJECTIVE	ADVERB
balance			
bulk			
deliberation	deliberate	deliberate	deliberately
	fill in		
finance	finance	financial	financially
finances			
		fiscal	fiscally
	flourish	flourishing	
fund	fund		
funds			
		graduated	
	make out		
		monetary	
		odd	
	pay back		
	pick up		
principal		principal	principally
proportion		proportional	proportionally
		disproportional	disproportionally
		proportionate	proportionately
		disproportionate	disproportionately
prospect	prospect	prospective	prospectively
prospects			
prospector			
			rather
			as a rule
	save up		
	settle up		
terms			

NOUN	VERB	ADJECTIVE	ADVERB
transaction	transact		
trend			
venture	venture		

Definitions and Examples

1. **pay back** {separable} (a) [to return money you have borrowed; to return a favor]

    He lent me five dollars last week, and I am going to **pay** him **back** today.
    Pay back everything you owe me as soon as possible.

    (b) [to treat someone in a similar way to the way he has treated you]

    Mr. Green always shouted at Jimmy when he walked through his yard. One night, the little boy **paid** Mr. Green **back** by throwing rocks on his grass.

2. **pick up** [to increase]

    Since the economy is improving, spending is **picking up**, and people are buying more products.
    Interest in learning foreign languages has **picked up** because more and more people want to travel.

3. **make out** {separable} (a) [to fill out a check]

    When the woman decided to buy the washing machine, the salesperson told her to **make out** a check for $759.39.
    I **made** the first check **out** for the wrong amount, so I had to **make out** another.

    (b) [6-7: to see or hear clearly]

    Please help me read this word on this old letter; I cannot quite **make** it **out**.

4. **save up** {separable} [to save money for a particular purpose]

    A: If you want to go to college, you had better begin to **save up** your money now.
    B: I started **saving** it **up** several years ago.

5. **settle up** [to pay the remaining part of an account]

    Before my aunt moved to Chicago, she **settled up** all her accounts in Pittsburgh.
    To keep a good credit rating, it is necessary to **settle up** your accounts promptly.

6. **fill in** (a) {separable} [to write information on a form or test]

   The students had to **fill in** the blanks with the right answers; however, one student did not study and **filled** them all **in** incorrectly.
   Please **fill in** your name, address, and social security number on the form.

   (b) **fill in (for)** [5-8: to substitute]

   Quinn **filled in for** me at work when I was sick.

7. **fund** [a collection of money to be used for a particular purpose]

   When the little girl needed an expensive operation, the townspeople began a **fund**.
   Sydney received money from a special **fund** in order to pay her tuition.

8. **funds** [money; cash]

   I would like to buy a new house, but I do not have any **funds**.
   The city council has voted to build another park, but there are no **funds** for the project.

9. **finance** [to provide funds for something]

   The city council is hoping that several wealthy businessmen will help **finance** the park project.
   When the young man started his business, his parents **financed** it for him.

10. **finances** [the money or resources of a government, business, group, or person]

    The government is investigating the **finances** of that business to find out if they have been cheating their customers.
    Her **financial** situation is good now that she has a job.

11. **fiscal** [having to do with finance]

    The **fiscal** year usually begins in July.
    Every department in a company must plan its **fiscal** needs carefully so it can work out a budget.

12. **transact** [to accomplish a piece of business]

    Many companies do not **transact** business on Saturday and Sunday.
    After completing their **transaction**, the two businessmen had dinner together.

13. **monetary** [referring to money]

    Since her business failed, Edith has had **monetary** problems.
    Because Uncle Joe helped to finance my new business, he has a **monetary** interest in it.

14. **deliberate** (a) [on purpose]

> The unhappy woman **deliberately** drove into her husband's parked car.
> The child claimed he broke the window by accident; however, the angry man was sure the child's action was **deliberate**.

(b) [to think carefully and for a long time about something]

> The bankers **deliberated** for several hours but decided they would not finance the man's new business.
> Joy **deliberated** for a long time about where she should go to college.

(c) [careful and slow in deciding; slow and unhurried]

> Bob was a **deliberate** man who never made a quick decision about anything.
> The old man walked **deliberately**; he did not want to slip on the ice.

16. **principal** (a) [primary; main; most important]

> The **principal** reason Andrew decided to buy a Toyota was the car's reputation for needing few repairs.
> Karen's need for more funds is the **principal** reason she changed jobs.

(b) [the main part of a financial amount, as contrasted to the interest]

> It is a good idea to invest your **principal** wisely. In that way, you can use the interest you make to pay for your expenses.

(c) [the head of a school]

> A **principal** must be a good organizer and must be able to get along with the teachers in his school.
> No child wants to be sent to see the **principal**; this usually means he is in trouble.

16. **balance** (a) [the amount of money in a bank account]

> The **balance** in my checking account is $261.16.
> If you keep a certain **balance** in your account, some banks will pay you interest.

(b) [the remainder of an amount]

> You can pay half of the money now and pay the **balance** in 30 days.

17. **proportion** [a part considered in relation to the whole]

> How well students do is usually in direct **proportion** to the amount they study.
> A greater **proportion** of money will be spent to improve safety in that company during this fiscal year compared to last year.

18. **proportionate** [in the proper proportion; fair]

> The little boy did not feel he got a **proportionate** share of the cake, so he tried to take some from his sister.
> One of the employees claimed that he was given a **disproportionate** share of work in the office. He asked his boss to give some of his duties to other workers.

19. **terms** [conditions]

> The **terms** of the loan are that I cannot spend any of the principal during the first month. After that, I can use the money as I wish.
>
> A: What are the **terms** for buying the house?
> B: I must give the seller ten percent of the price immediately. The bank will pay the rest, and I will pay the bank over 30 years.

20. **trend** [tendency; direction of movement]

> The **trend** in many financial institutions is to be very conservative.
> There is a growing **trend** in the United States to exercise regularly and eat wisely.

21. **venture** [an undertaking in which the result is dangerous or uncertain]

> Jerry asked Sam to finance his new business **venture**, but Sam was worried that it would not succeed.
> The man decided not to **venture** driving up the mountain because it was snowing very hard.

22. **flourish** [to prosper; to grow well]

> Lorien's business venture **flourished** after a very short time, so she is going to expand.
> Plants will **flourish** if they are given the proper amount of light and water.

23. **prospect** (a) [something possible in the future]

> The **prospect** of breaking a leg while skiing causes many people to avoid the sport.

    (b) [a candidate who is likely to succeed]

> Ms. Jones is a good **prospect** for mayor and will no doubt win the election.

    (c) [to search for gold or other metals]

> Many people moved to California in 1849 to **prospect** for gold.
> Few of the **prospectors** were successful.

24. **prospective** [expected; hoped for]

> Ever since she opened her bakery, my aunt sees all her relatives and friends as **prospective** customers.
> My **prospective** plans for the summer are to finish writing my book.

25. **prospects** [chances for success]

> A: What are your **prospects** for passing the exam?
> B: Not very good if I don't study!

26. **rather** [instead]

> A: Let's go to the movies tonight.
> B: Actually, I would **rather** stay home and watch TV.
> A: Here's the TV schedule; do you want to see a funny program or a serious one?
> B: A funny one, please. I enjoy laughing **rather** than crying.

27. **bulk** [the major portion of something]

> Unfortunately, he spent the **bulk** of his principal and has few funds left.
> The **bulk** of the renters did not like the terms of the new rental agreement and moved out of the apartment.

28. **graduated** [divided into marked intervals, especially for use in measurement]

> The scientist wanted to measure the substance carefully, so he poured it into a **graduated** container.
> In some states, there is a **graduated** income tax; this means that the higher your income, the higher the percentage you have to pay.

29. **as a rule** [usually; most of the time]

> **As a rule**, cats and dogs do not get along well together.
> Banks, **as a rule**, prefer to finance businesses which have good prospects for success.

30. **odd** (a) [not even]

> One, three, and five are **odd** numbers.
> An **odd** number is not divisible by two.

> (b) [1-25: strange]

>> That man is behaving in an **odd** way; he keeps looking at the bottom of his shoes.

> (c) [5-20: chances]

>> The **odds** that they will win are not good.

Introductory Exercises

A.   Match each word or phrase with its definition.

____ **1.** expected; hoped for	**a.** as a rule
____ **2.** having to do with finances	**b.** bulk
____ **3.** to return money you have borrowed	**c.** deliberate
____ **4.** to increase	**d.** fill in
____ **5.** on purpose	**e.** finance
____ **6.** to write information on a form or test	**f.** fiscal
____ **7.** primary; main	**g.** flourish
____ **8.** to fill out a check	**h.** funds
____ **9.** to save money for a particular purpose	**i.** graduated
____ **10.** money; cash	**j.** make up
____ **11.** to provide funds for something	**k.** odd
____ **12.** conditions	**l.** payback
____ **13.** a part considered in relation to the whole	**m.** pick up
____ **14.** tendency; direction of movement	**n.** principal
____ **15.** usually; most of the time	**o.** proportion
____ **16.** to prosper; to grow well	**p.** prospective
____ **17.** instead	**q.** rather
____ **18.** not even	**r.** save up
____ **19.** an undertaking in which the result is dangerous or uncertain	**s.** settle up
	t. terms
	u. trend
	v. venture

B.   Answer each question with a word from the word form chart.

1. What do you do to blanks on a form?
2. What do you call the money in your bank account?
3. If you have an important decision to make, what will you do?
4. When you want to buy something, what do you need?
5. Who is the chief authority at a school?
6. If you plan to use a check to pay someone, what must you do?
7. When you borrow money, what should you do as soon as possible?
8. If your flowers are growing well, how might you describe them?
9. What should you do if you plan to buy a new car next year?
10. What three adjectives might you use if you were discussing money matters?
11. What does a loan or agreement usually have?
12. What do two sides have to do before they can reach an agreement?
13. If your interest in something increases, what does it do?
14. How can you describe the number seven?

Study Exercises

C. Write **T** if the sentence is true and **F** if it is false.

_____ 1. A flourishing business is unsuccessful.

_____ 2. People who do not have many funds may seek financial help.

_____ 3. It is difficult to make out a check.

_____ 4. Eleven and thirteen are odd numbers.

_____ 5. Banks deal with monetary matters.

_____ 6. People usually do not get married deliberately.

_____ 7. Businesses usually investigate prospective employees carefully.

_____ 8. Merchants usually decide to close their stores when business picks up.

_____ 9. Most people would like to be rich rather than poor.

_____ 10. Careful people usually like to venture into dangerous places.

_____ 11. A person who has monetary interests might be involved in fiscal matters.

_____ 12. If you do a proportion of the work, it means you do the bulk of it.

_____ 13. As a rule, people who move to another city have to settle up their accounts before they leave.

_____ 14. People rarely follow fashion trends.

D. Match each two- or three-word verb with its synonym.

_____ 1. pay back

_____ 2. pick up

_____ 3. put up

_____ 4. go out

_____ 5. back up

_____ 6. clear out

_____ 7. take back

_____ 8. save up

_____ 9. clear off

_____ 10. stand for

_____ 11. think over

_____ 12. fill in

_____ 13. fill in for

_____ 14. clear up

a. to become clear
b. to go backwards
c. to write information on a form or test
d. to substitute for
e. to build
f. to stop burning
g. to think about something
h. to remove trash from an enclosed area
i. to become
j. to become less severe
k. to increase
l. to save money for a particular purpose
m. to represent
n. to return something
o. to remove trash from a flat area
p. to return money you have borrowed
q. to go away without causing any problems

E.   Complete the analogies with a word or phrase from the word form chart.

      1. funds : money :: financial : _____

      2. stop : go :: die down : _____

      3. deliberate : unplanned :: _____ : rarely

      4. fill in : form :: _____ : check

      5. moist : damp :: instead : _____

      6. known : anonymous :: _____ : unmeasured

      7. vast : large :: expected : _____

      8. return : item :: _____ : money

      9. collect : things :: _____ : money

    10. hunter : animal :: _____ : gold

F.   In the blanks write the most appropriate word or phrase from the word form chart.

      After working for three years at a job she did not really like, Elizabeth Barry decided to start her own business. Unfortunately, the (1) _____ in her checking account was low, so Elizabeth had to figure out a way to get more (2) _____ . Her aunt had given her some money before she died, but Elizabeth was receiving interest on the (3) _____ and did not want to use it. Finally, Elizabeth went to a local bank for (4) _____ help. She had to (5) _____ quite a few forms, and the bank officers (6) _____ for a week about her request. They were concerned that her (7) _____ was a risk and that her (8) _____ might not be good. After their deliberations, the bankers called her back to the bank. They told her they had decided to lend her a (9) _____ of the amount she had asked for but that she would have to plan carefully and (10) _____ the rest. Elizabeth accepted the (11) _____ of the loan, and now, two years later, her business is (12) _____ . She is happy, and the bankers feel they made a wise (13) _____ .

Follow-up

G. Dictation: Write the sentences that your teacher reads aloud.

1. _____
2. _____
3. _____
4. _____
5. _____

H. Answer the following questions.

1. Does your bank require you to keep a minimum balance in your account? How much?
2. What was the amount of the largest check you ever made out? What was it for?
3. What kinds of things do people in your country save up for?
4. Do you have a prospective job waiting for you when you finish your studies?
5. Do you usually follow popular trends? What kind?
6. Have you ever been involved in a major financial transaction? Explain.
7. What happens in your country if a person doesn't pay back money that he owes?
8. Have you ever asked a bank to finance something for you? What?
9. Where did you receive the bulk of your education?
10. Do you feel people should be paid in proportion to the amount of education they have? Is this what is done in your country?

I. Do you consider yourself a deliberate person, or do you enjoy taking risks? Give examples to support your answer.

Farming

Word Form Chart

NOUN	VERB	ADJECTIVE	ADVERB
abundance	abound	abundant	abundantly
alternate	alternate	alternating	
	back up	backed up	
	bare	bare	barely
breed	breed (bred, bred)		
breeder			
	buy out		
	chop		
	come through		
creature			
cultivation	cultivate	cultivated	
	do away with		
erosion	erode	eroded	
generosity		generous	generously
grounds	grind (ground, ground)	ground	
migrant	migrate	migrant	
		migratory	
mill	mill	milled	
offspring			
slave	enslave	enslaved	
slavery	slave		
sparsity		sparse	sparsely
sparseness			
surplus		surplus	
surrender	surrender		

Definitions and Examples

1. **surplus** [extra; the amount above what you need]

    The farmers had so much **surplus** grain that they could not sell all of it. They shipped all the **surplus** overseas.

2. **slave** (a) [a person that is owned by another person for the purpose of work]

    The American Civil War was fought primarily over the question of **slavery**; after the war, the **slaves** were freed.

    (b) [to work very hard]

    He **slaves** all day in the fields and then comes home and must take care of all business transactions as well.

3. **enslave** [to make a person into a slave]

    Many Africans and native Americans were **enslaved** by the Europeans who traveled to the New World.

4. **grind** [to break a solid down into small particles]

    We **grind** our coffee at home so that it is fresher.
    Hamburgers are made out of **ground** beef.
    Corn, wheat, and other grains are **ground** to make flour.

5. **mill** (a) [a building with machinery for grinding grain]

    Farmers sell much of their grain to **mills**.

    (b) [a machine used for grinding, cutting, rolling, etc.]

    We have a pepper **mill** in the kitchen for grinding black pepper.

    (c) [a factory]

    The southern states are famous for their paper **mills** and their fabric **mills**. The northern states **are** noted for their steel **mills**.

    (d) [to grind, generally used for flour]

    That store sells freshly **milled** grain.

6. **migrant** [moving from one place to another, frequently according to the seasons]

    There are many **migrant** farm workers in the United States; they **migrate** from one region to another in search of work.
    Many **migratory** birds stay in the north during the summer but fly south for the winter.

7. **erosion** (a) [the process by which earth or rock is removed from any part of the earth's surface, usually by the force of wind or water]

    The cracks in the dry soil, as well as bare rock showing through, were the effects of **erosion**.

    (b) [a breaking down of any material, system, institution, etc.]

    Many of the old buildings are **eroding** because their stone walls cannot withstand the severe weather.

    The **erosion** of a strong national farming system has put many farmers out of business.

8. **cultivate** (a) [to prepare land for raising crops]

    They **cultivate** the fields in early spring so that they can plant the crops.

    (b) [to grow plants or crops]

    In winter certain vegetables are **cultivated** in special hothouses where the temperatures can be regulated.

9. **abundance** [a great quantity; a plentiful amount]

    We have an **abundance** of space in the farmhouse; invite as many people as you like.

    In summer the fields **abound** with wild flowers—flowers that are not cultivated by anyone.

10. **barely** [by very little; hardly]

    The farmers made **barely** enough money to survive the year.
    He **barely** let me explain my point of view.

11. **bare** [without the usual or appropriate covering]

    Once they harvest the crops in the fall, the fields lie **bare** until early spring.
    The baby ran around the room **bare** until his mother put his clothes on.
    The trees are **bare** in the winter.

12. **alternate** (a) [to use or place first one and then the other]

    Farmers **alternate** crops in the fields so the nutrients in the soil are not completely used up by one crop.
    They **alternated** the flowers in the garden. They had a row of red, a row of white, a row of red, and so on.

    (b) [a substitute]

    He went to the bank with a plan but had an **alternate** plan just in case the bank would not accept his first idea.

13. **generous** (a) [abundant; plentiful]

> He helped himself to a **generous** portion of meat and potatoes.

   (b) [giving or sharing without concern about whether you will receive something in return]

> Our neighbors are very **generous**; they always share with us whatever they can.
> It was through the **generosity** of our friends that we were able to keep our farm operating.

14. **back up** (a) {separable} [to support]

> The local government **backed up** its threats to the citizens by calling in the military.
> We **backed** the mayor **up** when he needed support for his urban preservation plan.

   (b) [5-19: {separable} to move in a backward direction]

> The farmer **backed** the wagon **up** into the barn.

15. **chop (into)** [to cut by striking with a heavy, sharp tool; to cut into small pieces]

> We need to **chop** some wood for the fire.
> Please **chop** it **into** small pieces.

16. **chop up (into)** (a) {separable} [to cut into small pieces]

> They **chopped up** the vegetables to make vegetable soup.

   (b) **chop down** {separable} [5-14: to cut a tree down]

> They **chopped** the Christmas tree **down** and dragged it home.
> To clear the fields, they **chopped** the trees **down** and then chopped them up into sections that were easy to carry away.

17. **offspring** [children]

> Cats and dogs can produce as many as twelve **offspring** at a time.
> Hundreds of years ago it was very common for people to have many **offspring** because fewer than half reached adulthood.

18. **breed** (a) [to keep and raise animals that will produce offspring, often as a business]

> My uncle **breeds** race horses on his farm.

   (b) [to produce offspring]

> A dog and a cat can never be **bred** together.

   (c) [a specific type of a given animal, particularly those animals kept by man]

> The German shepherd is the **breed** of dog that many police departments use.

19. **sparse** [growing or placed at widely spaced intervals; not crowded]

> Grass grows very **sparsely** in the drier regions of the United States.
> His hair is so **sparse** that he looks almost bald.

20. **come through (with)** [to succeed in doing or providing something]

> The bank **came through with** the money that we needed.
> They **came through with** the help that we asked for.
> We can always count on Jack; he always **comes through** when we
> need him.

21. **creature** (a) [an animal]

> All sorts of **creatures** come out of their hiding places at night.

(b) [a person especially one you dislike or feel sorry for]

> The rich people of this area frequently regard the very poor as nothing
> more than **creatures** of the street.

22. **surrender (to)** (a) [to give up possession of something]

> If you cannot pay your bank loan, you will have to **surrender** your car to
> the bank so that they can sell it for the money you owe.
> Many U.S. farmers had to **surrender** their farms because they could not
> make enough money to pay all their bills.

> > (b) [2-8: to give oneself up, as to an enemy]

> > > The enemy **surrendered** to us because they knew that they had
> > > lost the battle.
> > > The parents finally **surrendered** to their daughter's repeated
> > > demands.

23. **buy out** {separable} [to buy a business in order to take it over]

> The larger farms **bought out** all the smaller, struggling farms.
> It was easy to **buy** him **out**; he needed money so badly that he sold his
> business for the first offer despite how low it was.

24. **do away with** (a) [to eliminate; to omit]

> The farmer decided to **do away with** his idea of raising pigs; raising cattle
> would be more profitable.

(b) [to kill]

> We **did away with** all the pests that kept eating the horses' food.

Introductory Exercises

A.   Match each word or phrase with its definition.

____ 1. an animal or person		**a.** abundant
____ 2. to move around		**b.** alternate
____ 3. extra		**c.** back up
____ 4. to wear away the surface		**d.** barely
____ 5. a factory		**e.** breed
____ 6. one person owning another		**f.** chop up
____ 7. one, then the other, etc.		**g.** creature
____ 8. giving		**h.** cultivate
____ 9. to give up		**i.** do away with
____ 10. to make into powder		**j.** erode
____ 11. children		**k.** generosity
____ 12. a lot of		**l.** grind
____ 13. to produce offspring		**m.** migrate
____ 14. to support		**n.** mill
____ 15. to grow		**o.** offspring
____ 16. to eliminate		**p.** slavery
____ 17. hardly		**q.** sparsity
		r. surplus
		s. surrender

B.   Complete each sentence with a word from the word form chart.

1. Too much wind and water striking the earth can cause

   _____ .

2. The factory where grain is ground is a(n) _____ .

3. Another word for sons and daughters is _____ .

4. If you have no clothes on, you are _____ .

5. All animals, man included, can be called _____ .

6. If you like to share your things, you are _____ .

7. Growing plants is known as _____ .

8. If you do something one way, then a different way, then try the first
   way again, you are _____ methods.

9. The opposite of "to go forward" is to _____ .

10. If you are taken as a slave, you are _____ .

11. Birds that fly south for the winter are _____ .

12. People who move from region to region are _____ .

13. To give something up when you don't want to is to _____ it.

14. To cut something into very small pieces is to _____ it _____ .

15. To have enough or more than enough is to have a(n) _____ .

Study Exercises

C. Write **T** if the sentence is true and **F** if it is false.

_____ **1.** If you have a surplus of food, you should buy more.

_____ **2.** Birds, dogs, and lions are all living creatures.

_____ **3.** People surrender their belongings whenever they are asked to.

_____ **4.** Flour mills cultivate grain.

_____ **5.** Your offspring are your grandparents.

_____ **6.** If someone believes in you, he will back you up.

_____ **7.** To buy the bare necessities means to buy only the most necessary items.

_____ **8.** If trees grow sparsely, they are not crowded.

_____ **9.** People do away with things that they think are not useful.

_____ **10.** Migrants stay in the same place from month to month.

_____ **11.** You alternate feet as you walk.

D. Match each phrase on the left with the most appropriate set of examples on the right.

_____ **1.** Things you can grind

_____ **2.** Things you can chop up

_____ **3.** Things you can back up

_____ **4.** Things you can come through with

_____ **5.** Things you can cultivate

_____ **6.** Things that can erode

_____ **7.** Things that can migrate

_____ **8.** Things that can alternate

_____ **9.** Things you can surrender

_____ **10.** Things you might want to do away with

_____ **11.** Things you can breed

a. money, support, help

b. a temperature, prices, enthusiasm

c. someone's moods, an electrical current

d. vegetables, wood, meat

e. cows, dogs, horses

f. coffee, meat, grain

g. people, birds, animals

h. useless items, evil men, bothersome animals

i. your house, your car, your business

j. corn, flowers, plants

k. land, a mountain, a political system

l. people, a good idea, a politician, your car, a bus

E. Complete the analogies with a word or phrase from the word form chart.

1. to breed : animals :: to _____ : plants

2. few : many :: _____ : abundant

3. fire : burn :: wind : _____

4. chop up : wood :: _____ : flour

5. man : person :: dog : _____

6. stay : remain :: move : _____

7. adults : children :: parents : _____

8. not enough : lack :: more than enough : _____

F. Read the passage and answer the questions that follow.

In recent years, many U.S. farmers have found it difficult to make a living at farming. It has gotten increasingly more expensive to operate a farm, and many farmers, if they have not already lost their land, are continually threatened by the
5 possibility of losing their property.

The reasons for these difficulties can be found in events of a few years ago. At a time several years ago when farmers needed financial assistance, the government and banks came through with the support that they needed. Loans were extended so that farmers
10 could buy more equipment and machinery to increase farm production. They were advised to plant more and more crops because the forecast indicated that people would buy all that they grew and that what was not sold at home could be shipped abroad. Unfortunately, people did not buy as much as originally
15 anticipated, prices fell off, and farmers were left with tons of surplus crops and with incredible financial losses and worries. Their businesses were eroding right before their eyes, and there was little that they could do to prevent it. Most farmers, but particularly those owning small farms, were in critical financial
20 condition, much worse than before they had taken out their loans.

Despite barely making enough money to live on, the farmers still had to pay back the loans. As could be expected, the banks were not so generous when farmers were unable to meet their bank payments. Many farmers had to surrender their land to the
25 banks as repayment of their loans. Farms that had been in the family for generations were lost, either to the banks or to larger farms, whose owners could afford to buy them up. The smaller farmers were being bought out and essentially left with nothing.

While in the past year the crisis has fallen off somewhat—
30 that is, one does not hear daily on the news that dozens of Midwest farmers have lost their properties—the farmers cannot forget that financial problems still exist. They are aware that in this time of modern farming, when emphasis is placed on more

and better and faster production, conditions could at any time take
35 a turn for the worse and that they could once again be faced with
losing the farms which have always been their lives.

1. What threat do farmers always face? _____

   _____

2. How did the banks help the farmers? _____

   _____

3. Why were they advised to buy machinery and plant more? _____

   _____

4. How accurate was the financial forecast? _____

   _____

5. What happened that financially damaged the farmers' businesses? _____

   _____

6. Did the loans help the farmers? Why or why not? _____

   _____

7. What was the primary concern that the farmers then faced? _____

   _____

8. How did the banks react to farmers' inability to pay off the loans? _____

   _____

9. What were the larger farms doing during this period of financial
   uncertainty? _____

   _____

10. How is the farming situation today? _____

    _____

11. What do farmers always keep in mind these days? _____

    _____

Follow-up

G. Dictation: Write the sentences that your teacher reads aloud.

1. _____
2. _____
3. _____
4. _____
5. _____

H.   Answer the following questions.

1. What are some creatures that typically come out at night?
2. What types of things are sparse/abundant in your country? Think in terms of plants, industries, consumer products, etc.
3. Do any people in your country still mill flour by hand? If so, how do they do it? If not, how could you grind flour by hand?
4. What are the typical crops cultivated in this area? In your area or country? What makes this/that area suitable for these crops?
5. Does your country have a history of slavery? When was it common? Who were the slaves and who were the owners? When and how were they freed?
6. Are migrant farm workers common in your area? What are some problems that you would imagine migrant farm working families to have?
7. What are some problems that erosion can cause for farmers? How can erosion be controlled?
8. Sometimes erosion can cause wonderful geological structures. Have you seen or do you know of any famous cases of erosion? What does the area look like? What caused the erosion in that particular region?
9. What are some laws that the government has done away with? Whom has the elimination of these laws or regulations affected most? Has the change been harmful or helpful?
10. What are some examples of the generosity of the people in your area? On a personal basis? On a larger or public basis, such as providing money or property for certain causes or for establishing such things as museums, special schools, and so on?

Work

Word Form Chart

NOUN	VERB	ADJECTIVE	ADVERB
	account for		
arbitration	arbitrate		
arbitrator			
assessment	assess		
assessor			
burden	burden	burdensome	
chore			
colleague		colleagial	colleagially
colleagueship			
		elementary	
	engage in		
enterprise		enterprising	
exercise	exercise		
	get down to		
inclination	incline	inclined	
incline			
initiative	initiate		
	make up		
merit	merit	meritorious	meritoriously
monopoly			
monopolizer	monopolize		
monopolization			
officer			
	overwhelm	overwhelming	overwhelming
		overwhelmed	
post			
	see through		
	stand out		
subordinate	subordinate	subordinate	

NOUN	VERB	ADJECTIVE	ADVERB
	take off		
	tell off		
utopia		utopian	

Definitions and Examples

1. **chore** [a task, especially one which is not pleasant]

    Cleaning the house is a **chore** which no one enjoys.
    Each of the children has assigned **chores** to do each week.

2. **initiate** [to begin]

    Most changes which occur in that company are **initiated** by the president.
    She **initiated** a plan to save money during production.

3. **initiative** [the personal characteristic of acting independently of outside control or influence]

    They hired her because she demonstrated a lot of **initiative** in her last job by reorganizing the office.

4. **colleague** [an associate at one's work place]

    He was fired because he was too dependent on his **colleagues** and did not show enough initiative.
    He is praised by his **colleagues** for his excellent work.

5. **stand out** [to be very visible because of one's achievements]

    She **stands out** among her colleagues because of the many research papers she has published.
    The applicants who **stand out** during the interview process will be hired.

6. **subordinate** [a person of lower position]

    That boss does not treat his **subordinates** very well.
    He did not feel that he had any influence over the decision because of his **subordinate** position.

7. **tell off** {informal} {separable} [to speak angrily to someone and make negative comments]

    I wanted to scream at my boss and **tell** him **off**, but I was afraid that he would fire me.
    He **told off** his brother last week, and they are still not speaking to each other.

8. **take off** {separable} (a) [to not go to work]

    I plan to **take** Monday **off** so that I can have a three-day weekend.
    Japanese workers hardly ever **take** days **off**.

    (b) [5-15: to remove]

    He **took off** his boots before entering the house.

9. **post** [a job; a position]

    She is starting a new **post** in New York next week.
    The soldier was put on trial because he left his **post** during the battle.
    There are many teaching **posts** available in rural areas.

10. **see through** {separable} [to complete]

    My boss expects us to **see** this **through** before we leave tonight.
    He promised to **see** this project **through** although he wants to quit.

11. **assess** [to determine the importance, size, or value of]

    The supervisor must **assess** the job performance of each worker to decide
    whom to promote.
    The city tax office **assesses** the value of each property in order to
    determine how much tax is owed by the owner.

12. **burden** (a) [a duty or responsibility]

    Supporting his family is a heavy **burden** for him.
    The **burden** of completing the project on time was too great for him.

    (b) [a load]

    The horse was carrying such a large **burden** that it could not continue up
    the hill.

13. **elementary** (a) [basic; simple; on an easy level]

    We have to learn to solve the **elementary** problems before we try the
    difficult ones.
    She is taking an **elementary** Spanish course.

    (b) [1-1: the first six years of school]

    My son entered **elementary** school when he was six years old.

14. **make up (for)** [to take some action because another action was not done]

    She **made up for** missing work last week by working late every night this
    week.
    You will have to **make up for** your poor grade on the last test by getting
    an A on the final.

15. **merit** [to deserve; to have value]

> She **merits** a raise in pay, but the company seniority system may prevent her from getting it.
> Your plan has **merit**; we will have to consider it carefully.

16. **inclination** (a) [a tendency; what someone likes to do]

> Her **inclination** is to take off on Mondays and Fridays.
> He is **inclined** to talk too much; he is always talking.

(b) [a slope]

> The **inclination** of this road is very steep.
> We could not ride our bicycles up the **incline**.

17. **enterprise** (a) [a business organization]

> Their new **enterprise** is doing rather well; they are planning to open two new stores next month.

(b) [initiative]

> She showed a lot of **enterprise** when she founded that company.

(c) [a project which is especially difficult or complicated]

> This new **enterprise** is taking all of our time; we should never have tried to fix the roof by ourselves.

18. **monopoly** [the total control of the sale of a product by one person or by a group of people who cooperate]

> There are laws against the forming of **monopolies** in the United States because a **monopoly** can charge excessively high prices.
> There is only one grocery store in this town, so its owners have a **monopoly** on food sales.

19. **monopolize** [to control totally]

> He **monopolized** our conversation by talking more loudly than everyone else.

20. **overwhelm** [to defeat; to crush]

> I have been **overwhelmed** by work recently; I have not had time to sleep.
> She found the task to be **overwhelming** and quit.

21. **utopia** [an imaginary place of ideal perfection]

> He dreams of living in a **utopia** where he would not have to work.
> The new owner's **utopian** ideas about how to run the factory soon changed when he saw the realistic problems.

22. **exercise** (a) [something done repeatedly in order to develop or improve a specific skill or power]

> The boss has us do **exercises** each day to improve our skills at using the new machinery.
> The math teacher assigned three **exercises** for homework.

> > (b) [2-6: something which makes your body physically stronger]

> > > Running is excellent **exercise**.

23. **account for** [to give an adequate explanation]

> The inefficiencies in that factory **account for** its low production.
> I cannot **account for** his strange behavior recently. I have no idea what is wrong with him.

24. **arbitration** [the process of settling a controversy by using an outside judge who is acceptable to those on both sides of the controversy]

> The labor union leaders have entered a period of **arbitration** with the company executives.
> The **arbitrator** decided that the workers' wages should be raised but that they should receive fewer vacation days.
> The outside **arbitrators** were called in when labor and management could not reach a decision on their own.

25. **engage in** [to begin and carry on an enterprise; to participate in]

> She is **engaged in** the study of the causes of that disease.
> They are **engaged in** designing a new type of automobile.

26. **get down to** [to give one's attention or consideration]

> After lunch, we will **get down to** business.
> They quickly **got down to** their tasks and began to work.

27. **officer** (a) [an executive in a company]

> The **officers** of the company are meeting now to decide how to meet the union's demands.
> The **officers** of the bank make the decisions about loans.

> > (b) [2-8: a person of high rank in the military]

> > > Generals, majors, captains, and lieutenants are all **officers** in the army.

> > (c) [5-12: a policeman]

> > > The **officer** asked to see my driver's license.

Introductory Exercises

A. Match each word or phrase with its definition.

_____	1. to begin and carry on an enterprise	**a.**	account for
_____	2. something done repeatedly in order to develop or improve a specific skill or power	**b.**	arbitration
		c.	assess
		d.	burden
		e.	chore
_____	3. the total control of the sale of a product by one person or a group of people who cooperate	**f.**	colleague
		g.	elementary
		h.	engage in
_____	4. a tendency; what someone likes to do	**i.**	enterprise
_____	5. basic; simple; on an easy level	**j.**	exercise
_____	6. to complete	**k.**	get down to
_____	7. to speak angrily to someone and make negative comments	**l.**	inclination
		m.	initiative
		n.	make up for
_____	8. an associate at one's work place	**o.**	merit
_____	9. a task, especially one which is not pleasant	**p.**	monopoly
		q.	officer
_____	10. to be very visible because of one's achievements	**r.**	overwhelm
		s.	post
_____	11. to not go to work	**t.**	see through
_____	12. to determine the importance, size, or value of	**u.**	stand out
		v.	subordinate
_____	13. to take some action because another action was not done	**w.**	take off
		x.	tell off
_____	14. a business organization	**y.**	utopia
_____	15. to defeat; to crush		
_____	16. an imaginary place of ideal perfection		
_____	17. to deserve		
_____	18. a duty or responsibility; a load		
_____	19. a job; a position		
_____	20. a person of lower position		
_____	21. the personal characteristic of acting independently of outside control or influence		

B.   Answer each question with a word or phrase from the word form chart.

   1. Whom does a boss give orders to?
   2. What kind of place do people dream about?
   3. Whom do you work with?
   4. What kind of group can completely control prices?
   5. What are the executives in a company?
   6. What can help you learn to do a task better?
   7. What is something that you must carry?
   8. Why do you need to do things by yourself?
   9. What should you do to a chore? (two actions)
   10. What does a supervisor do to a subordinate's work?
   11. What does someone who is excellent at his job do?
   12. Who can help you if you are unable to settle some argument?
   13. How can you describe something that is very simple?
   14. How can you describe a task that is too difficult to do?

Study Exercises

C.   Write **T** if the sentence is true and **F** if it is false.

   _____   **1.** A utopia is a nice place.

   _____   **2.** If a person's work stands out, he does not merit what he earns.

   _____   **3.** People usually find elementary tasks overwhelming.

   _____   **4.** When an employee takes off from work, he may later have to make up for the work he missed.

   _____   **5.** A boss will be happy when a subordinate tells him off.

   _____   **6.** An arbitrator initiates arguments.

   _____   **7.** Customers like to buy from monopolies.

   _____   **8.** An employee who sees an overwhelming job through deserves merit.

   _____   **9.** An officer's post in a company is a relatively high one.

   _____   **10.** People's responsibilities are often burdens.

   _____   **11.** Colleagues need an arbitrator when they agree.

   _____   **12.** Bosses usually want workers to account for their mistakes.

D. Complete the analogies with a word or phrase from the word form chart.

1. junior : senior :: _____ : superior

2. school : friend :: work : _____

3. judge : trial :: _____ : negotiation

4. judge : judgment :: supervisor : _____

5. rule : a country :: _____ : an industry

6. join : a club :: _____ : a business

E. Circle the letter of the word or phrase which does not fit.

1. tell off   **a.** your boss
                 b. your employee
                 c. your child

2. take off   **a.** a day
                 b. a week
                 c. a second

3. see through   **a.** the project
                 b. the task
                 c. the solution

4. make up for   **a.** your absence
                 b. your idea
                 c. your mistake

5. get down to   **a.** business
                 b. work
                 c. breakfast

F. In each blank, write the most appropriate word or phrase from the word form chart.

My first post in the business world was certainly not utopian. I was hired as a manager in a clothing factory. Unfortunately, many of the workers were (1) _____ to be lazy. For example, they often (2) _____ days from work for no good reason. Also, they often ignored their assigned (3) _____ to talk to their friends.

My (4) _____ of the situation was that major changes were needed in the factory and its staff, so I began to (5) _____ some changes. I told the employees that they would have to (6) _____ each of the days which they missed. Workers who did good work and who (7) _____ as better than their (8) _____ would be rewarded.

I know that many of my (9) _____ did not welcome these

changes. Some were very angry, but none of them dared to

(10) _____ me _____ . The changes occurred slowly,

but I was very determined to (11) _____ my plans

_____ . Finally, the situation which had seemed so

(12) _____ at first became less of a burden. My first job was a

success, although it was difficult.

Follow-up

G. Dictation: Write the sentences that your teacher reads aloud.

1. _____

2. _____

3. _____

4. _____

5. _____

H. Answer the following questions.

1. What chores did your parents require you to do around the house when you were a child?
2. For what reasons do you take days off from school?
3. Have you ever found any of your classes to be overwhelming? Explain.
4. What is the greatest burden that your parents carry?
5. Are monopolies permitted in your country? In what areas are there monopolies?
6. What are you inclined to do when you have free time?
7. Explain your idea of utopia.
8. What is the most difficult thing that you have ever seen through?
9. Tell about a time when you took initiative.
10. In what situations are professional arbitrators used in your country?
11. How is the performance of a student assessed in this class?

I. Tell about the life of someone who became a business success in your country.

Health

Word Form Chart

NOUN	VERB	ADJECTIVE	ADVERB
acuteness		acute	acutely
agony	agonize	agonizing	agonizingly
anesthesia	anesthetize	anesthetic	
anesthesiology			
anesthesiologist			
anesthetic			
antidote			
	bring to		
cough	cough	coughing	
deficiency		deficient	deficiently
deprivation	deprive	deprived	
fatigue	fatigue	fatigued	
		fatiguing	
	follow		
hygiene		hygienic	hygienically
	let out		
organ		organic	organically
	pass away		
performance	perform		
prescription	prescribe	prescriptive	
	pull through		
remedy	remedy		
senility		senile	
sterilization	sterilize	sterile	
		sterilized	
surgeon		surgical	surgically
surgery			
	throw up		
toxin		toxic	toxically

173

NOUN	VERB	ADJECTIVE	ADVERB
transplant	transplant	transplant	
		widespread	
wrinkle	wrinkle	wrinkled	

Definitions and Examples

1. **acute** (a) [sharp; severe]

    That illness is characterized by a high temperature and **acute** pain in the ears.

    (b) [very perceptive]

    He has an **acute** sense of hearing; he can hear almost anything.

    (c) [reaching a severe or dangerous stage rapidly, as in a disease or medical emergency]

    A heart attack is an example of an **acute** medical problem.

2. **cough** [to force air from the lungs suddenly and noisily in order to remove unwanted fluids or objects from the lungs or throat]

    Too much pollution in the air can cause people to **cough**.
    If you have a piece of food stuck in your throat, you can **cough** to try to remove it.

3. **fatigue** [a condition of being weaker or tired as a result of hard work, exercise, stress, etc.]

    He was so **fatigued** that he slept for twelve hours.
    Fatigue can be a serious problem for those who work in manual labor jobs.

4. **follow** (a) [to obey]

    We **followed** the doctor's orders exactly.

    (b) [3-7: to come or go after]

    That illness is characterized by a high temperature **followed** by acute stomach pains.
    The parents **followed** the doctor to the conference room where they discussed their son's problems.

5. **pass away** [to die]

    My grandfather **passed away** five years ago.
    Saying that someone **passed away** is a gentler way of saying the person has died.

6. **bring to** {always separated} [to bring someone from an unconscious or nearly unconscious state to a conscious state]

   They **brought** the patient **to** after about five minutes.
   They threw the drunk under the cold shower to **bring** him **to**.

7. **let out (of)** {separable} [to permit a person to leave the hospital, jail, etc.; to release from a place]

   The doctors **let** my father **out** of the hospital this morning.
   They **let** me **out** after I signed the necessary insurance forms.
   The teachers **let out** the students a few minutes early.

8. **pull through** {separable} [to get through the worst part of an illness; to get well]

   The doctors **pulled** the patient **through** the acute stages of the disease.
   With the proper medical treatment, he was able to **pull through**.

9. **remedy** [something that will reduce pain, cure a disease, or correct a disorder; anything that corrects a problem; a solution]

   Proper exercise and diet is a sure **remedy** for overweight people.
   Chicken soup is a common **remedy** for a cold or sore throat.

10. **prescribe (for)** [to order or recommend a remedy or treatment]

    The doctor **prescribed** three different types of medicine and six weeks in bed **for** his back problem.
    I took the **prescription** to the drugstore to get my medicine.

11. **surgery** [a form of medical treatment by instrumental operations]

    Heart **surgery** is much more common these days than it was even ten years ago.

12. **surgeon** [the doctor who performs surgery]

    The **surgeon**, despite all his efforts, was unable to save the accident victim.

13. **perform** (a) [to carry out; to do an activity; to fulfill a responsibility]

    The surgeon carefully **performed** the delicate eye surgery.
    Nurses **perform** a wide variety of duties in the hospital.

    (b) [2-23: to give a public presentation of music, theater, etc.]

    They **performed** a new play by Alex Moffit.

14. **transplant** [to transfer one body part to another body area or to a different body]

> Dr. Christian Barnard performed the first heart **transplant** in the late sixties.
>
> Presbyterian Hospital in Pittsburgh is famous worldwide for its **transplant** surgery.

15. **agony** [intensive physical or mental stress or pain]

> The car accident victim was in such **agony** that the doctor prescribed a strong pain killer.
>
> The family **agonized** over the death of their beloved grandmother.

16. **throw up** {informal} {separable} [to vomit]

> He did not want to eat anything because he knew he would **throw up**.
>
> The patient **threw** the medicine **up**; it irritated his stomach too much.

17. **anesthetic** [something given to purposely cause total or partial loss of feeling]

> The doctor gave her an **anesthetic** near the injury so that she would not feel any pain during the surgery.
>
> For certain surgeries the patient needs an **anesthetic** which will make him unconscious.

18. **sterile** [completely free of anything that can cause disease; extremely clean]

> Doctors and nurses must wear **sterile** clothing when performing surgery in the operating room.
>
> Medical instruments must be **sterilized** so that they do not pass infection from one patient to another.

19. **toxic** [harmful; deadly; poisonous]

> Many products used to clean the house are highly **toxic**.
>
> The smoke and gas that are produced by industries can contain **toxins**.

20. **senile** [a mental weakening that frequently accompanies old age]

> Not all elderly people become **senile**.
>
> **Senility** is usually characterized by forgetfulness but can also be characterized by other problems, for example moments of anger or intense sadness.

21. **wrinkle** [lines in the skin that accompany old age; unwanted lines in fabric or other soft materials]

> She sat in the sun so much that her skin has become **wrinkled** very early.
>
> Sleeping in your clothes will cause them to **wrinkle**.

22. **widespread** [very common; occurring or accepted widely]

> Drug abuse is a **widespread** problem in the world today.
> The use of computers in business and education has become **widespread**.

23. **deficient (in)** [lacking an essential element; inadequate; insufficient]

> Many students in the United States are **deficient** in math and science.
> The doctors found that she had a **deficiency** of three essential nutrients.

24. **organ** [a part of the body adapted to perform specific duties]

> The heart, lungs, and stomach are all examples of internal **organs**.
> The eye is the **organ** adapted for vision.

25. **antidote** [a remedy for a poison]

> Toxic cleaning products almost always have the **antidote** printed on the
>   bottle.
> Some poisons are so fast-acting that no **antidote** will work against them.

26. **deprive (of)** [to keep or take away from someone something that he wants or has the right to have]

> The accident **deprived** him **of** his sight and of the use of his legs.
> If you **deprive** a plant **of** light and water, it will certainly die.

27. **hygiene** [the science of the principles of health and the prevention of disease; cleanliness]

> Personal **hygiene** is taught to children at a very young age; they are
>   taught to brush their teeth, wash their hands, and keep their hair and
>   bodies clean.
> Doctors and nurses pay close attention to **hygiene**.

Introductory Exercises

A. Match each word or phrase with its synonym.

—— 1. tired	**a.** acute
—— 2. cleanliness	**b.** agony
—— 3. sharp	**c.** anesthesia
—— 4. a doctor in an operating room	**d.** antidote
—— 5. a poison	**e.** bring to
—— 6. lacking	**f.** cough
—— 7. severe pain	**g.** deficient
—— 8. to obey	**h.** deprived
—— 9. a remedy that works against poison	**i.** fatigued
—— 10. common	**j.** follow
—— 11. to die	**k.** hygiene
—— 12. to release	**l.** let out
—— 13. to vomit	**m.** pass away
—— 14. to move from one area to another	**n.** perform
—— 15. a pain killer	**o.** prescription
—— 16. to complete an activity	**p.** pull through
—— 17. to make conscious	**q.** remedy
—— 18. lines in the skin	**r.** surgeon
	s. throw up
	t. toxic
	u. transplant
	v. widespread
	w. wrinkles

B. Write **T** if the sentence is true and **F** if it is false.

—— 1. Doctors have found a remedy for passing away.

—— 2. You deprive someone when you take away something he likes or wants.

—— 3. You can become ill if your body is deprived of certain nutrients.

—— 4. An antidote is given to reduce pain.

—— 5. Acute pain does not hurt a lot.

—— 6. A patient will die if he pulls through a surgical procedure.

—— 7. Senility is an illness of the mind.

—— 8. Fatigue can be a problem among people who work long hours.

—— 9. Most people want wrinkled skin.

—— 10. A disease is widespread when many people have it.

—— 11. Doctors frequently transplant prescriptions for remedies.

—— 12. Food that is left unrefrigerated for long periods of time can develop toxins.

_____ **13.** Everything in an operating room should be sterilized.

_____ **14.** The lungs are organs adapted for breathing.

_____ **15.** Deprivation of certain nutrients can cause problems for a person.

Study Exercises

C. Match the first half of each sentence with its appropriate second half.

_____ **1.** The doctor prescribed an antidote

_____ **2.** During periods of war,

_____ **3.** One week after her surgery,

_____ **4.** Many older people develop

_____ **5.** A prescription tells the people at the drugstore

_____ **6.** Fatigue can be caused

_____ **7.** The heart, brain, lungs, and stomach are

_____ **8.** A surgeon is the doctor who

_____ **9.** If you follow the doctor's suggestions,

_____ **10.** With proper medical attention

_____ **11.** If someone gets sick to his stomach,

_____ **12.** The nurses gave the patient an anesthetic

a. agony is extremely widespread.

b. by too much of any strenuous mental or physical activity.

c. you will probably get better more quickly.

d. to work against the toxic liquid the child drank.

e. he might have to throw up.

f. performs surgery.

g. so that he would not feel any pain during surgery.

h. the problem of senility.

i. all examples of internal organs.

j. the doctors let her out of the hospital.

k. people can pull through even the most serious of illnesses.

l. what kind and how much of a medicine you need.

D. Paraphrase the underlined words in each sentence using a word from the word form chart.

1. The patient was experiencing <u>very severe</u> pain.

_____

2. Lifting heavy boxes in the store all day long can be <u>extremely tiring</u>.

_____

3. The doctors found a <u>lack</u> of white blood cells in the patient's blood.

_____

4. Doctor Johnson <u>did</u> the throat surgery.

_____

5. Certain chemical mixtures will produce <u>poisonous</u> substances.

_____

6. Personal <u>cleanliness</u> is very important for good health.

_____

7. The parents did not <u>obey</u> the doctor's instructions.

_____

8. They <u>took</u> <u>away</u> <u>from</u> her all her privileges.

_____

9. They just could not believe the <u>severity</u> of the disease.

_____

10. Despite their extreme efforts, the patient <u>died</u> shortly after midnight.

_____

11. People constantly try to invent a <u>solution</u> for old age.

_____

12. She has many thin <u>lines</u> around her mouth from smoking so much.

_____

13. The doctor <u>recommended</u> a week's rest from strenuous work for my backache.

_____

14. The couple <u>experienced</u> <u>extreme</u> <u>stress</u> over the death of their daughter.

_____

15. Visitors must put on <u>specially cleaned</u> clothes before entering the transplant patient's room so that they do not infect the patient.

_____

E. In each blank, write the most appropriate word or phrase from the word form chart.

1. For the comfort of the patients, visitors must _____ the rules of the hospital.

2. Among the people who are present during surgery are the _____ , who performs the actual operation; the nurses, who assist the doctor; and a(n) _____ , who controls the amount of anesthetic the patient receives.

3. _____ transplants are becoming more and more common every year—especially heart transplants.

4. A drugstore will not sell you certain medicines without a(n) _____ from a doctor.

5. He began to _____ when the food caught in his throat.

6. That poison has no _____ ; if you happen to eat it, you will surely die.

7. The patient had a(n) _____ pain in his side; every time he moved, it felt as if a knife were cutting him.

8. A simple _____ for the common cold is to stay warm, get plenty of rest, and drink lots of fluids.

9. The patient is experiencing the most dangerous stage of the disease; he may not _____ .

10. _____ is frequently characterized by forgetfulness.

11. Her husband slept all night in the hospital waiting room, so his clothes were all _____ when he awoke.

12. Her teeth are very soft because her body is _____ in the minerals which give teeth and bones their strength.

13. They _____ the patient _____ by putting cold water on his face and calling his name loudly.

14. He was in so much pain that he was in _____ .

15. Food at picnics must be kept on ice or else it can become _____ .

F. Read the passage and answer the questions that follow.

    Because of modern technology, organ transplants have become a relatively common occurrence in recent years. Heart transplants, for example, are performed much more frequently than even five years ago. While patients are excited about being able to extend

5 their lives through a transplant operation, they are also aware that they will pass through many agonizing physical and psychological phases during the process.

    Before a surgeon will decide to perform a heart transplant, he will have tried all other methods of treating his patient's heart

10 disease. When prescription medicines do not have any effect and all other types of heart operations are inappropriate or have failed, a heart transplant is the only means available to save the patient's life.

    During the pre-transplant stage, the patient is often very

15 fatigued. Because his heart is deficient, his body does not receive an adequate supply of blood, and, therefore, even the simplest of tasks becomes a chore. Walking even short distances becomes difficult, causing shortness of breath and acute chest pains as the heart overworks itself to send blood through the body. At this

20 stage the patient is tired of taking all the medicine that has been prescribed in an attempt to avoid operations. He is in constant

agony, worrying about the condition of his heart and wondering when it will finally stop beating, cutting short his life.

When the doctor finally decides that a heart transplant is the
25 only remedy for his patient's heart problems, he discusses with the patient the various phases he will go through. He is very honest with his patient, telling him that he has only a short time to live and that he has a decision to make—that of accepting or rejecting the heart transplant. The fact that the patient has to make the
30 final decision puts an extreme amount of pressure on him.

Once the patient decides to have the heart transplant, he experiences an even higher degree of anxiety than he had earlier. His name is placed on a list of patients waiting for a donor heart, and he is never sure if the heart will arrive in time to save his life.
35 This is when he needs an extra amount of emotional support from doctors, family, and friends.

Just before the operation, the patient has concerns about the transplant itself. He worries about the procedures and wonders if he will really pull through the surgery. He wonders if he made the
40 right decision. After surgery, the patient feels separated from his family as they are not permitted in the intensive care unit to visit him. He must begin his recovery stage alone.

The transplant patient at this point is surprised at just how physically well he feels. He is no longer fatigued, and does not
45 experience the acute chest pain as he did before the operation. He knows that the transplant has saved his life, but at the same time is aware that his difficulties are not over. He must deal with the possibility of organ rejection. At any time, his body may find the new heart unacceptable, and he will die. To help prevent this
50 rejection, the patient must take all types of prescription drugs which leave him open to illness and infection. In addition to his own concerns, he must also deal with the emotions of friends and family. They no longer view him as quite healthy and are constantly observing him and his every move. He has to work very
55 hard to make them feel comfortable about his condition.

While heart transplant surgery has been employed to save many lives, it does not come without a price. The patient will encounter a series of difficulties through every stage of the transplant process. He and his family must be strong if the patient
60 is expected to pull through the physical and emotional strain that transplant surgery places on him.

1. What treatments can doctors provide before deciding on a transplant? ____

_____

2. How does a patient who is suffering from chronic heart disease feel? ____

_____

3. What effect does a deficient heart have on the body? _____

_____

4. Why is the doctor so honest with the patient? _____

_____

5. Why does the patient feel so much pressure when he is deciding on whether to proceed with the transplant? _____

_____

6. Why does the waiting list produce even more anxiety? _____

_____

7. What will help the patient pull through the anxiety he experiences at this stage? _____

_____

8. What are the patient's concerns immediately before the transplant? _____

_____

9. Why does he begin the recovery stage alone? _____

_____

10. What are the immediate physical effects of the transplant? _____

_____

11. What new difficulties does the patient face at this point? _____

_____

12. Why are people uncomfortable with the transplant patient? _____

_____

Follow-up

G. Dictation: Write the sentences that your teacher reads aloud.

1. _____

2. _____

3. _____

4. _____

5. _____

H. Answer the following questions.

1. What does an anesthetic do? What are some ways to give a person an anesthetic? Have you ever been under an anesthetic? When? Why?
2. What does it mean to be deficient in something? What are some effects on the bones, skin, and teeth when a person is deficient in certain nutrients? Health is not the only area in which a person can be deficient. What are some other areas of deficiency a person might have?
3. What are some examples of widespread health problems in your country or around the world?
4. Why do certain medicines require a prescription? What is the procedure in your country for getting prescription drugs?
5. What are some ways of sterilizing objects or food? Why is sterilization important?
6. Every culture has folk remedies for curing diseases. What are some folk remedies that you know for a cold, toothache, or other pains, for a burn, for wrinkles?
7. What are some characteristics of senility? What types of problems can senility cause for family members?
8. What can cause fatigue? What is the most fatiguing thing you have ever done?
9. What kinds of things will make a person cough?
10. Every culture has its own way of dealing with death. What are the typical procedures—legal, medical, and so on—that you must follow when a person has passed away?
11. What are your views on transplant operations? What do you see as the most serious problems involved in transplants—physical, emotional, legal, or ethical?

Government (B)

Word Form Chart

NOUN	VERB	ADJECTIVE	ADVERB
acceptance	accept	acceptable	acceptably
		unacceptable	
alliance	ally	allied	
ally			
ballot			
bid	bid		
bidding			
counsel	counsel		
counselor			
discrimination	discriminate	discriminatory	
		indiscriminate	indiscriminately
draft	draft		
draftee			
empire			
emperor			
empress			
explication	explicate		
		explicit	explicitly
exposure	expose	exposed	
		external	externally
form	form		
formation			
		internal	internally
leaning	lean		
minister			
perspective			
		premature	prematurely
republic		republican	

NOUN	VERB	ADJECTIVE	ADVERB
	see about		
	send back		
turnout	turn out		
welfare		welfare	
	write down		

Definitions and Examples

1. **turn out** (a) [to result, to end up]

    A: How did the discussion **turn out**?
    B: Not very well. Everyone argued about everything, so we accomplished very little.

    (b) [to arrive or to assemble at a gathering]

    They were very disappointed at the small number of people who **turned out** for the concert.

2. **turnout** [the number of people at a gathering; attendance]

    The **turnout** for the football games is decreasing with every additional loss.

3. **write down** {separable} [to make a written note of something]

    He **wrote** the information **down** on a piece of paper.
    Be sure to **write down** my phone number before you go.

4. **see about** (a) [to check into; to investigate, generally on an informal basis]

    We have to **see about** buying a new car this year.

    (b) [take care of]

    The boss **sees about** locking up the building after office hours.

5. **send back** {separable} [to ask or make someone return to where he came from; to return something]

    They **sent** him **back** to the store to get the things that he had forgotten.
    The post office will **send** letters **back** to their source if the mailman cannot deliver them.

6. **lean** (a) [to have a tendency toward]

The government in that country **leans** to the right; the leaders are rather conservative.

(b) [to not be vertical; to be in a position at a slight angle; to support one's weight in this nonvertical position]

That tree is not growing straight. It's really **leaning** to one side.
He **leaned** against the wall while waiting for the bus.

(c) [to rely on for assistance or support]

It's good to know that you have friends you can **lean** on when you need help.

7. **counsel** [advice or guidance; to advise]

We followed the **counsel** of the mayor, and conditions in the town began to improve.
They **counseled** us to sell our house and move to a drier climate.

8. **explicit** [clear and specific]

I **explicitly** stated how we planned to carry out the investigation.
His duties are very **explicit**; he knows exactly what he has to do each day.

9. **explication** [an explanation, especially in detail]

The president demanded an **explication** in writing of the cause of the problem.

10. **premature** [prior to the customary or correct time; too early]

The baby was born six weeks **prematurely**.
It would be **premature** to say who will be representing the party in the presidential election.

11. **external** [on the outside; acting or coming from the outside; not domestic; foreign]

Many **external** factors affect the market in this country.
Externally he appears really calm, but on the inside he is as worried as anyone else is.

12. **internal** [on the inside; domestic]

The manager decided that the problem was no longer only **internal**, so he called in an outside consultant.
Some countries have a Minister of **Internal** Affairs who is responsible for domestic matters.

13. **expose** (a) [to make visible or known; to reveal]

> The police **exposed** a whole group of art thieves after a three-month investigation.

(b) [to put in a position so that external factors could have an effect]

> They experienced all kinds of health problems after being **exposed** to the toxic gas.

(c) [to allow light to act upon photographic film]

> I accidentally opened the camera and **exposed** all the film; our pictures were ruined.

14. **perspective** [a point of view; opinion]

> From the **perspective** of the president, the country is in top condition, but it's the people, not the president, who are experiencing the difficulty. Their **perspective** would certainly differ.

15. **discriminate** (a) [to make a clear distinction; to differentiate]

> The colors are so similar that it is difficult to **discriminate** which one is darker.

(b) [to act on the basis of prejudice]

> The poor are **discriminated** against in that town.
> That law is very **discriminatory**; it operates in favor of one group and against another.

16. **discriminating** [to be very selective, usually in the direction of good quality]

> He has very **discriminating** taste; he will wear only certain clothes and drinks only the best wines.

17. **welfare** (a) [health, happiness, and general well-being]

> The laws were passed by the government for the **welfare** of all.

(b) [government financial assistance for the poor]

> When families have no source of income, they frequently have to turn to **welfare** programs provided by the government.

18. **ally** [to unite with another in a formal or personal relationship, generally for a common cause; a friend in a cause]

> The smaller companies **allied** with the stronger, more established companies so that they would not go out of business.
> The United States, France, Russia, and England formed the **Allied** forces in World War II. The Axis forces were formed by the **alliance** of Germany, Italy, Japan, and other nations opposing the **Allies**.

19. **empire** (a) [a political unit, usually larger than a kingdom and frequently made up of a number of territories or nations, ruled by a single authority]

> The Spanish **Empire** once consisted of Spain itself plus most of South America and a portion of North America.
>
> Napoleon Bonaparte was one of the most famous **emperors** in the world.

(b) [an extensive enterprise]

> After years of hard work, he built a very successful business **empire**.

20. **draft** (a) [the selection of personnel from a group, particularly in the case of the military]

> Many young men in the United States who wanted to avoid the **draft** in the late 1960s and early 1970s moved to Canada.
>
> **Draftees** must report to the military office on June 4.

(b) [the preliminary outline, version, or design of something]

> People rarely write anything perfectly the first time; they generally write a number of **drafts** and make revisions.

21. **republic** [a government which is not ruled by a king or emperor and which generally has a president and laws set down by the people through elected officials]

> The United States is a **republic** whose basic laws were drafted in 1787.
>
> The people prefer a **republican** form of government.

22. **bid** [to attempt to win or attain something; to offer an amount as a price]

> **Bidding** is common in many card games in which money is involved.
>
> Before I awarded the construction job to anyone, I took **bids** from different companies. The company that **bid** the lowest, that is, the company that could complete the job for the least money, got the job.

23. **ballot** (a) [a paper or ticket used to register a vote]

> After the **ballots** were all counted, Johnson was announced the winner.

(b) [the process or act of voting]

> We have to hold a **ballot** in order to decide who should run the corporation.

(c) [the list of candidates running for office]

> There was no one on the **ballot** that I was really in favor of.

24. **accept** [to receive or take (something offered) because you want to]

> After reviewing all the reasons, we finally **accepted** his decision.
> We **accept** what you say as the truth, but you need to clarify this last point.

> > **[1-1: to admit to a place or to a group]**

> > > We were **accepted** at the University of Pittsburgh.
> > > They **accepted** only five candidates for the ballot.

25. **acceptable** [satisfactory]

> They reached an **acceptable** agreement on the issue.

26. **minister** (a) [a diplomat; a high officer of state appointed to head an executive or administrative department of government; a person working on behalf of someone else by carrying out specified orders]

> They fired the **minister** of the interior and appointed someone else.
> The prime **minister** of Great Britain is its chief political leader.

(b) [a person working in religious service]

> We talked to our **minister** after church today.
> The **minister** gave a very meaningful sermon in church today.

27. **form** (a) [a document with empty spaces in which to write requested information]

> We filled out all the necessary **forms** when applying for our driver's licenses.
> Hospitals must deal with endless health insurance **forms**.

(b) [the shape of something; to shape or make something; to develop something]

> We made a cake in the **form** of a guitar for our musician friend.
> She **formed** the snow into a huge snowball.
> Please let me **form** my own opinion of people.

(c) [to be a part of]

> The fifty states **form** the United States.

Introductory Exercises

A. Match each word with its definition.

____ 1. to uncover	**a.** accept
____ 2. person entering the military	**b.** acceptable
____ 3. to be inclined toward	**c.** alliance
____ 4. a government with an elected leader	**d.** ballot
____ 5. satisfactory	**e.** bid
____ 6. to check	**f.** counsel
____ 7. the making of something	**g.** discriminatory
____ 8. viewpoint	**h.** draftee
____ 9. advice	**i.** empress
____ 10. result	**j.** explicit
____ 11. to return	**k.** expose
____ 12. a vote	**l.** external
____ 13. to make a note of	**m.** formation
____ 14. too early	**n.** internal
____ 15. specific	**o.** lean
____ 16. favoring one group over another	**p.** minister
____ 17. to make a formal offer of	**q.** perspective
____ 18. from the outside	**r.** republic
____ 19. from the inside	**s.** premature
	t. see about
	u. send back
	v. turn out
	w. welfare
	x. write down

B. Answer each question with a word from the word form chart.

1. Who is the head of an empire?
2. What do you fill out if you want to get a credit card?
3. What do you do if you do not want to forget something?
4. If your legs are tired, what can you do to rest them?
5. What is another name for a formal friendship?
6. Who would you go to if you needed advice?
7. What do you call not hiring someone for a job because of his religion?
8. What is another word for the creation of something?
9. If you want to know if a public event was really successful, what could you count?
10. If the dinner you ordered arrived at your table cold, what would you do?
11. If the apartment you are living in were really terrible, what could you do?
12. What could cause a burn to the skin?
13. What would you call a person who favors a government with elected officials and a president?
14. If you have no money, what kind of agency might you have to seek help from?

Study Exercises

C. Write **T** if the sentence is true and **F** if it is false.

———   **1.** A republic has an emperor as its leader.

———   **2.** If you disagree with someone, it is because you have differing perspectives on the subject.

———   **3.** An explication is usually detailed.

———   **4.** You can get a draft from a school counselor.

———   **5.** People generally will not accept things they do not believe.

———   **6.** A minister frequently speaks on behalf of another person.

———   **7.** In order to elect a president, people make their bids.

———   **8.** Constant exposure to cold and damp weather could make you sick.

———   **9.** If a person leans toward a certain political group, he is more in favor of that group than of others.

——— **10.** A person can make a bid for an elected position.

——— **11.** A dinner party can turn out well, poorly, or somewhere in between.

——— **12.** If a baby is born early, he is premature.

——— **13.** Explicit instructions are necessary for anyone who is trying to do something for the first time.

——— **14.** Shouting in the middle of a theater during a performance would be unacceptable behavior.

——— **15.** You can generally trust your allies.

D. Match the first half of each sentence with its appropriate second half.

_____ 1. The marriage counselor

_____ 2. The newspapers exposed

_____ 3. If you do not feel well,

_____ 4. Politicians try to protect

_____ 5. After they completed the investigation,

_____ 6. Prematurely releasing information from the police investigation

_____ 7. If you receive broken merchandise,

_____ 8. People who do not accept the political beliefs of their party

_____ 9. If you need emotional support,

_____ 10. They counted all the ballots

a. all the corruption in the town council.

b. it turned out that they had forgotten to cover an important point.

c. could give the people time to escape.

d. advised us to listen to each other more.

e. you should send it back to the store.

f. the welfare of the citizens they represent.

g. you can usually lean on your friends.

h. you should see about making an appointment with a doctor.

i. to find out who won the election.

j. might form another with slightly different ideas.

E. In each blank, write the most appropriate word from the word form chart.

1. The _____ sent out ministers to all areas of his empire.

2. _____ to the public will help make a candidate better known.

3. The council members _____ the preliminary version of the new laws last week.

4. He lost his bid for the presidency; his party would not _____ him as their official candidate.

5. The secretary _____ everything that was said at the council meeting so that there would be a formal record.

6. He decided to seek legal _____ because he knew he was going to have a lot of problems.

7. The two political parties became _____ just before the election in order to gather more strength.

8. He stated his ideas very _____ in the hope that people would understand them better.

9. It is _____ to enter restaurants in the United States without your shoes or shirt on.

10. They had to live on _____ for six months until he could find a job.

11. On subway cars, trains, and buses it is unsafe to _____ against the doors.

12. He said he saw a ghost. Did it have a(n) _____ , or was it shapeless?

F. Complete the analogies with a word or phrase from the word form chart in this unit.

1. love : hate :: _____ : enemy

2. president : _____ :: emperor : empire

3. _____ : refuse :: take : leave

4. confusing : unclear :: _____ : clear

5. covered : _____ :: clothed : bare

6. king : queen :: emperor : _____

7. teacher : education :: _____ : religion

8. domestic : foreign :: _____ : external

G. Match each word or phrase with its opposite.

____ 1. acceptable	**a.** unclear	
____ 2. creation	**b.** hide	
____ 3. discrimination	**c.** internal	
____ 4. ally	**d.** shapeless	
____ 5. external	**e.** send back	
____ 6. explicit	**f.** unsatisfactory	
____ 7. having form	**g.** keep	
____ 8. accept	**h.** enemy	
____ 9. expose	**i.** destruction	
____ 10. send back	**j.** lack of prejudices	

H. Read the passage and answer the questions that follow.

When the time for government elections is near, candidates begin to prepare their plans on how to gain the acceptance of the majority of the population. When making a formal bid for the position of president, prime minister, or whatever the main
5 executive position of the country might be, the candidate must be very careful about which themes he discusses so that he can please as many people as possible and thereby win their votes.

A candidate employs the help of many counselors who advise him on the formation of a plan which will ensure the winning of

10 the election. When drafting the plan, the candidate and his counselors must take the perspective of the voters and consider which way they lean on a variety of political matters. How would the voters think, for example, about doing away with the military draft or perhaps about instituting a draft if one did not already

15 exist? The side the candidate took on this matter would affect the number of votes he would receive from such groups as young people ready for military service or people against war. Or, how would voters feel about certain decisions affecting the nation's welfare programs? A decision to reduce funding of programs for the

20 poor would certainly reduce the number of votes that the candidate received from lower income voters. In his plan, the candidate must consider questions of internal matters, such as laws, taxes, and business, as well as external affairs with other countries. The stand the candidate chooses to take on all matters

25 of interest to the people will determine the number of political alliances he can make, that is, which people, which organizations, which companies will support him in the election. The plan, then, which essentially shares with the public the candidate's perspective on all important political matters, must be very

30 carefully formulated. This plan serves one purpose, and that is to make the candidate acceptable to the majority of the people who can vote in the election.

Once the candidate's plan is complete, he tries to get as much public exposure as possible. He speaks in person to large groups of

35 people of all kinds. He also employs the public media—
newspapers, television, and radio—in order to gain the acceptance of the public. When speaking, he presents his plans to the public and explains the benefits of each point. At the same time, it is common for the candidate to expose the faults in his opponents'

40 plans and illustrate how those plans will not serve to benefit the people. If the candidate has prepared carefully and has presented his plans clearly to the public, he probably will have gained the acceptance of enough voters to win the election. All he will have to do is wait until the ballots have been counted to see how the

45 election turns out.

1. Why do candidates formulate a plan before they run for office? _____

_____

2. Who assists the candidate in making his plans? _____

_____

3. How does the candidate have to think when deciding on his plan? _____

_____

4. How can the candidate's plan affect the people's vote? _____

_____

5. What types of matters must the candidate take into consideration? _____
_____

6. What does the plan tell the public? _____
_____

7. What does a candidate do after he has prepared his plan? _____
_____

8. How can he reach more people more effectively? _____
_____

9. What does the candidate do in his speeches to the public? _____
_____

10. If the candidate has done an excellent job of predicting the political climate, what will he gain in the end? _____
_____

11. What will tell the candidate how the election has turned out? _____
_____

Follow-up

I. Dictation: Write the sentences that your teacher reads aloud.

1. _____
2. _____
3. _____
4. _____
5. _____

J. Answer the following questions.

1. What are three things that you might make a bid for?
2. What is the purpose of going to a counselor?
3. What are several types of discrimination?
4. If someone is giving you an explication, what is he doing?
5. What kinds of things might you send back?
6. Why would you write something down? What types of things do people commonly write down?
7. What are some ways in which welfare programs can help low income families?
8. If you ask someone if you can borrow his car for a week and he says that he will see about it, what is he telling you?

9. What does it mean to be indiscriminate?
10. What is the difference between a republic and an empire?
11. What are some things that you can expose?
12. What are some things that you can draft?

K. Answer the following questions.

1. How does a person make a bid for an elected position in your country?
2. What types of discrimination have you witnessed or do you know about?
3. How could discrimination be reduced?
4. What types of welfare programs are offered by your government? How do they function? Are they successful? Do people abuse them? How?
5. Who are your country's closest allies, and what types of services or products do they offer your country?

Nature

Word Form Chart

NOUN	VERB	ADJECTIVE	ADVERB
crudeness		crude	crudely
decay	decay	decayed	
disintegration			
disintegrator	disintegrate	disintegrated	
dump	dump		
element		elemental	
elements			
		elementary	
evolution	evolve	evolved	
		evolutionary	
exhibit	exhibit	exhibited	
exhibition			
extract	extract	extracted	
extraction			
extractor			
		extraordinary	extraordinarily
fluid		fluid	
fluidity			
		formidable	formidably
	give out		
gulf	engulf	engulfed	
insect			
insecticide			
intervention	intervene		
phase	phase		
sacrifice	sacrifice	sacrificial	sacrificially
savage		savage	savagely
shell	shell		
	stand up		

NOUN	VERB	ADJECTIVE	ADVERB
		thermal	thermally
		unique	uniquely
universe		universal	universally
vulnerability		vulnerable	vulnerably

Definitions and Examples

1. **exhibit** [to show or display, particularly for public viewing]

   The museum **exhibited** a collection of rare South American birds.
   The **exhibit** of Picasso paintings drew crowds to the museum.

2. **unique** [being the only one of its kind; being very different without anything to equal it]

   These birds are **unique** because they are the only ones in this region with this type of coloring.
   He is a **unique** person; I have never met anyone with as many talents as he has.

3. **extraordinary** [beyond what is ordinary or usual; exceptional]

   The Badlands in the United States are an **extraordinary** example of wind and water erosion.
   What an **extraordinary** pattern of clouds! I've never seen so much red and gray in the clouds before.

4. **insecticide** (a) [a poison used to kill insects]

   We put a powdered **insecticide** in the corner to kill the insects that kept coming in the house.
   Some **insecticides** used to kill insects on food plants have been found to have a negative effect on people's health.

   (b) **insect** [4-4: a very small animal, usually with no backbone, having three pairs of legs and a body that is made up of three parts; frequently with wings]

   The child screamed when he saw the black **insects** climbing up the wall.

5. **extract** [to remove from; to take out; to pick out]

   They **extracted** many tons of gold from that mine.
   The dentist will **extract** two of my back teeth next Monday.

6. **vulnerable** [exposed to injury; unprotected from danger; easily hurt physically or emotionally]

> Riding a motorcycle on the highway without wearing any head protection makes you **vulnerable** to head injury.
>
> Because the town was located near the water, it was **vulnerable** to floods during the rainy season.

7. **gulf** [a large area of ocean or sea partially enclosed by land]

> The **Gulf** of Mexico is surrounded by land on three sides, Mexico to the west, several southern U.S. states to the north, and the Florida peninsula to the east.

8. **engulf** [to cover on all sides]

> The fire **engulfed** the entire building in a matter of minutes.
>
> The waves **engulfed** the small child as she ran through the water.

9. **shell** (a) [the hard external covering of eggs, nuts, and many types of sea animals]

> You have to know how to open the **shell** in order to eat that seafood.
>
> The **shells** of chicken eggs are usually white or light brown.

(b) [to remove the shells of nuts and seafood]

> They **shelled** the nuts with a nutcracker.
>
> She **shelled** the oysters quickly.

10. **fluid** [anything that is in liquid form and can flow]

> People were not permitted to enter the building because there was an unidentifiable **fluid** coming from the pipes in the basement.
>
> Water, milk, gasoline, and oil are all examples of **fluids**.

11. **disintegrate** [to break into many tiny pieces or particles]

> The smaller plane practically **disintegrated** when it collided with the larger plane.
>
> The leaves that fell from the trees **disintegrated** into a powder within a matter of a week.

12. **crude** (a) [in a natural state]

> **Crude** oil needs to be processed in order to make gasoline.

(b) [roughly made]

> The house was very **crudely** made from pieces of old wood, mud, and dried plants for the roof.
>
> They found a **crude** form of writing on the cave wall.

13. **intervene** [to come in or between in order to affect a situation]

> When the pollution in the city became too great, the government **intervened** and required the factories to adopt pollution controls.
> After Keith **intervened**, the situation deteriorated.

14. **formidable** [causing a certain amount of fear, dread, or concern]

> The clouds that were blowing in from the west were **formidable**; a severe storm was surely on the way.
> The citizens had to work hard to prevent the companies from destroying the area. The companies had gained such power that they were very **formidable** opponents.

15. **sacrifice** [to give up one thing of high value for the gain or benefit of something or someone more highly valued]

> They decided to **sacrifice** a section of the city park in order to build a much-needed library.
> He made a big **sacrifice** in terms of pay when he moved to the South to work, but his health has improved radically because his work environment is calmer.

16. **decay** [to decompose or rot; to break down]

> Leaves that fall from trees eventually **decay** and turn into soil.
> The **decayed** part of a tooth is known as a cavity. This is the part that the dentist removes before he fills the hole with metal or plastic.
> Because of all the corruption, the Roman Empire began to **decay** until it finally lay in ruins.

17. **phase** (a) [a stage of development]

> The moon passes through a number of **phases** before it reaches the full moon **phase**, and then it begins its cycle all over again.
> Children pass through a **phase** during which they are afraid to talk to people they do not know very well.

   (b) **phase (in, out)** {separable} [to begin a new program in gradual stages; to end a program in gradual stages]

> They could not make the changes in the procedures in one day. They **phased** them **in** over a period of six months. The old procedures will be **phased out**.

18. **give out** [to become exhausted; to quit functioning]

> The mines finally **gave out**; there was no more coal left to be mined.
> The horses worked day and night until they finally **gave out**.
> I walked so far that my legs **gave out** and I had to take a rest.

19. **stand up (under, against)** (a) [to be able to tolerate or last under certain circumstances]

> Despite the crudeness with which the houses are constructed, they are able to **stand up against** the severest of weather conditions.
> I do not know how he **stands up under** all that pressure that he has at work.

>> (b) **stand up to** [6-1: to defend your position against someone else's]

>>> He always **stands up to** her and won't let her tell him what to do all the time. He tells her when she's gone too far.

>> (c) **stand up for** [6-1: to protect or support someone or something]

>>> If you don't **stand up for** your rights, people will take advantage of you.
>>> I **stood up for** him and told the judge that he certainly couldn't have done what they thought.

>> (d) **stand up** {separable} [6-5: to fail to keep an appointment]

>>> I don't make special appointments for him anymore because he always **stands** me **up**.

20. **evolve** [to develop or achieve gradually]

> After many years of hard work, the government ministers **evolved** an extraordinary plan.
> The **evolution** of animals is studied by many biologists to predict how these animals might further **evolve**.

21. **savage** [wild, uncivilized, and dangerous]

> The explorers encountered many **savage** animals on their journey through the wilderness.
> The young man was **savagely** murdered in the downtown area of the city.

22. **thermal** [referring to, producing, using, or caused by heat]

> There are many **thermal** areas of water and land in Yellowstone National Park.
> In winter we wear **thermal** underwear under our clothes to stay warm.
> That bottle has a **thermal** covering so that its contents will remain at their original temperature despite the external temperature.

23. **universal** [affecting the entire world; applicable to all purposes, conditions, or situations]

> Poverty and hunger are **universal** problems.
> There is no **universal** language, that is, one which everyone in the world can understand.

24. **element** (a) [a basic or essential part of something]

> The basic **elements** to a happy family are love, understanding, and communication.
>
> If you don't understand the basic **elements** of the subject, you shouldn't take that class.

(b) [the basic chemical particles (atoms) that combine to form all substances in the universe]

> Oxygen and hydrogen are the **elements** that combine to form water.
>
> In chemistry class we had to learn the names and structures of all the **elements**.

25. **elements** {generally plural} [the natural forces that together make up the weather]

> The crudely made house was not strong enough to stand up against the **elements**.
>
> Wind, rain, snow, and hot and cold temperatures make up the **elements**.

26. **dump** [to drop things, frequently a large quantity, in a pile]

> They kept **dumping** their garbage in the woods until the local police intervened.
>
> The factories **dumped** so much waste material into the rivers that the water soon become polluted.

Introductory Exercises

A.   Match each word or phrase with its definition.

—— **1.** liquid	**a.** crude
—— **2.** open to danger	**b.** decay
—— **3.** in a natural state	**c.** disintegrate
—— **4.** causing fear or worry	**d.** dump
—— **5.** to come between	**e.** element
—— **6.** related to heat	**f.** evolve
—— **7.** to change gradually from one thing to another	**g.** exhibit
—— **8.** to remove from	**h.** extract
—— **9.** stage	**i.** fluid
—— **10.** a basic part of something	**j.** formidable
—— **11.** to rot	**k.** give out
—— **12.** to become tired	**l.** gulf
—— **13.** to show on a formal basis	**m.** insecticide
—— **14.** a body of water	**n.** intervene
—— **15.** a hard covering of certain fish	**o.** phase
—— **16.** poison for insects	**p.** sacrifice
—— **17.** to break into very small pieces	**q.** savage
—— **18.** to give up something of value	**r.** shell
—— **19.** to tolerate	**s.** stand up under
	t. thermal
	u. vulnerable

B.   In each blank, write the most appropriate word or phrase from the word form chart.

1. They put _____ on the plants to protect them from insects.

2. The fishermen took their boat out into the _____ where they could catch more fish._____

3. We went to see the art _____ that was at the university.

4. We removed the _____ from the fish before we cooked it.

5. These land formations are _____ to this area; they do not occur anywhere else in the country.

6. In areas where it is very cold people use special _____ clothing so that their body heat will not escape through their clothing.

7. Many parents make great financial _____ so that they can put their children through college.

8. They use the fluid that they _____ from that plant to treat burns and other types of injuries.

9. The plants cannot _____ under the dry weather conditions.

10. Smaller animals are very _____ to the attack of large animals.

11. Many Indians in the Americas were considered _____ by the explorers.

12. The modern day horse _____ from a smaller similar animal that lived on the earth millions of years ago.

13. The repairs on his car were very _____ ; you could tell he did not know what he was doing when he made them.

14. Her mother gets angry when Mary _____ all of her dirty clothes in the middle of her bedroom.

15. It is a _____ fact that brothers and sisters tend to fight with each other.

16. They predict that the supply of metal in that mine will _____ within ten years.

17. Reading, writing, speaking, and listening are all basic _____ in learning a language.

18. Children pass through various _____ as they grow from a baby to an adult.

19. This hot weather is _____ for the middle of winter.

Study Exercises

C. Write **T** if the sentence is true and **F** if it is false.

_____ 1. A fluid will be able to flow.

_____ 2. Insecticides are used to do away with insects.

_____ 3. The universe includes all objects.

_____ 4. A dentist might extract your tooth if it is extremely decayed.

_____ 5. If your leg gives out, you have a lot of strength left in it.

_____ 6. It is extraordinary to see people with black hair in China.

_____ 7. Once people die, their bodies will eventually decay.

_____ 8. If a river floods, water can engulf the houses that are nearby.

_____ 9. Trying to finish 24 hours of work in less than 10 hours is a formidable task.

_____ 10. Wood is a fluid.

_____ 11. A dump is very neatly organized.

_____ **12.** If someone is savage, he is very calm and controlled.

_____ **13.** If there is a big fight in the street, the police might intervene to break it up.

_____ **14.** The purpose of a shell is to protect whatever is inside the shell.

_____ **15.** Too much sugar can cause excessive tooth decay.

D. Match each word or phrase with its purpose.

_____ **1.** intervention	**a.** to gain greater benefit
_____ **2.** an exhibit	**b.** to keep hands very warm
_____ **3.** an insecticide	**c.** to protect contents
_____ **4.** a shell	**d.** to show people things
_____ **5.** sacrifice	**e.** to affect a situation
_____ **6.** thermal gloves	**f.** to kill insects

E. Match each word or phrase with its opposite.

1. vulnerable	**a.** solid
2. unique	**b.** not become involved
3. savage	**c.** processed
4. intervene	**d.** many of a kind
5. fluid	**e.** not wild
6. evolve	**f.** common, usual
7. crude	**g.** safe, secure
8. extraordinary	**h.** remain the same

F. Circle the correct answer(s) for the following questions.

1. Which things cannot be a fluid?
   a. oil   **b.** stone   **c.** an insecticide   **d.** blood   **e.** wood

2. Which things do not decay?
   a. leaves   **b.** teeth   **c.** metal   **d.** dead animals   **e.** glass

3. What would you not see in the middle of a gulf?
   a. ship   **b.** a boat   **c.** a sailor   **d.** a house   **e.** fish

4. Which things can give out?
   a. the sky   **b.** a mine   **c.** a wall of an old building
   d. someone's heart   **e.** a paragraph

5. Which things have shells?
   a. eggs   **b.** books   **c.** certain sea creatures
   d. dogs   **e.** trees

6. Which things would be formidable?
   a. speaking in front of 2,000 people   b. a severe storm
   c. a difficult job   d. taking a vacation

7. Which would be a savage act?
   a. kissing someone   b. studying a difficult subject
   c. killing someone   d. working hard   e. loudly calling someone

8. Which of the following would be extraordinary?
   a. blond people in Sweden   b. snow in summer
   c. clouds on a rainy day   d. green ivory

G.   In each blank, write the most appropriate word from the word form chart.

1. The factory _____ so much waste into the river that the fish died.

2. She has a(n) _____ personality; I do not know anyone quite like her.

3. When the spaceship entered the earth's atmosphere, the temperature was so hot that the ship _____ into particles.

4. A _____ lake is one whose water is heated by the earth.

5. _____ is the process of gradually changing over a long period of time.

6. The part of the tree that was in constant contact with the water began to _____ .

7. In ancient Greece, it was common practice to _____ an animal or a person in honor of the gods.

8. The United States is gradually changing over to the metric system. Instead of changing all at once, however, the government is _____ the system in little by little.

9. The waters in the _____ are warmer than the waters in the ocean.

10. Because the boat was so _____ made, it was unable to stand up against the elements during the long journey.

11. The _____ on many sea animals make it difficult for other sea animals to injure them.

12. After his wife died, he was emotionally very _____ ; if someone said the wrong thing, he would get very upset and hurt.

H.   Read the passage and answer the questions that follow.

All the plants and animals of our universe have evolved over millions of years from plants and creatures of long ago that they do not even resemble. Very gradually, changes took place to allow the different forms of life to adapt to changes in the environment.

5   If the environment became drier, for example, plants developed ways to gain access to water. Over the years a plant might have developed special roots capable of growing deeper in search of water. Or perhaps the plant developed special leaves that were able to store large quantities of liquid to help them stand up

10 against long periods of severe dryness. If the environment in which the plants were growing became less savage, so that fewer creatures depended on the plant for food, the plant lost special protection over the years. For example, a plant that once had on its branches long, sharp points as a means of protection would lose

15 these points as fewer animals depended on it as a food source. A plant which needed light but was constantly shadowed by the trees above would gradually evolve into another form capable of reaching the sunlight. Perhaps it developed larger leaves more capable of processing sunlight for its much needed energy, or

20 perhaps it evolved into a vine, a long thin plant that is able to grow up trees, walls, etc. As a vine, the plant no longer had to remain on the floor of the woods. It could now climb to the top of the trees and reach the sunlight.

    Many animals of millions of years ago also evolved into the

25 creatures we know today. As with plants, they evolved out of necessity. They developed certain abilities in order to adapt to the ever-changing environment. Fish of long ago, for example, developed legs which allowed them to leave the water in search of food. Because they were now able to leave the water, they

30 gradually evolved into air-breathing animals, developing lungs which permitted them to stay on land permanently. With this change, however, came the sacrifice of not being able to stay under water for long periods of time as they once had been able to. Animals which once had bodies that were suitable to a thermal

35 environment either died or evolved and adapted as the atmosphere changed to a less thermal one. Thick skin, for example, which had served as a protective layer to help maintain body fluids in the heat gradually evolved into a thinner layer better suited to a cooler environment. Also, if the environment became less dangerous,

40 creatures' bodies would change. Animals which once had shells to protect them against attack would gradually lose them as they became less vulnerable in the world. Gradually their shells would soften and their bodies would evolve into one which reflected the safer environment. As plant life changed, animals found ways of

45 reaching it. For example, if the food were no longer located near the ground, an animal found ways of reaching higher into the trees. Perhaps the creature's front legs gradually evolved into

wings, allowing it to fly to the food source. Or, perhaps it
developed feet uniquely suited to climbing up the tree.

50   Not all animals and plants, of course, were able to adapt or
evolve as the environment changed. Many which could not stand
up to the different temperatures and circumstances simply died.
These plants and animals, although they are not in living form, are
still part of the universe today. After they died, they eventually

55 decayed and disintegrated into tiny particles of soil. The decayed
plant and animal life of millions of years ago has become some of
the different rock and layers of the earth today.

1. Why did plants and animals change over the years? _____

_____

2. How did some plants adapt to a drier climate? _____

_____

3. How did some plants evolve as the environment became less savage? ____

_____

4. What changes took place to enable some plants to reach sunlight? _____

_____

5. Why did some fish develop legs and lungs? _____

_____

6. What sacrifice came with the development of legs and lungs in some

fish? _____

_____

7. What was the purpose of thick skin on certain animals? _____

_____

8. Why did some animals lose their shells? _____

_____

9. How did some animals reach plants if the plants were no longer located

near the ground? _____

_____

10. What happened to the animals and plants that could not adapt to the

atmospheric changes? _____

_____

Follow-up

I.   Dictation: Write the sentences that your teacher reads aloud.

  1. _____
  2. _____
  3. _____
  4. _____
  5. _____

J.   Answer the following questions.

  1. What are you if you are in a position of danger?
  2. What is the hard covering on an egg called?
  3. How do you describe a situation which scares you or makes you nervous?
  4. What do you call an environment that is very wild?
  5. If you have given up something you love for the benefit of someone else, what have you done?
  6. Where would you go to see a lot of special art work?
  7. What is the purpose of a garbage dump?
  8. What are you doing when you are intervening?

K.   Answer the following questions.

  1. What, in your opinion, are the elements of a savage environment?
  2. What are some things in our universe that nature is particularly vulnerable to? That is, what things can harm our plant and animal life?
  3. Think of some plants and animals that you know. How are they uniquely suited to the environment in which they live?
  4. What are some eventual problems of dumping pollutants into our atmosphere? Describe a series of events which might occur.
  5. What is the most extraordinary thing you know of in nature?

Military

Word Form Chart

NOUN	VERB	ADJECTIVE	ADVERB	PREPOSITIONAL PHRASE
ammunition				
blast	blast	blasting		
conflict	conflict	conflicting		
discharge	discharge	discharged		
dressing down	dress down			
enforcement	enforce	enforced		
force	force	forced		in force
		forceful	forcefully	
		forcible	forcibly	
fort				
	give back			
guerrilla		guerrilla		
halt	halt	halting	haltingly	
holdout	hold out			
hostility		hostile	hostilely	
	lie down			
missile				
occupation	occupy	occupied		
		occupying		
patrol	patrol			
refuge		refuge		
refugee				
repulsion	repulse	repulsed		
		repulsive	repulsively	
revolution	revolt	revolutionary		
		revolting		
seizure	seize	seized		
status				

NOUN	VERB	ADJECTIVE	ADVERB	PREPOSITIONAL PHRASE
strategy		strategic	strategically	
tactic		tactical	tactically	
veteran		veteran		
	wipe out			

Definitions and Examples

1. **halt** [to stop]

   > The soldiers told the enemy to **halt**.
   > The train came to a sudden **halt**.

2. **halting** [hesitant; nervous]

   > He spoke in a **halting** voice.
   > The old man crossed the street very **haltingly**.

3. **patrol** [to move around an area for purposes of observation or security]

   > The soldiers **patrolled** the city in search of the enemy.
   > The guards **patrolled** the prison walls to make sure no prisoners escaped.
   > The general sent six soldiers out on **patrol**.

4. **guerrilla** [a member of a group that engages in battle with the group in power in order to overthrow that group]

   > The **guerrillas** hid in the mountains and attacked the government troops by surprise.
   > **Guerrillas** frequently have less military equipment than the government they are fighting against.

5. **revolt (against)** [to rebel against an authority]

   > The army **revolted** against the president's government.
   > The workers **revolted** and almost went on strike when they heard the company's new regulations.

6. **revolting** [extremely unpleasant; almost sickening]

   > She found the murder scenes in the movie **revolting**.
   > His behavior is absolutely **revolting**.

7. **fort** [a structure built to protect an area from attack]

   > The enemy tried to burn down the walls of the **fort**.
   > The **fort** was built on top of a hill so that the soldiers could see in all directions.

8. **conflict** [a disagreement or problem between two groups]

> What began as a small **conflict** turned into a six-year war.
> Those two countries always have **conflicts** at the border.
> We have **conflicting** points of view.

9. **veteran** (a) [someone who finished serving in the military]

> The government built a monument in honor of the many **veterans** who served during the war.

(b) [experienced in a skill]

> Our swimming instructor is a **veteran** swimmer.

10. **ammunition** [anything that can be fired from guns; explosive materials used in war]

> Guns are useless to soldiers in war if there is no **ammunition**.
> The patrol captured a large portion of the enemy's **ammunition**.

11. **discharge** (a) [to release officially from an obligation or situation]

> After four years of service, he was honorably **discharged** from the army.
> The patient was **discharged** from the hospital.

(b) [to fire a weapon]

> The soldiers **discharged** the explosives just as the enemy was passing along the road.

12. **refuge** [protection from danger; anything that offers help, relief, or escape]

> The people in the war-torn country found **refuge** in the neighboring countries.
> By drinking alcohol he tried to find **refuge** from his problems.

13. **refugee** [a person seeking refuge]

> The **refugees** found life in the new country to be very difficult but certainly much safer than in the war-torn area they had left.

14. **hostility** [a feeling of dislike or hatred, particularly between enemies]

> The countries were so **hostile** that they finally declared war on each other.
> Her **hostility** toward her neighbors was obvious in the impolite way she talked to them.

15. **missile** [a weapon that is shot through the air and explodes upon striking an object]

> The debate over **missiles** is a particularly heated topic.
> Our enemies fired so many **missiles** that we simply could not protect the region and had to surrender it.

16. **blast** (a) [to fire weapons on]

They **blasted** the fort until the wall finally gave out.

(b) [to make an explosion; an explosion or the noise of an explosion]

The miners **blasted** a hole in the wall of the mine so that they could get through.
The **blast** was so loud that he permanently lost his hearing.

(c) [to attack very strongly with words]

She was so angry that she **blasted** him with insults and loudly mentioned all his faults.

17. **strategy** [a plan of action]

Their **strategy** of attacking from the rear proved to be successful.
There are many **strategies** you can use to improve your reading ability.

18. **tactic** [strategy]

General McDonald was an expert in military **tactics**.
What **tactics** will they use to overpower the enemy?

19. **seize** [to take or grab, especially rapidly or by force]

The army **seized** control of the city.
He **seized** the handle of the door to keep himself from falling down.
The enemy tried to **seize** our capital.

20. **give back** {separable} [to return]

When she finished reading my book, she **gave** it **back** to me.
After the war, they **gave back** all the land they had seized.

21. **wipe out** {separable} [to destroy]

The enemy completely **wiped out** our troops.
The blast **wiped** our communication system **out** for two days.

22. **status** (a) [the state of affairs]

The general wanted to know the **status** of the wounded. The doctors informed him that three soldiers had severe wounds and ten had minor wounds.

(b) [the level of one thing in relation to another]

The rich often have a higher social **status** than the poor.

23. **occupy** [to seize possession of an area or a region and maintain control over it]

The troops had to stay in that country all during the **occupation**.
The army **occupied** the country until the war ended.

[3-2: to keep busy; to fill or take up space or time]

She **occupied** herself with cleaning the house.
The table and chairs **occupied** the whole corner of the room.

24. **force** (a) [strength; power]

He used all his **force** to open the door.

(b) [to use strength or power to make something or someone do something]

They **forced** the enemy to surrender.

(c) [a group of persons organized for a given purpose, particularly a military purpose]

He was a member of the armed **forces**.

25. **in force** [in effect; in use]

They put all new laws **in force** after they defeated the government and enforced them to the last detail.

26. **repulse** (a) [to force something back]

Our attack **repulsed** the enemy; they could not gain any more territory.

(b) [to cause extreme dislike; to sicken]

His behavior was so **repulsive** I had to leave the room.

27. **lie down (on)** [to put oneself in a horizontal position]

The soldiers **lay down on** the ground to avoid getting hit with enemy fire. We have to **lie down** to rest before we go on.

28. **hold out (against)** (a) [to fight against to prevent surrender]

They **held out against** the enemy for a week but finally gave up when their ammunition ran out.

(b) [to wait for a better offer]

When we sold our house, we **held out** for the best offer we could get.

29. **call up** {separable} [to call on the telephone]

The general **called up** the president to let him know the status of the battle.
I have to **call** her **up** before I leave.

30. **dress down** {separable} (a) [to criticize sharply; to reprimand]

The general **dressed** the soldiers **down** for their behavior.

(b) [to wear less formal clothing than usual]

They **dressed down** for the party because it was supposed to be an informal affair.

Introductory Exercises

A. Match each word or phrase with its definition.

_____	**1.** a structure built to protect an area	**a.** ammunition
_____	**2.** to watch over	**b.** blast
_____	**3.** sickening	**c.** conflict
_____	**4.** to go against authority	**d.** discharge
_____	**5.** state of a situation	**e.** force
_____	**6.** an explosive weapon	**f.** fort
_____	**7.** explosives used in guns	**g.** give back
_____	**8.** a person looking for a safe place	**h.** guerrilla
_____	**9.** an old soldier	**i.** halt
_____	**10.** to destroy	**j.** hold out
_____	**11.** to attempt to not give up	**k.** hostility
_____	**12.** the capture and control of an area	**l.** missile
_____	**13.** to return	**m.** occupation
_____	**14.** to take by force	**n.** patrol
_____	**15.** an argument, large or small	**o.** refugee
_____	**16.** the nosie of an explosion	**p.** repulsive
_____	**17.** to stop	**q.** revolt
_____	**18.** a plan of attack	**r.** seize
_____	**19.** hatred	**s.** status
_____	**20.** strength	**t.** strategy
		u. veteran
		v. wipe out

B. In each blank, write the most appropriate word from the word form chart.

1. If two people disagree, there is a(n) _____ between them.

2. If something explodes, you will hear a(n) _____ .

3. If someone is making you do something you do not want to do, he is _____ you to do it.

4. If you have borrowed something from a friend, you should _____ it _____ as soon as possible.

5. If you want to fire a gun, you will need _____ .

6. If you have served in the military, you are a(n) _____ .

7. To keep city streets safe, the police _____ the neighborhoods.

8. A country that is governed temporarily by another country, particularly after a war, is a(n) _____ nation.

9. When you have finished your military duty, the army will _____ you.

10. To take something by force is to _____ it.

11. If you are trying to get away from an unsafe situation, you look for _____ .

12. If someone doesn't like you, he might treat you with _____ .

Study Exercises

C. Match each word with its opposite.

_____ 1. veteran

_____ 2. seize

_____ 3. lie down

_____ 4. compliment

_____ 5. go

_____ 6. halting

_____ 7. occupied

_____ 8. hostility

_____ 9. get discharged

_____ 10. hold out

_____ 11. conflict

_____ 12. repulsion

a. confident
b. love
c. enter
d. agree
e. surrender
f. dress down
g. free, not busy
h. attraction
i. halt
j. give back
k. inexperienced
l. get up

D. In each blank, write the most appropriate word or phrase from the word form chart in this unit.

1. Because the citizens disagreed with the government in power, they started a(n) _____ .

2. He went into the army in 1941 and was _____ in 1946.

3. The enemy troops _____ control of all radio communications.

4. They sent a(n) _____ out to make sure that the area was secure.

5. They fired _____ from the planes in an attempt to force the enemy out of the region.

6. The two countries were involved in a(n) _____ as to who had control over the gulf.

7. Not sure whether the enemy was inside the building, the soldiers entered very _____ .

8. To protect the people, they built a _____ around the town.

9. The _____ from the explosion was heard over a mile away.

10. They had a parade in honor of all the _____ who had fought in World War II.

11. Their _____ failed, and they were taken prisoner. Instead of attacking at night, they should have waited until morning.

12. The people found _____ in the old church, where they knew they would be safe.

13. There is such _____ between those two; every time they talk, they start to fight.

14. The soldiers at the line of fire need more _____ to continue the battle.

15. He _____ on the bed so that the doctor could examine the wound.

16. The _____ had been trained by another country in order to overthrow the government of their own country.

E. Write **T** if the sentence is true and **F** if it is false.

—— **1.** If you do something good, you will be dressed down.

—— **2.** A veteran is very good at what he does.

—— **3.** It is common for soldiers to patrol an occupied territory.

—— **4.** Hostility is something people want to achieve.

—— **5.** A forceful voice would be a strong, loud voice.

—— **6.** If something repulses you, you really do not like it.

—— **7.** If something is strategically located, it is in a perfect location.

—— **8.** If people are unhappy with a situation, they might revolt.

—— **9.** A strike could halt production at a factory.

—— **10.** If someone discharges explosives, you will hear a blast.

—— **11.** Soldiers hold out so that the enemy can seize them.

—— **12.** If someone wants to know the status of a situation, he wants to know what is happening.

—— **13.** People like to have conflicts with others.

—— **14.** People enjoy being refugees.

—— **15.** You wipe a country out if you want to make its citizens free.

F.   Complete the analogies with a word or phrase from the word form chart.

1. seize : take :: explode : _____

2. attract : toward you :: _____ : away from you

3. status : level :: tactic : _____

4. wait : give up :: _____ : surrender

5. veteran : old soldier :: _____ : rebel

6. vulnerable : danger :: safe : _____

7. build : construct :: destroy : _____

8. confident : uncertain :: sure : _____

G.   Read the passage and answer the questions that follow.

       In many countries when the citizens do not agree with the group in power, they plan a revolution to overthrow the government. The hostility between the groups grows until it develops into a conflict that is actually a war against the group in

5   power. In such a case, it is not uncommon to hear of guerrillas attacking government troops by surprise and seizing and occupying government buildings to try to gain control.

       The government, in the meantime, tries to halt the guerrilla attacks. Patrols go out in search of the revolutionaries, and

10 generals experienced in military tactics plan strategies to fight against the guerrillas. They look for ways to force the guerrillas out of their hiding places or holdouts. The government in power also plans strategies to deal with the help that guerrillas might receive from outside sources, that is, help from other countries

15 that send weapons, ammunition, and other equipment to the guerrillas or that might train the guerrillas in military warfare and tactics.

       As with any type of conflict, there are many innocent people who are caught in the middle. They look for refuge away from the

20 blasts of the battles and the repulsive acts of war. Many try to avoid the struggle between the revolutionaries and the government forces by looking for refuge in areas of their own country. Others leave the country entirely to escape the horrors of the conflict.

       If the revolutionaries win the war, they occupy all the

25 positions of importance in the government or wipe out the old system completely and institute a new one. The new government must have its strategies well thought out so that it can enforce new laws and regulations without creating hostility among the people. If the revolution is successful, the government will be able

30 to stay in power without making the citizens feel that they are living in an occupied nation.

1. What might people do if they do not agree with the government? _____

_____

2. What kind of soldiers are commonly involved in revolutions? _____

_____

3. How do guerrillas frequently fight? _____

_____

4. What kinds of plans does the government have to make? _____

_____

5. Who frequently helps guerrillas? _____

_____

6. What kind of help do they receive? _____

_____

7. Why do people look for refuge? _____

_____

8. Where might they find refuge? _____

_____

9. What might the revolutionary government do when it comes to power?

_____

_____

10. What does the new government have to be careful not to do? Why? _____

_____

Follow-up

H.   Dictation: Write the sentences that your teacher reads aloud.

1. _____
2. _____
3. _____
4. _____
5. _____

I. Answer each of the following questions with a word or phrase from the word form chart.

 1. If looking at something makes you ill, how would you describe that thing?
 2. If someone is always mean and aggressive toward you, how would you describe him?
 3. If you are tired, what can you do to rest?
 4. If the police are chasing a criminal and want him to stop, what will they scream?
 5. If you want to leave the military, what do you ask for?
 6. What do you call the building that protects an area?
 7. What kind of soldiers have already had military experience?
 8. What do you call a person who is running away from danger?
 9. If you want to make sure that an area is safe, what do you do?
10. If someone in authority has criticized you severely, what has he done?
11. What do you need to put in your guns so that you can use them?
12. What is a loud noise?
13. What is another word for "strategy"?
14. What is another word for "destroy"?

J. Answer the following questions.

 1. How does this/your country treat its veterans? Are there any special services that veterans receive?
 2. What famous revolutions have taken place in your country/around the world? What was the cause? What took place during the revolt? What was the result?
 3. What are some strategies that are common to guerrilla warfare? What do you know about guerrillas and their tactics?
 4. What are some common regulations during a period of occupation of a country?

UNIT
21

Morality

Word Form Chart

NOUN	VERB	ADJECTIVE	ADVERB
	bear on		
	break in on		
convention	convene	conventional	conventionally
		unconventional	unconventionally
	cut in		
domination	dominate	dominant	
		dominating	
dominance			
eternity		eternal	eternally
ethics		ethical	ethically
		unethical	unethically
fundamental			
fundamentals		fundamental	fundamentally
funeral			
	hand down		
		inherent	inherently
integrity			
	let down		
	live up to		
	look down on		
mercy		merciful	mercifully
		unmerciful	unmercifully
mission			
missionary			
myth		mythical	mythically
		mythic	
predomination	predominate	predominant	predominantly
restraint	restrain		
rite			

222

NOUN	VERB	ADJECTIVE	ADVERB
submission	submit	submissive	submissively
	withstand		
	(withstood, withstood)		

Definitions and Examples

1. **look down on** [to feel superior to]

   That famous professor **looks down on** people who are not as smart as he is.

   Please do not **look down on** my car; it is the only one I had enough money to buy.

2. **myth** [an old story about imaginary people]

   Hundreds of years ago, primitive people often developed **myths** to explain things they did not understand, like weather.

   Often, people from early civilizations believed in **mythical** animals; one, called a centaur, had the head and upper body of a man and the lower body of a horse.

3. **funeral** [the ceremony when someone who has died is buried]

   Funerals are often occasions when relatives who live far away return to comfort other family members.

   Most religions have special **funeral** customs.

4. **convention** (a) [a custom]

   Until recently, it was a **convention** in the United States for people to wear black to a funeral.

   In fact, in some ethnic groups, wearing black or dark colors is still **conventional** at funerals, and people who wear bright colors are looked down on.

   (b) [a formal meeting of members or representatives of a group]

   Conventions are usually held in large cities which have good transportation systems and interesting sights to see.

   Hotels try to attract **conventions** because they bring a lot of business.

5. **unconventional** [not following custom; departing from the ordinary]

   Teenagers often dress very **unconventionally** by adult standards.

   When an actor does something **unconventional**, people find it interesting; however, when an ordinary person does the same thing, people tend to look down on him.

6. **fundamental** [basic; essential]

   Eating nutritious food is **fundamental** to good health.
   Freedom of speech is a **fundamental** right in the United States.

7. **dominant** [having the most control or influence]

   In the struggle for world power, both the United States and the Soviet
      Union would like to be **dominant**.
   Certainly the leaders of the two countries have different opinions about
      which one is in a position of **dominance**.

8. **dominate** [to be dominant in position or authority; to control by superior
   power]

   Often older children **dominate** their younger brothers and sisters.
   Some people have the ability to **dominate** a conversation and do not
      permit other people to talk.

9. **predominate (over)** [to be of greater power, importance, or quantity]

   In many lakes today, the kinds of fish which have adjusted to pollution
      predominate over other kinds.
   In the southern part of the United States, very hot weather **predominates**
      during the summer.
   In a basketball game, the team with the tallest players often
      predominates over the other team.

10. **rite** [the customary way to conduct a religious or other serious ceremony]

    Marriage **rites** differ from country to country.
    Most religions have some kind of funeral **rites**.

11. **eternity** [an endless period of time]

    Christians believe that if they follow God's laws, they will live with him
       for **eternity**.
    Eternity has neither a beginning nor an end.

12. **ethical** [following the accepted standards of right and wrong of a particular
    group]

    People do not want their leaders to behave in an **unethical** way.
    Stealing is not **ethical** in most countries.

13. **mercy** [kind treatment of a person under one's power, such as a prisoner or
    enemy]

    That judge behaved unethically when he showed **mercy** to his friend.
    The captured soldier begged his enemy to be **merciful**.

14. **submit** (a) [to surrender to the authority of another]

> After a short fight, the robber **submitted** to the police.
> Before the man **submitted**, he asked his captors for mercy.

   (b) [to offer something to the consideration or judgment of another]

> Before a student can be considered by a university, he has to **submit** an
>   application.
> In order to earn a Ph.D. degree, students must **submit** a long paper called
>   a dissertation.

15. **submissive** [dutiful; obedient]

> Parents who dominate their children expect them to be **submissive.**
> When the teacher told the class to be quiet, the **submissive** children
>   stopped making noise.

16. **live up to** [to maintain a standard that has been demanded]

> It is not always easy to **live up to** what our parents expect.
> John's new job did not **live up to** his expectations, and he soon left it for
>   another.

17. **let down** (a) {separable} [to disappoint]

> Many Americans felt **let down** by President Nixon and thought he had
>   behaved unethically during the Watergate affair.
> The mother told her son that if he always did his best he would never **let**
>   her **down**.

   (b) [5-15: to make a piece of clothing longer]

> The new trend in fashion is longer skirts, so I need to **let** some
>   of mine **down**.

18. **restrain** [to control or limit; to deprive of freedom or liberty]

> Children must be **restrained** from doing wrong until they are old enough
>   to make their own moral decisions.
> The prisoner had many **restraints**; he was not permitted to see, telephone,
>   or even write to his family.

19. **cut in (on)** [to interrupt]

> When the adults were talking, the child rudely **cut in** and asked for a
>   cookie. His mother angrily told him that it was impolite to **cut in on**
>   people who were talking. However, the child was unable to restrain
>   himself and **cut in** again.

20. **break in** (on) (a) [to interrupt; to cut in]

> The woman's husband wanted to tell the story in his own way and kept **breaking in on** his wife. When he **broke in** for the third time, his wife angrily told him to tell the story himself.

> (b) **break into** [5-10: to enter a car or building by force]

> > The thieves **broke into** my house late last night.

> (c) **break in** [5-19: to use until it is comfortable]

> > If you do not **break in** new shoes slowly, you will have sore feet.

21. **bear on** [to be related to; to be connected with]

> The manager told the employee that his unethical behavior had a **bearing on** his being fired.
> The university told the student that his GRE scores would **bear on** his being accepted.

22. **mission** [a group sent to do some special work; a special task]

> The farmers sent a **mission** to the president to request financial aid.
> His **mission** is to live up to what his parents expected of him.
> A **missionary** is a person who does religious work, often in a foreign country, and who tries to change people's beliefs to be the same as his own.

23. **integrity** [strict obedience to moral standards of behavior]

> A good judge must act with **integrity** at all times and not be guilty of unethical behavior.
> People who lie, cheat, and steal have little **integrity**.

24. **withstand** [to oppose something with force; to resist successfully]

> The small group of soldiers **withstood** the enemy troops as long as possible, but finally they had to submit.
> The young man was unable to **withstand** the suggestions of his immoral friends and began to steal money from his company.

25. **inherent** [existing as an essential part]

> The prisoner's **inherent** goodness caused the judge to be merciful.
> The king was **inherently** evil, and all the people were glad when he died.

26. **hand down** (a) [to give a court decision]

> The Supreme Court often deliberates for a long time before **handing down** a decision.
> The decision on that case has not been **handed down** yet.

> (b) {separable} [5-17: to leave something to someone at the time of your death]

> > This silver spoon was **handed down** to me by my grandmother.
> > I plan to **hand** it **down** to my oldest daughter.

Introductory Exercises

A. Match each word or phrase with its definition.

____ 1. to feel superior to

____ 2. the ceremony when someone who has died is buried

____ 3. basic; essential

____ 4. the customary way to conduct a religious ceremony

____ 5. following the accepted standards of right and wrong of a particular group

____ 6. to surrender to the authority of another

____ 7. to maintain a standard that has been demanded

____ 8. having the most control or influence

____ 9. to interrupt

____ 10. the endless period of time following death

____ 11. to be of greater power, importance, or quantity

____ 12. to disappoint

____ 13. to control or limit

____ 14. a group sent to do some special task

____ 15. kind treatment of a person under one's power

____ 16. strict obedience to moral standards of behavior

____ 17. to resist successfully

____ 18. an old story about imaginary people

____ 19. not following custom; departing from the ordinary

a. bear on
b. break in on
c. dominant
d. eternity
e. ethical
f. fundamental
g. funeral
h. hand down
i. inherent
j. integrity
k. let down
l. live up to
m. look down on
n. mercy
o. mission
p. morality
q. myth
r. predominate
s. restrain
t. rite
u. submit
v. unconventional
w. withstand

B.   Answer each question with a word from the word form chart.

1. If you show kindness toward an enemy, what are you?
2. What does a person who lies, cheats, and steals lack?
3. What is a sad ceremony after someone dies?
4. What do people with similar interests often go to?
5. What is a person called who goes to a foreign country to teach about his religion?
6. If two people are talking, what should you avoid doing? (two answers)
7. If one person predominates over another in a fight, what must the second person do?
8. What might our needs for food and sleep be called?
9. If you are unhappy with a class you are taking, how will you feel?
10. What does a court do when it has decided a case?
11. What is a country that has power over another?
12. What do you need if you are trying to lose weight?
13. What is the marriage ceremony?
14. Describe a person who doesn't always act in the ways most others do.

Study Exercises

C.   Write **T** if the sentence is true and **F** if it is false.

_____ 1. Parents try to restrain their children from doing wrong.

_____ 2. If something is eternal, it will never end.

_____ 3. A cow is a mythical animal.

_____ 4. A criminal hopes the judge at his trial will be merciful.

_____ 5. An inherently good person has integrity.

_____ 6. A person who studies ethics is interested in morals.

_____ 7. One of our fundamental rights is to cut in on others' conversations.

_____ 8. We look down on people who are ethical.

_____ 9. Our study habits usually bear on our grades.

_____ 10. It is somehow difficult to withstand people who are dominating us.

D. Match each two- or three-word verb with its definition.

_____ 1. cheer up
_____ 2. feel up to
_____ 3. clear up
_____ 4. let up
_____ 5. dress up
_____ 6. call up
_____ 7. clean up
_____ 8. write up
_____ 9. fix up
_____ 10. give up
_____ 11. blow up
_____ 12. tie up
_____ 13. turn up
_____ 14. fill up
_____ 15. live up to

a. to prepare a report or document
b. to make clear
c. to become less severe
d. to repair
e. to discover; to find
f. to fill completely
g. to maintain a standard that has been demanded
h. to substitute for
i. to become cheerful
j. to make clean
k. to cause to explode
l. to leave an activity to do something
m. to have the strength or ability to do something
n. to put on special or formal clothes
o. to become ill with
p. to telephone
q. to tie tightly
r. to surrender
s. to clean the inside of
t. to visit someone casually without planning first

E. Complete the analogies with a word or phrase from the word form chart.

1. black : white :: cruel : _____
2. up : down :: _____ : submissive
3. car : automobile :: basic : _____
4. rob : steal :: _____ : dishonest
5. listen : polite :: _____ : impolite
6. truth : fiction :: history : _____
7. happy : wedding :: sad : _____
8. submit : fail :: _____ : succeed
9. release : go :: _____ : stop
10. man : God :: hour : _____
11. rules : game :: _____ : ceremony
12. weak : strong :: _____ : dominate

F.   In each blank, write the most appropriate word or phrase from the word form chart.

Studies have shown that criminals often had unhappy childhoods. Sometimes their parents were too (1) _____ and never let them make any decisions for themselves. Others never took the time to teach their children the (2) _____ difference between right and wrong, and so they never developed a system of (3) _____ . Still other parents had such high standards that their children could not (4) _____ them. These children felt that nothing they did was ever good enough and that their parents (5) _____ them. As these children grew up, they rebelled in different ways. Some rejected their parents' way of life and chose to act as (6) _____ as possible. Others, who had never developed a strong idea of right and wrong, found they could not (7) _____ the bad suggestions of their friends and got into trouble. If we look back at the childhoods of some of these criminals, we find that most are not (8) _____ evil; rather, they had a bad beginning.

Follow-up

G.   Dictation: Write the sentences that your teacher reads aloud.

1. _____
2. _____
3. _____
4. _____
5. _____

H.   Answer the following questions.

1. Do you feel a judge should be rigid or merciful? Why?
2. Do you think you are predominantly conventional or unconventional? Explain.
3. Describe a funeral in your country.
4. Does your religion teach eternal life? Describe your ideas about it.
5. Is there something special in your family that has been handed down? What?
6. Describe the rite of marriage in your country.

7. Is there anything that you try to restrain yourself from doing? What?
8. Does your culture have any stories about mythical animals? Describe one of the animals.
9. From whom did you learn your system of ethics?
10. Do people in your country look down on those who behave or dress unconventionally? Give examples.

I.   Tell about a myth that you know, especially one that teaches a lesson.

Transportation

Word Form Chart

NOUN	VERB	ADJECTIVE	ADVERB
barrier			
consequence		consequent	consequently
degree			
departure	depart	departing	
device			
	enable		
		forward	forward(s)
	get off		
	go over		
	hang up		
hazard		hazardous	hazardously
		mere	merely
	pull in		
	pull out		
	run down		
	slow down		
	slow up		
split	split	split	
	(split, split)		
	still	still	still
strain	strain	straining	
		strained	
ticket	ticket	ticketed	
transformation	transform	transformed	
transformer		transforming	
trip	trip		
vibration	vibrate	vibrating	
	wipe off		

Definitions and Examples

1. **hang up** {separable} [to replace a telephone receiver on its hook]

   When the caller found out that he had reached a wrong number, he **hung up**.
   John **hung** the telephone **up** after he finished his call.

2. **pull in** [to arrive (used for vehicles)]

   The bus **pulled in** about fifteen minutes ago and left again a few minutes later.
   That train always **pulls in** exactly on time.

3. **pull out** (a) [to leave (used with vehicles)]

   The train was supposed to **pull out** at 4:05 P.M., but it was almost an hour late in leaving.
   The second bus **pulled out** only a few minutes after the first one left.

   (b) [to withdraw from a situation or commitment]

   He had promised to take the job, but he **pulled out** at the last minute.

4. **run down** (a) {separable} [to hit someone with a vehicle]

   The drunk driver **ran down** a man on a bicycle.
   Fortunately, he **ran** the man **down** in front of a hospital.

   (b) [to lose power; to be in a weakened condition]

   If I do not wind my clock once a week, it **runs down**.
   When people do not eat properly, they often become **run down** and sick.

5. **slow down** {separable} [to go more slowly; to cause to go more slowly]

   The car **slowed down** when it reached the stoplight.
   The boy's mother made him **slow** the car **down**; she told him he was driving too fast.

6. **slow up** [to reduce speed]

   The child asked her father to **slow up** because she could not walk that fast.
   It is a good idea to **slow up** when driving through busy parts of town.

7. **wipe off** {separable} [to clean a surface with something like a cloth]

   She **wiped off** the table before putting a clean tablecloth on it.
   She used a clean rag to **wipe** it **off**.

8. **get off** (a) {separable} [to send]

> This letter is important, and I need to **get** it **off** right away.
> I try to **get off** my rent check early, but I am not always successful.

> (b) [5-19: to leave a vehicle]

>> We need to **get off** the bus when it reaches the corner.

9. **go over** [to succeed]

> A: How did your speech **go over**?
> B: Quite well, I think. The professor seemed to like it.

> My dinner party didn't **go over** very well; the fish I served made one of
> the guests sick!

>> [5-4: to cover]

>>> The reporter from the paper **went over** the story with me
>>> carefully.

10. **device** [something made to do a particular job]

> Housework is easier than it used to be because many helpful **devices** have
> been invented.
> The washing machine, for example, is a **device** that takes the difficulty
> out of washing clothes.

11. **strain** (a) [to have difficulty doing something]

> The man **strained** to pick up the heavy box, and he was unable to do so.
> It is a **strain** to study and work at the same time; I think I will take fewer
> courses.

> (b) [to separate liquids from solids by using a device with small holes]

> It is necessary to **strain** the mixture to remove all the seeds.
> If the soup isn't **strained** carefully, it will not be smooth.

12. **barrier** [an obstacle]

> Because work was being done on the road, **barriers** were put up to prevent
> people from driving in that area.
> Patricia did not let her lack of money become a **barrier** to getting a good
> education; she borrowed $10,000 from the bank to pay her tuition.

13. **hazard** [something dangerous]

> That old building is a **hazard**; they should put barriers around it before it
> collapses on someone.
> Smoking cigarettes is **hazardous** to your health.

14. **vibrate** [to move very quickly alternating in two directions; to shake]

> The train I took to work yesterday seemed hazardous; it **vibrated** terribly for an hour.
> During rush hour, the traffic is so heavy that the bridge on the highway seems to **vibrate**.

15. **forward(s)** [the direction that is opposite to reverse]

> The official stopped the man **at** the barrier, checked his passport, and then permitted him to go **forward**.
> My aunt tried to back up her car; instead, it went **forwards** and hit a tree.

16. **enable** [to make it possible to do something]

> The telephone is a useful device which **enables** us to communicate quickly with one another.
> The loan Melissa received from the bank **enabled** her to finish school.

17. **merely** [only]

> The child did not mean to break the window; he **merely** wanted to see how far he could throw the ball.
> Mrs. Jones never called first when she wanted to visit someone; she **merely** dropped in.

18. **split** [to break into parts or pieces]

> The boys **split** the pie into three equal portions.
> When the man put on the jacket, it was so tight that it **split** across the back.

19. **transform** [to change or cause to change]

> In five years the strain of her father's sickness **transformed** the happy young girl into a sad and distressed woman.
> When the new road was built, the small town was **transformed** into a large city.
> Through their love, the new parents **transformed** the sad, adopted baby into a happy, strong child.

20. **consequence** [the result]

> If you do not eat correctly, the **consequence** will be poor health.
> He did not study for his exam; **consequently** he failed.

21. **trip** (a) [to fall or almost fall]

> John did not notice the low barrier in front of his car, and he **tripped** over it.
> The road there is very uneven; be careful not to **trip**.

> (b) [1-2: a journey]

> > Last summer, we took a **trip** to Florida.

22. **still** [calm; not moving]

   I do not like to sail unless the bay is **still**; too many high waves frighten me.

   When the lake is **still**, you can look into the water and see your reflection.

23. **ticket** (a) [a legal paper given by an official which explains that you have broken a traffic or parking law and tells you how much you must pay]

   If you don't stop at a stop sign, a policeman can give you a **ticket**.

   If you receive too many speeding **tickets**, your driver's license can be taken away.

   (b) [1-2: a paper that shows payment for transportation]

   I bought the plane **ticket** for my trip yesterday.

24. **degree** (a) [amount; extent]

   That course has a high **degree** of difficulty, and students hesitate to take it.

   Everyone worries about money to some **degree**.

   (b) [2-15: a measure of temperature]

   When the temperature is ten **degrees** Fahrenheit (10° F), people try to stay inside and keep warm.

25. **station** (a) [a place that sends radio or television signals]

   Advertisers like to advertise their products on popular radio **stations**.

   A: Which television **station** is your favorite?
   B: None of them. I'd rather read than watch television.

   (b) [1-2: a building where people wait for a bus or train]

   The train will arrive at the **station** at 1:04 P.M.

26. **depart** [to leave]

   The train will **depart** from the station at 5:05 P.M.
   There are ten **departures** for Chicago from the station every day.

Introductory Exercises

A. Match each word or phrase with its definition.

____ **1.** to arrive, especially a vehicle	**a.** barrier
____ **2.** to hit someone with a vehicle	**b.** consequence
____ **3.** to cause to go more slowly	**c.** degree
____ **4.** to succeed	**d.** depart
____ **5.** something made to do a particular thing	**e.** device
____ **6.** an obstacle	**f.** enable
____ **7.** to reduce speed	**g.** forward
____ **8.** to send	**h.** get off
____ **9.** to move very quickly alternating in two directions; to shake	**i.** go over
	j. hang up
____ **10.** amount; extent	**k.** hazard
____ **11.** to leave, especially a vehicle	**l.** merely
____ **12.** something dangerous	**m.** pull in
____ **13.** only	**n.** pull out
____ **14.** the direction that is opposite to reverse	**o.** run down
____ **15.** calm	**p.** slow down
____ **16.** to change or cause to change	**q.** slow up
____ **17.** the result	**r.** split
____ **18.** to make it possible to do something	**s.** station
	t. still
	u. strain
	v. ticket
	w. transform
	x. trip
	y. vibrate

B. Answer each question with a word or phrase from the word form chart.

  1. When a bus leaves the station, what does it do? (two answers)
  2. When you finish talking on the telephone, what do you do?
  3. What do you do to dusty furniture?
  4. What is a machine that washes clothes?
  5. How could you describe a road which is covered with snow?
  6. In what direction do you usually drive a car?
  7. If I share an apple with you, what must I do first?
  8. Before you decide to do something dangerous, what should you consider first?
  9. What do drivers hate to receive?
 10. What do you want to avoid doing if you are carrying a box of expensive glasses?
 11. What do you call something that prevents you from doing what you want?
 12. How can you make food smooth enough for babies to eat?

Study Exercises

C. Write **T** if the sentence is true and **F** if it is false.

———— **1.** A train pulls in when it departs.

———— **2.** It makes a person feel good when something he does goes over well.

———— **3.** Before you call someone, you have to hang up.

———— **4.** Policemen give drivers tickets for speeding because they slow up.

———— **5.** Taking care of small children can be a strain.

———— **6.** When something vibrates, it is still.

———— **7.** It is a good idea to do things which are hazardous.

———— **8.** Removing barriers enables a person to do something.

———— **9.** When something is transformed, there are usually no major changes.

———— **10.** If you walk in the dark, it is easy to trip.

———— **11.** Most students enjoy taking tests which have a high degree of difficulty.

———— **12.** A televison station is a place that sells televisions.

———— **13.** It is against the law to drive forwards.

———— **14.** It is necessary to write a letter before getting it off.

D. In each blank, write the most appropriate two- or three-word verb from the following list. Be sure to use the correct form.

pull out	look forward to	feel up to	use up
look up to	look back on	fall back on	slow down
come up with	throw away	use up	break down
keep up with	go in for	face up to	lie down
drop out of	go on with	run down	come up to
catch on	come down with	work out	grow up

1. Because the student could not _____ his work, he had to _____ school.

2. It is a good idea to _____ all your food before you take a vacation, or you might have to _____ it _____ when you return.

3. When Bill was young, he often could not _____ his problems; now that he has _____ , however, he is able to _____ them _____ .

4. Mary was really _____ to the concert, but when the day arrived, she became sick and did not _____ going.

5. After the cyclist _____ the flu, he could not

_____ the week-long race.

6. The train _____ a man who jumped onto the track as it was

_____ of the station.

7. The train's engineer _____ the train _____ as
soon as he realized he had hit something.

E. Complete the analogies with a word or phrase from the word form chart.

1. plans : problem :: road : _____

2. put away : clothes :: _____ : telephone

3. up : down :: reverse : _____

4. river : pool :: moving : _____

5. come : arrive :: go out : _____

6. do : act :: result : _____

7. car : slow down :: battery : _____

8. bus : vehicle :: dishwasher : _____

9. sweep : floor :: _____ : table

F. In each blank, write the most appropriate word or phrase from the word form chart.

Yesterday afternoon, we received an exciting telephone call from my
cousin. After my mother (1) _____ the telephone, she told me
cousin Sarah would arrive at 7:00 P.M. and that we needed to work quickly to
finish cleaning up the house. We had already done everything but the kitchen
and dining room. Housework is not too much of a (2) _____
because luckily we have a dishwasher and a vacuum cleaner, which are
useful (3) _____ and (4) _____ us to do our work
quickly. After we put the dishes in the dishwasher, we (5) _____
the stove and dining room table. Then my mother announced that it was
time to (6) _____ for the train station. The station is a long drive
from our house, and the roads are narrow and rather (7) _____ .
For this reason my mother (8) _____ the car at every curve. I
thought we would never get there! Finally, we arrived at the station just as
the train was (9) _____ , and when cousin Sarah got off, we
greeted her with two smiling faces.

Follow-up

G. Dictation: Write the sentences that your teacher reads aloud.

1. _____
2. _____
3. _____
4. _____
5. _____

H. Answer the following questions.

1. For what kinds of things can the police give you a ticket in your country?
2. If you do not get enough rest, do you feel any consequences? What kind?
3. What kinds of situations cause a strain for you?
4. Have you ever been transformed by an event in your life? What?
5. What kinds of machinery vibrate a lot?
6. What things can cause you to trip?
7. Do you enjoy doing work that has a high degree of difficulty?
8. What enables you to overcome your problems?
9. What devices help you the most?
10. Describe some situations that are hazardous.
11. What would you do if you ran down someone with your car?

I. Describe the most serious barrier you have ever had to overcome in your life. What happened?

Business

Word Form Chart

NOUN	VERB	ADJECTIVE	ADVERB	PREPOSITIONAL PHRASE
adversity		adverse	adversely	
	back out			
	brush off			
	count in			
	cross out			
display	display	displayed		
		eventual	eventually	
exertion	exert			
extent		extensive	extensively	
falling out	fall out with			
fluctuation	fluctuate	fluctuating		
industry		industrious	industriously	
industriousness				
modification	modify	modified		
			moreover	
			nevertheless	
				owing to
		prior		prior to
		rough	roughly	
security	secure	secure	securely	
		insecure		
	seek			
	(sought, sought)			
warranty				

Definitions and Examples

1. **modify** [to change]

   After a person has a heart attack, his doctor usually tells him to **modify** his eating and exercise habits.

   People often make **modifications** when they buy a home.

2. **owing to** [because of]

   Owing to the old man's poor health, his family hired a nurse to stay with him.

   University students often have little free time **owing to** the amount of work they have to do for their courses.

3. **rough** [approximate]

   We need to get a **rough** estimate of the cost of modifications we want to have made to the house.

   The engineers think it will take **roughly** three years to complete the project, but they are not absolutely sure.

   [5-19: not smooth]

   The road was very **rough** and full of holes, so we did not have a smooth ride.

4. **prior** [before; preceding in time or order]

   I can't go to the movies; I have a **prior** commitment.

   Prior to my marriage, I lived in New York; now I live in Florida.

5. **display** [to show]

   Stores try to **display** their merchandise attractively so that people will buy it.

   Although the man must have been in pain, his face **displayed** no emotion.

6. **warranty** [guarantee]

   Today many products have a **warranty** that guarantees the company will fix them free for a certain period of time.

   When Michael began having trouble with his brakes, he was glad the car was still under **warranty**.

7. **exert** [to try hard]

   Sally had to **exert** herself to study for her exam because she wasn't feeling very well.

   It takes a lot of **exertion** to play some sports. For example, playing football requires a lot of **exertion**.

8. **industrious** (a) [hardworking]

Although studying is not easy for him, he has exerted himself and has been very **industrious** this term.

When Mrs. Brown came home, she was surprised to find her children working **industriously** in their rooms; she had expected to find them watching television.

(b) [2-20: a business that produces a large number of things to sell]

There are many **industries** in the United States; it is an **industrial** nation.

9. **adverse** [opposed to one's interests]

In the nineteenth century, factory workers often worked under **adverse** conditions; they worked long hours with little heat and poor light.

Some people face **adversity** well, but others lose their courage and just give up.

10. **back out (of)** (a) [to decide not to do something you have promised to do]

The man signed the contract to buy the house on Friday; two days later, however, he decided to **back out**.

United States law permits you to **back out of** some contracts within a three-day period without a penalty.

(b) {separable} [to exit from an area by moving backwards]

John carefully **backed** his car **out of** the narrow driveway into the street.

When the man became angry, the child quickly **backed out of** the room.

11. **fluctuate** [to vary irregularly; to change]

In spring, the temperature **fluctuates** from day to day, and it is difficult to dress appropriately.

My friend's ideas about the career he will choose keep **fluctuating**; he cannot seem to make a firm decision.

12. **eventual** [occurring at some later time or at a time in the future]

After her **eventual** graduation from college, Carol will try to find a job with an architect.

Robert traveled to Europe first, and **eventually** he went to Asia.

13. **seek** [to try to find]

He has been **seeking** a new place to live for several months, but he has not found anything he can afford.

She **sought** a new partner for her business for a long time before finally finding one.

14. **seek to** [to try to do something]

> All businesses **seek to** make a high profit, but some are more successful than others.
>
> He **sought to** enter the race, but it was too late.

15. **nevertheless** [however]

> She really wanted to go to the movies; **nevertheless**, she decided to stay home and do her homework instead.
>
> The man's salary was not very high; **nevertheless**, he spent a lot of money on expensive clothes.

16. **moreover** [in addition to what has been stated; also]

> I absolutely cannot go to the party because I have to clean the kitchen; **moreover**, I have an important exam to study for.
>
> There are several reasons why Richard studies so hard. He likes to make good grades; **moreover**, he wants to go to graduate school.

17. **extent** [the distance over which a thing extends; scope]

> The townspeople were surprised at the **extent** of the disaster; they had not expected the damage to be so great.
>
> Before we can seek a solution, we must first understand the **extent** of the problem.

18. **secure** (a) [to obtain]

> Bill wants to expand his business; first, however, he needs to **secure** a loan from the bank.
>
> He has already **secured** a piece of property where he can put up another building.

(b) [safe]

> It is wise to keep your money in a **secure** place; for example, keep large amounts of money in the bank, not in your wallet.

19. **brush off** (a) [to clean with a brush or one's hand]

> Sarah carefully **brushed off** the back of her skirt when she stood up.
> Before the party, all the leaves need to be **brushed off** the chairs.

(b) {separable} [to not permit oneself to be upset by something]

> Daniel's business lost money the first year; nevertheless, he **brushed** it **off** and said that he knew the second year would be a success.

(c) {separable} [to be unfriendly to a person; to ignore or not pay attention to someone]

> I tried to get Bonnie's attention, but she **brushed** me **off** and kept walking.

20. **fall out with** [to disagree so strongly that you break off the relationship]

> After the man changed jobs, he **fell out with** his new boss almost immediately and decided to return to his prior position.
>
> The two sisters had a major **falling out** and haven't spoken to each other for twenty years.

21. **cross out** {separable} [to cancel by drawing a line through]

> First, Lisa made a list of everything she wanted to buy; then she **crossed out** the items she really could not afford.
>
> The Carters called and cannot come to the party; when you find their name on the guest list, please **cross it out**.

22. **count in** {separable} [to include]

> The general asked for volunteers for the dangerous mission, and more than thirty soldiers asked to be **counted in**.
>
> A: We're going to the movies tonight. Do you want to come along?
>
> B: If you're going to see that new one, please **count** me **in**! I've been wanting to see it for weeks.

23. **pass out** (a) {separable} [to distribute]

> The professor asked a student in the front row of the class to help **pass out** the papers.
>
> It did not take the student long to **pass** them **out**.

(b) [to become unconscious]

> The woman was so weak from her illness that she **passed out**.
>
> Mountain climbers must be careful when they climb high mountains; if the level of oxygen is too low, they might **pass out**.

Introductory Exercises

A.   Match each word or phrase with its definition.

_____ **1.** to change
_____ **2.** guarantee
_____ **3.** occurring at some time in the future
_____ **4.** hardworking
_____ **5.** to try to find
_____ **6.** approximately
_____ **7.** because of
_____ **8.** to vary irregularly
_____ **9.** to try hard
_____ **10.** in addition to what has been stated
_____ **11.** opposed to one's interests
_____ **12.** to disagree and stop a relationship
_____ **13.** however
_____ **14.** scope
_____ **15.** to show
_____ **16.** safe
_____ **17.** to exit from an area by moving backwards

a. adverse
b. back out (of)
c. brush off
d. count in
e. cross out
f. display
g. eventual
h. exert
i. extent
j. fall out with
k. fluctuate
l. industrious
m. modify
n. moreover
o. nevertheless
p. owing to
q. prior
r. roughly
s. secure
t. seek
u. warranty

B.   Answer each question with a word or phrase from the word form chart.

1. How should we do our work in school?
2. If our plans do not work out, what can we do?
3. When temperatures change a lot during the day, how can we describe them?
4. What do stores have in their windows?
5. If your research has a large scope, how can you describe it?
6. When one person disagrees with another, what might they do?
7. How can you describe a job you had before your present one?
8. If you get dirt on your clothes, what can you do?
9. What is another word for "obtain"?
10. If you have to make an estimate that is not exact, how can you describe it?
11. If a task is difficult, what must you do?
12. If you need to remove items from a list, what can you do?
13. How can you get your car out of a garage?

Study Exercises

C. Write **T** if the sentence is true and **F** if it is false.

_____ **1.** A person who wants to be counted in does not want to be included.

_____ **2.** Stores often display new merchandise in their front windows.

_____ **3.** When something fluctuates, it means it is stable.

_____ **4.** When we modify something, we change it.

_____ **5.** An industrious student usually pleases his professors.

_____ **6.** A person who feels insecure feels safe.

_____ **7.** When someone buys a new car, he usually does not want a warranty.

_____ **8.** People are unhappy when they fall out with their friends.

_____ **9.** Most people enjoy working under adverse conditions.

_____ **10.** A person who seeks to do something has already finished it.

_____ **11.** If you exert yourself to do something, you try very hard.

_____ **12.** Someone who passes out may be advised to see a doctor.

D. Match each two- or three-word verb with its synonym.

_____ **1.** draw up

_____ **2.** pass out

_____ **3.** cut up

_____ **4.** cut in on

_____ **5.** pass away

_____ **6.** brush off

_____ **7.** count in

_____ **8.** fall out with

_____ **9.** fall off

_____ **10.** do away with

_____ **11.** count out

_____ **12.** figure on

_____ **13.** figure out

_____ **14.** fall through

_____ **15.** count on

a. to use completely
b. to decline or become less
c. to not happen although expected or planned
d. to plan for
e. to prepare a document
f. to find a way; to solve a problem
g. to kill
h. to die
i. to distribute
j. to cut into small pieces
k. to disagree
l. to include
m. to succeed in doing or providing something
n. to not consider or include
o. to clean with a brush or one's hand
p. to emphasize
q. to anticipate as certain
r. to interrupt

E. Complete the analogies with a word or phrase from the word form chart.

1. closed : hide :: open :_____

2. wipe off : furniture :: _____ : clothes

3. now : before :: present :_____

4. positive : negative :: _____ : lazy

5. exact : knowledge :: _____ : guess

6. present : now :: later : _____

7. accept : count in :: reject : _____

8. rough : smooth :: _____ : favorable

9. stable : unchanging :: unstable : _____

F. In each blank, write the most appropriate word or phrase from the word form chart.

The history of the United States is filled with the stories of poor immigrants who were able to establish successful businesses after years of difficult and (1) _____ conditions. (2) _____ to coming to this country, many immigrants had been poor in their native lands and came to (3) _____ a new life for themselves and their families. Many (4) _____ became their own boss instead of working for others. Their businesses often began in small ways: making and selling clothes from their homes or selling vegetables from door to door. Perhaps for a number of years, their income would have (5) _____ greatly. (6) _____ , they would continue to work hard, and (7) _____ their (8) _____ would be rewarded. Andrew Carnegie, for example, who was a steel manufacturer, entered the United States from Scotland as a poor boy. However, by the time he reached middle age, he had become one of the richest men in the world.

Follow-up

G. Dictation: Write the sentences that your teacher reads aloud.

1. _____

2. _____

3. _____

4. _____

5. _____

H. Answer the following questions.

1. Have you ever passed out? What happened?
2. Is there anything about yourself that you would like to modify? What?
3. In what activities do you have to exert yourself most?
4. Are you basically an industrious person?
5. Have you ever had a serious falling out with a friend?
6. Does the economy in your country fluctuate a great deal? Explain.
7. Prior to using this book, how did you learn new English words?
8. Have you ever applied for and secured a loan for anything? What?
9. Do you own any items, such as a car or watch, that came with a warranty? Have you ever had to use your warranty?
10. Have you ever backed out of a contract? What kind? Why?

I. Using as many words from the word form chart as possible, discuss the development of your career goals and what you plan to do eventually.

UNIT
24

Science (B)

Word Form Chart

NOUN	VERB	ADJECTIVE	ADVERB
circuit		circuitous	circuitously
combustion		combustible	
combustibility			
compression	compress	compressed	
compressibility		compressible	
compressor			
crystal			
crystallization	crystallize	crystalline	
		crystallized	
distillation	distill	distilled	
distillate			
empiricism		empirical	empirically
empiricist			
		finite	
fraction		fractional	
genetics		genetic	genetically
geneticist			
grant	grant		
hydroelectricity		hydroelectric	
inducement	induce	induced	
infinity		infinite	infinitely
intensity	intensify	intense	intensely
		intensive	
magnet	magnetize	magnetic	magnetically
magnetism			
optics		optical	
optician		optic	
		organic	organically
		inorganic	

NOUN	VERB	ADJECTIVE	ADVERB
space			
specimen			
sphere		spherical	spherically
stimulus	stimulate		
stimulation			
stimulant			
superstition		superstitious	superstitiously
trait			

Definitions and Examples

1. **crystal** [a solid material with regularly shaped angles and flat surfaces]

   Crystals of ice formed on the cold windows.
   Diamonds have a **crystalline** surface.

2. **trait** [a quality or characteristic, especially of people or animals]

   Patience is a desirable **trait**.
   Endurance is an important **trait** for long-distance runners.

3. **sphere** (a) [a round body whose surface is at all points equally distant from the center]

   A soccer ball is a **sphere**.

   (b) [a region or surrounding area]

   Although Dick Hammond was a local politician, his **sphere** of influence extended across a wide area.

4. **superstition** [a belief or practice that is not based on known facts]

   Superstitious people consider some numbers to be unlucky.
   There is no place for **superstition** in science.

5. **hydroelectric** [having to do with the production of electricity by water power]

   Hydroelectric power is common in mountainous areas.
   Hydroelectricity is safe, dependable, and inexpensive.

6. **fraction** (a) [a small part]

   Only a **fraction** of this class passed the test.

   (b) [a number that expresses the parts of a whole. Example: one-third]

   Fifty <u>percent</u> expressed as a **fraction** is <u>one-half</u>.

7. **combustion** [the process of burning]

   Natural gas is a highly **combustible** substance.
   Careless use of some chemicals can produce **combustion**.

8. **compress** [to make smaller by pressing together]

    Some machines are driven by **compressed** air.
    It is difficult to **compress** water.

9. **magnet** [a stone or piece of iron or steel that attracts pieces of iron or steel]

    The **magnetic** North Pole is not the same as the geographic North Pole.
    An electric current can produce a **magnet**.
    Children enjoy using **magnets** to pick up metal objects.

10. **intense** [very great; very strong]

    Intense pain can indicate serious injury.
    You can **intensify** the heat by adding more wood to the fire.

11. **finite** [having limits]

    There is a **finite** number of possibilities that we can choose from when
        planning a career.
    Nursing is an **infinitely** rewarding profession.

12. **genetics** [the branch of biology that deals with variation in plants and animals
    and the traits they will inherit]

    Research in **genetics** could lead to the elimination of certain inherited
        diseases.

13. **stimulate** [to increase temporarily the activity of an organ or organism; to
    excite]

    Warm temperatures can **stimulate** a plant to grow faster.
    Coffee acts as a **stimulant** to the body.

14. **optics** [the science that deals with light and vision]

    A telescope is an **optical** instrument used for looking into the sky.
    An **optician** is a person who makes or sells eyeglasses.

15. **specimen** [an example of a kind; one of a group taken to show what the
    others are like]

    This rare snake is a prized **specimen**.
    The biology laboratory contained many **specimens** in clear bottles.

16. **induce** [to cause, persuade or produce]

    It can be dangerous to use drugs that **induce** sleep.
    Soft music **induces** some people to relax.

17. **circuit** (a) [a route or trip around]

    The plants travel in regular **circuits** around the sun.

    (b) [a complete path which electricity flows through]

    When the wire is cut, the **circuit** is interrupted.

18. **grant** (a) [to give what is asked; to allow or admit]

    The boss will not **grant** permission for us to leave early.

    (b) [the thing that is granted, such as a privilege, a sum of money, an area of land]

    Scientists often use government **grants** to pay for their research.

19. **organic** (a) [characteristic of or coming from plants or animals]

    Only **inorganic** materials are found on the moon.
    Organic fertilizer contains no artificial chemicals.

    (b) [having to do with the bodily organs]

    Some **organic** problems, like heart disease, have no simple cure.

20. **space** (a) [the unlimited area in which the universe exists]

    The earth moves through **space** in a regular pattern.
    Space ships carry scientists through outer **space**.

    (b) [1-12: a place for something]

    Big houses have **space** for entertaining.

21. **empirical** [based on experiment, observation, or practical experience]

    Do you have **empirical** data to support your theory?
    Professor Jones believes that **empiricism** is the only way to advance
    scientific knowledge.

22. **distill** [to make a liquid pure by heating it until it becomes a gas and then cooling it to a liquid again]

    Distilled water is often used in delicate equipment.
    The **distillation** process involves both heating and cooling.

Introductory Exercises

A. Match each word or phrase with its definition.

——	1. the unlimited area in which the universe exists	**a.** circuit
——	2. based on experiment	**b.** combustion
——	3. a quality or charactistic	**c.** compress
——	4. a stone or piece of iron or steel that attracts pieces of iron	**d.** crystal
——	5. the process of burning	**e.** distill
——	6. to excite	**f.** empirical
——	7. a round body	**g.** finite
——	8. a belief not based on facts	**h.** fraction
——	9. a branch of biology	**i.** genetics
——	10. a small part	**j.** grant
——	11. a trip around	**k.** hydroelectric
——	12. very strong	**l.** induce
——	13. to cause or persuade	**m.** intense
——	14. to give what is asked	**n.** magnet
——	15. an example of a kind	**o.** optical
——	16. having limits	**p.** organic
——	17. to make smaller	**q.** space
		r. specimen
		s. sphere
		t. stimulate
		u. superstition
		v. trait

B. Answer each question with a word from the word form chart.

1. What is the approximate shape of the earth?
2. Name one source of electric power.
3. Who makes the special glass for telescopes?
4. Where are the stars and planets found?
5. How can we purify a liquid?
6. Describe the structure of a diamond.
7. Who studies genetics?
8. What is another way to express one-third?
9. What do we see when we light a match?
10. What do we inherit from our parents?
11. How many numbers are in our number system?
12. What do we use to attract pieces of iron?
13. How can you describe a strong emotion?
14. What kind of evidence do you get from observation?

Study Exercises

C. Write **T** if the sentence is true and **F** if it is false.

_____ 1. Crystals are commonly gaseous materials.

_____ 2. A sphere has no flat surfaces.

_____ 3. Hydroelectric power depends on oil.

_____ 4. Only a fraction of the earth's surface is covered with ice.

_____ 5. A scientist who studies insects probably has many interesting specimens.

_____ 6. It is usually not possible for parents to grant their child's every wish.

_____ 7. Organic chemists study rare metals.

_____ 8. Modern medicine relies heavily on superstition.

_____ 9. All mammals have certain traits in common.

_____ 10. Wood is a combustible material.

_____ 11. Magnets are sometimes made of paper.

_____ 12. Scientists can use genetics to predict the characteristics of some plants.

_____ 13. If a circuit is broken, the electric current is interrupted.

_____ 14. Distilled water is cleaner than river water.

_____ 15. Empirical data come mainly from logic and reasoning.

D. Circle the word(s) or phrase(s) that do not fit.

1. to induce	a drug a cure a current a stomach ache	**6.** an infinite	distance plan amount number
2. to grant	a wish a privilege some money a dilemma	**7.** optical	instrument illusion telescope ballot
3. hydroelectric	power water installation plant	**8.** a magnetic	force biology material attraction
4. a fraction	of the capacity of the distance of the capitalism of the population	**9.** organic	conflict chemistry materials spoon
5. intense	thermometer heat emotions desire	**10.** empirical	evidence data motor crystal

E. Complete the analogies with a word from the word form chart.

   1. square : cube :: circle : _____

   2. ship : ocean :: rocket : _____

   3. sun : solar :: water : _____

   4. music : relax :: coffee : _____

   5. watch : jeweler :: glasses : _____

   6. modern : science :: primitive : _____

   7. pie : piece :: sum : _____

   8. road : endless :: number: _____

F. Read the passage and answer the questions that follow.

        Modern science is a mix of empiricism and theoretical ideas. Government and industrial grants have made it possible for scientists to develop some very useful instruments and techniques.

        One example of this is the purification of sea water by means
5 of distillation. Water-poor countries require large amounts of fresh water for agriculture and human needs and the supply of sea water is nearly infinite.

        Genetic engineering is another rapidly developing field of research. Through the study of genes, geneticists have been
10 learning more about inherited traits. They are using this science to develop new varieties of agricultural products and man-made drugs to fight some diseases better.

        Modern optics has produced the laser, a ray of high-intensity light in a very narrow frequency range. For a laser to work, more
15 than just a fraction of the atoms must be stimulated to produce visible light in an organized fashion. Lasers are being used in medicine for certain kinds of surgery.

        High-intensity magnets, which produce a very strong magnetic field, are used in devices which are a substitute for X-ray pictures.
20 The devices can help examine specimens and body organs for diseases.

        The space program is dependent on the development of man-made crystals, which are used in the computers that guide the spaceships. Also, empirical methods play an important role in the
25 development of crystallization processes.

        The practical results of scientific research are interesting and exciting and have improved the quality of our lives. Dedicated researchers, with the help of grants from agencies, have brought us out of the age of superstition and into the age of science.

   1. Where does the money for research come from? _____

_____

2. What process can be used to purify sea water? _____

_____

3. What useful advances have come from genetic engineering? _____

_____

4. Where are lasers being used? _____

_____

5. What can be used as a substitute for an X-ray picture? _____

_____

6. How are crystals used in the space program? _____

_____

Follow-up

G. Dictation: Write the sentences that your teacher reads aloud.

1. _____
2. _____
3. _____
4. _____
5. _____

H. Answer the following questions.

1. Which traits have you inherited from your parents?
2. Do you have any superstitions? Describe them.
3. Are there any hydroelectric plants in your country? Where?
4. Describe two practical uses for a magnet.
5. What are some common combustible materials?
6. What kinds of specimens might a biologist keep?
7. Where might you apply to receive a research grant?
8. What is located in outer space?
9. What do you think will come next in the exploration of outer space?
10. What common items have a spherical shape?
11. At what age do school children in your country usually learn about fractions?
12. What can be done to relieve intense pain?
13. What benefits can genetics bring?

I. What recent scientific advancement do you think has been most important? Why?

Media (B)

Word Form Chart

NOUN	VERB	ADJECTIVE	ADVERB
commentary			
commentator	commentate		
conception	conceive	conceivable	conceivably
concept		inconceivable	inconceivably
critic	criticize	critical	critically
critique			
criticism			
emergence	emerge	emerging	
grasp	grasp	grasping	
ignition	ignite		
imagination	imagine	imaginable	
		unimaginable	
		imagined	
		imaginary	
		imaginative	
		unimaginative	
instance			for instance
magnitude			
	pick up		
	play down		
	play up		
precision		precise	precisely
		imprecise	
profundity		profound	profoundly
rationalization	rationalize	rational	rationally
rationale			
rationalism		irrational	
rationalist			
remark	remark	remarkable	remarkably

NOUN	VERB	ADJECTIVE	ADVERB
	run down		
shift	shift		
	show up		
substance		substantive	substantively
		substantial	substantially
survey	survey		
surveyor			

Definitions and Examples

1. **magnitude** [size; importance; degree of brightness]

   A star of a certain **magnitude** can be seen without a telescope.
   The **magnitude** of the problem was not completely understood at first.

2. **precise** [exact; accurate; definite]

   Scientific instruments can make **precise** measurements.
   I told my doctor **precisely** where my pain was.

3. **emerge** [to come out; to come into view]

   The crowd cheered as the king **emerged** from the church.
   Many theories are likely to **emerge** after such an interesting observation.

4. **ignite** [to set on fire or catch fire]

   Wood **ignites** easily if it is dry.
   The **ignition** system of my car is in need of repair; the car does not start easily.

5. **imagine** (a) [to guess; to suppose]

   I cannot **imagine** who the author could be.
   Can you **imagine** why this is such a popular book?

   (b) [to think; to believe]

   Mr. Calkins **imagined** that his boss was pleased with his work.
   I would prefer to **imagine** that my job is secure.

   (c) [2-23: to picture in one's mind; to have an idea]

   It is hard to **imagine** a civilization without laws.

6. **imaginary** [existing only in the mind, not real]

   The equator is an **imaginary** line around the center of the earth.
   Children enjoy stories about **imaginary** beings.

7. **shift** [to change in some way, for example from one place, position, or person to another]

    When I **shift** my car into reverse it makes a strange noise.
    We expect a **shift** in wind direction during the night.

8. **conceive** (a) [to have an idea or feeling; to think in one's mind]

    It is difficult to **conceive** of a plan to end hunger.
    I think it is **conceivable** that Ralph will change his plans after serious
        discussion with me.
    The artist's **conception** of heaven included angels and music.

    (b) [to become pregnant]

    A woman who cannot **conceive** might have a serious medical condition.
    For humans, birth occurs approximately nine months after **conception**.

9. **show up** (a) [to arrive, to appear]

    My brother **showed up** late at the graduation.
    It is not polite to **show up** without an invitation.

    (b) {separable} [to reveal the true character or nature of something or someone,
        often a negative aspect]

    We thought we were stronger, but the other team **showed** us **up**.
    Do not **show up** the boss. He doesn't like it.

10. **play up** {separable} [to emphasize; to give more importance to]

    Some newspapers **play up** stories about murder and disaster.
    If a newspaper **plays** those stories **up**, I usually buy a different newspaper.

11. **criticize** (a) [to disapprove; to find fault with]

    It is difficult to **criticize** someone who is trying to do his best.
    The boss was **critical** of some employees who were slow and careless.

    (b) [to make judgments about the merits and faults of artistic productions, for
        example, books, music, art, movies, or plays]

    I usually agree with the movie **critic** in this magazine.
    Literary **criticism** is a form of scholarly writing.

12. **critical** [very serious or dangerous]

    Some forests have suffered a **critical** loss of trees as the result of acid rain.
    After major surgery, the patient's condition was described as **critical**.

13. **rational** [sensible; reasonable; able to think and reason clearly]

    Rational people prefer compromise to war.
    It is difficult for an angry child to behave **rationally**.

14. **rationale** [a basis for belief or action]

> I understand why she is changing her major, but I do not feel her **rationale** is logical.
> His **rationale** for moving is that he needs a larger house.

15. **play down** {separable} [to minimize; to give less emphasis to]

> The reporters **played down** the ambassador's contribution to the trade agreement.
> I think they **played** it **down** at the request of the president.

16. **profound** [very deep]

> The children felt a **profound** sorrow when their grandmother died.
> My philosophy professor is the author of a very **profound** book.

17. **substantial** [important; large; real; firm]

> We have seen **substantial** progress in the negotiations.
> I would feel safer if this were a more **substantial** building.

18. **remark** [to say; to comment]

> Did you hear the president's **remarks** at the press conference?
> Our guests **remarked** on the unexpected cold weather here.

19. **remarkable** [not common; extraordinary]

> A diamond of that size is quite **remarkable**.
> The injured child was **remarkably** calm in the emergency room.

20. **run down** (a) {separable} [to speak against strongly; to speak badly about]

> If you **run down** your employer you might not get a promotion.
> Andrew constantly criticizes his enemies and **runs** them **down** at every opportunity.

> (b) [6-22: to hit someone with a vehicle]

> > The truck **ran** the pedestrian **down** at the intersection.

> (c) [6-22: to lose power]

> > My radio battery **ran down**, making the volume too low.

21. **pick up** {separable} (a) [to learn or get casually and without particular effort]

> Children **pick up** foreign languages easier than adults.
> When I lived in Paris, I **picked up** some hints for good cooking.
> I **picked** some good cheese **up** when I was downtown yesterday.

> (b) [6-14: to increase]

> > Since the economy is improving, spending is **picking up** and people are buying more products.

22. **grasp** (a) [to understand]

These are difficult concepts for beginning students to **grasp**.
As children mature, they learn to **grasp** abstract ideas.

(b) [to take and hold something by closing the fingers around it]

A curious baby will **grasp** at any colorful object.
It is proper to **grasp** the baseball bat with both hands.

23. **instance** [an example, a case]

This is the most severe **instance** of censorship we have ever seen.
Many nutrients are essential to good health. **For instance**, proteins are
  needed for cell repair.

24. **survey** (a) [to gather information]

Companies sometimes need to **survey** their employees to learn about
  working conditions.

(b) [to look over; to examine]

The engineers were asked to **survey** the damage done by the flood.
I need to **survey** the literature before I write my book.

25. **commentary** [a series of comments or notes]

I sometimes listen to the editor's **commentary** after the evening news.
A **commentator** discusses the implications and significance of a news
  story.